Palgrave Studies in Classical Liberalism

Series Editors
David F. Hardwick, Department of Pathology and Laboratory Medicine, The University of British Columbia, Vancouver, BC, Canada
Leslie Marsh, Department of Economics, Philosophy and Political Science, The University of British Columbia, Okanagan, BC, Canada

This series offers a forum to writers concerned that the central presuppositions of the liberal tradition have been severely corroded, neglected, or misappropriated by overly rationalistic and constructivist approaches.

The hardest-won achievement of the liberal tradition has been the wrestling of epistemic independence from overwhelming concentrations of power, monopolies and capricious zealotries. The very precondition of knowledge is the exploitation of the epistemic virtues accorded by society's situated and distributed manifold of spontaneous orders, the DNA of the modern civil condition.

With the confluence of interest in situated and distributed liberalism emanating from the Scottish tradition, Austrian and behavioral economics, non-Cartesian philosophy and moral psychology, the editors are soliciting proposals that speak to this multidisciplinary constituency. Sole or joint authorship submissions are welcome as are edited collections, broadly theoretical or topical in nature.

Alice L. Kassens · Joshua C. Hall
Editors

Challenges in Classical Liberalism

Debating the Policies of Today Versus Tomorrow

palgrave
macmillan

Editors
Alice L. Kassens
Business & Economics Department
Roanoke College
Salem, VA, USA

Joshua C. Hall
Business and Economics
West Virginia University
Morgantown, WV, USA

ISSN 2662-6470 ISSN 2662-6489 (electronic)
Palgrave Studies in Classical Liberalism
ISBN 978-3-031-32892-3 ISBN 978-3-031-32890-9 (eBook)
https://doi.org/10.1007/978-3-031-32890-9

This Palgrave Macmillan imprint is published by the registered company Springer Nature Switzerland AG
The registered company address is: Gewerbestrasse 11, 6330 Cham, Switzerland

Contents

Contributors

Samuel E. Abrams Teachers College, Columbia University, New York, NY, USA

Brian J. Asquith W.E. Upjohn Institute for Employment Research, Kalamazoo, MI, USA

Margaret C. Bock Goucher College, Baltimore, MD, USA

Ryan Calo University of Washington, Seattle, WA, USA

Tina Marsh Dalton Wake Forest University, Winston-Salem, NC, USA

Ronald B. Davies University College of Dublin, Dublin, Ireland

Corey A. DeAngelis American Federation for Children, San Antonio, TX, USA

Angela K. Dills Western Carolina University, Cullowhee, NC, USA

Joshua C. Hall West Virginia University, Morgantown, WV, USA

Alice L. Kassens Roanoke College, Salem, VA, USA

Jeffrey A. Miron Harvard University, Cambridge, MA, USA

Amanda Novello Economic Policy Researcher, Jersey City, NJ, USA

Peter F. Orazem Iowa State University, Ames, IA, USA

Arvind Panagariya Columbia University, New York, NY, USA

Soumyadip Roy Jindal School of Banking and Finance, Jagdishpur, India

Jenny Schuetz Brookings Institution, Washington, DC, USA

Adam Thierer Street Institute, Washington, DC, USA

Patrick J. Wolf University of Arkansas, Fayetteville, AR, USA

Aaron Yelowitz Gatton College of Business and Economics, University of Kentucky, Lexington, KY, USA

Armineh Zohrabian University of Arkansas for Medical Sciences, Little Rock, AR, USA

List of Figures

List of Tables

1

Introduction

Joshua C. Hall and Alice L. Kassens

Overview

Historically, classical liberalism has presented a vision of how a society comprised of free and responsible individuals will create institutions that allow us to live together better. While many scholars have contested this optimism about the ingenuity and initiative of the individual, classical liberals have paid little attention to the issues raised by individuals concerned about the here and now. Namely, how do dynamism and creative destruction disrupt communities and may lead to a variety of worse outcomes for some?

J. C. Hall (✉)
West Virginia University, Morgantown, WV, USA
e-mail: joshua.hall@mail.wvu.edu

A. L. Kassens
Roanoke College, Salem, VA, USA
e-mail: kassens@roanoke.edu

A. L. Kassens and J. C. Hall (eds.), *Challenges in Classical Liberalism*, Palgrave Studies in Classical Liberalism,
https://doi.org/10.1007/978-3-031-32890-9_1

The volume you hold in your hands aims to deepen our understanding of this key challenge to a free society. It does so by focusing on seven of the most important areas of debate in society today: land use, education, trade openness, labor markets, health care, technology, and recreational alcohol and drugs. Not only are these areas in the news daily, but each of them can involve trade-offs between the world we live in and the world we hope to live in.

These are not your typical pro-con essays. The authors are not responding to one another. Instead, the authors were chosen because of their previous work, that while respecting individual autonomy and the role of markets, differ in terms of trade-offs between today and tomorrow. Each section begins with an essay from a scholar making a case for a dynamic, open society in the area under discussion. The other essay is from a scholar favoring the status quo or incremental, guided change. When paired together, the goal of the essays is not to score points or to win a debate but rather to illuminate important challenges to classical liberalism, such as overlooked or ignored trade-offs, disagreements about the magnitude of benefits and costs, and differences in values.

An important feature unique to this volume is that while the scholarship of the other author in each section might have been known in advance, each essay was written in isolation. By letting each side state their case without direct knowledge of the specific arguments of the other essayist, these tensions and disagreements come to the forefront. We do so to encourage you, the reader, to read closely and engage with the debate. What do the authors agree on? Why do they disagree? Is it because of empirical arguments? And if the arguments are largely empirical and still disagree, why is that? Is some literature privileged because of its focus? Are there any important arguments unstated? Are the authors closer or farther away in their views than expected?

Given this goal, we will briefly sketch the arguments presented by the authors in each area. We hesitate to highlight too many areas of disjoint, however, as we want to avoid our views overtaking reader reactions to the essays.

Land Use

Land use is one of the most contentious areas of debate in the United States, especially since COVID-19 disrupted our work and home life. Working from home, rising real estate prices, and continued job growth in large cities has led to considerable dissatisfaction with the status quo. The durability of housing and the need to coordinate economic and personal activities suggest some role for planning, especially as consumer tastes evolve faster than the housing stock depreciates. Land use is an area where we are in the area of second-best policy, and these two chapters highlight this fact.

Brian Asquith and Margaret Bock begin by explaining the status quo in the United States. In "The Case for Dynamic Cities," Brian Asquith and Margaret Bock begin by explaining the status quo in the United States. They highlight how past government interventions designed to make cities more livable instead often led to increased congestion, greater racial and ethnic segregation, and concentrated poverty. The aging of the population and the rise of remote work are at the core of a set of challenges to cities moving forward. These challenges require policies that will allow for adaptation to the way citizens will live, work, and play. Asquith and Bock suggest two policy options that will help cities adapt to the changing needs of citizens: annexation of inner ring suburbs and allowing for the development of housing options such as accessory dwelling units and multi-family housing to increase population density.

Like Asquith and Bock, Brookings Institution scholar Jenny Schuetz begins by explaining the status quo, focusing on who regulates land use and how it is done. Schuetz discusses the economic argument for zoning laws and building codes designed to mitigate negative externalities. Overly strict land use, however, can lead to high housing costs, environmentally harmful development, and economic mobility issues for households of modest means. This is often driven by land use governance being too local and ignoring the effect of their decisions on the entire region. For example, almost no one wants a grocery store right next door, but everyone wants to be able to get quickly and easily to a grocery store. Schuetz's essay highlights how the status quo often reflects power and money differentials in society and that much of what seems "market-driven" reflects vested interests.

Education

Corey DeAngelis and Patrick Wolf begin their essay in favor of dynamism in education markets by noting how robust private education has been in the United States historically. Given that 90% of students are enrolled in public (government) schools, any changes from the status quo toward educational freedom will affect the students in public schools. Therefore, DeAngelis and Wolf spend considerable time presenting evidence on the effects of school choice on the public school system. They argue that the evidence shows that public schools often have more resources per pupil after school choice programs are introduced. In addition, the students in public schools often learn more due to the increase in competition from private schools and charter schools. With students using school choice often better off in terms of education and other outcomes parents care about (safety, values, etc.), more education freedom seems to be leading toward more dynamic education markets that more quickly respond to family needs, without any downside.

Samuel Abrams presents a very different viewpoint on the effect of school choice on students and communities. To begin, the focus and evidence presented by Abrams are much more philosophical and international in scope. Institutional details and how school choice is implemented matter for their effects on students and communities. He presents evidence from countries like New Zealand, Chile, Sweden, and the United States to show that not everything is rosy when some families exercise choice. Abrams's essay demonstrates concern over how school choice is implemented to mitigate downside risks, from greater income segregation and racial segregation to lower test scores for those who remain in public schools. In addition, he argues that school choice is one of many possible policy prescriptions to lead to improved outcomes.

Trade Openness

Arvind Panagariya makes a case for trade openness in his essay "Free Trade as a Key to Economic Development." He begins by walking through a history of free trade post-World War II and how the experience of East Asian countries that adopted outward-oriented trade policies has informed debate among economists since then. Panagariya argues that free trade is important to economic growth and development, especially for developing countries. By engaging in free trade, countries use comparative advantage to advance economically. The remainder of the essay is devoted to specific countries, and how they are not evidence for protectionism but rather how a little bit of free trade goes a long way.

Economist Ron Davies highlights the trade-offs with free trade in his essay. He begins by discussing the effects of increased exports on a country, such as a reduced demand for domestic production in industries facing increased competition. This competition can lead to a loss of jobs, decreased wages, and wage inequality as the sectors benefitting from trade advance faster than those exposed to international competition. Davies then highlights several additional effects of trade openness that are concerns, such as increased pollution and cultural homogeneity. In addition, ethical and national security issues may be at play, such as in the case of child labor or the production of critical national defense infrastructure.

Labor Markets

Peter Orazem and Soumyadip Roy discuss the benefits of unfettered labor markets in their essay, focusing on how government regulation affects labor markets' efficiency. Employing a cross-country analysis, they highlight how labor freedom is related to a higher return on human capital. This leads to higher incomes and economic growth for society. Employment protections can slow productivity by stopping the reallocation of individuals from low productivity work to high productivity work. In addition, protections for vulnerable populations, like youth, can sometimes lead to higher youth employment by raising the cost of hiring. The remainder of their essay focuses on issues like monopsony, minimum wages, and occupational licensure. Overall, labor market restrictions raise the cost of employing labor and distort the flow of labor to its highest and best use.

In her essay, Amanda Novello focuses on the United States labor market, which focuses on the case for greater labor market restrictions to assist individuals facing low and stagnating wages today. She discusses how inflation has eroded the real value of the minimum wage and how the United States has the lowest minimum wage relative to median pay. Poverty reduction and a narrowing in gender and racial wage gaps would occur if the minimum wage were increased to at least $15 an hour. Novello then makes a case for greater collective bargaining to minimize workplace issues such as unfair dismissal and to reduce income inequality. She concludes by discussing labor union organizing and problems associated with the gig economy. Due to the prevalence of women, people of color, and immigrants in the gig economy and working at the minimum wage, labor market protections protect the most vulnerable in society today.

Health Care

In "Should We Trust Consumers or Bureaucrats with Health Insurance Choices?" Aaron Yelowitz focuses on health insurance. He begins by noting how the market for health insurance has several economic issues, such as adverse selection and moral hazard. In the United States, government plays a large role in health insurance through the tax treatment of employer-provided insurance as well as government programs such as Medicare and Medicaid. Given the number of issues individuals face in choosing health insurance and the government's large role in the sector already, some argue for greater government involvement in the health insurance market, such as by changing default enrollment choices. Yelowitz argues that government officials are not infallible in making default choices and that consumers typically make better choices when given the opportunity to learn. He argues that allowing consumers to learn from mistakes by allowing more frequent open enrollment periods would lead to more robust outcomes in the long run.

Christina Dalton looks at the topic of health care in her essay. She notes several economic problems with health-care provision and insurance throughout the paper. For consumers, information asymmetries concerning quality are large. Dalton argues for centralized information or mandated standards to improve health care, given medical literacy in the population. Adverse selection exists on both the public and private provider sides of health care. A key issue to Dalton is how individuals can influence their health and the incentive problems created with our current focus in insurance markets of less than a year. Even if people can influence their own health, the financial benefits are often in the distant future, making it very difficult to align incentives for proper health care over the life cycle.

Technology

Adam Theirer makes a case for innovative dynamism concerning technological advances in his essay "Coping with Technological Disruption." He begins by listing all the ways technological innovation has improved people's lives. It has led to higher income, longer life expectancy, greater access to cultural goods, etc. It has also empowered individuals by giving more individuals the time and the tools to create new music, games, or online communities focused on shared interests. Theirer also argues that technological innovation has often served as a check on both public and private power by giving citizens new tools to push back against entrenched interests. While technology can lead to job loss and anxiety, history has shown the tremendous benefits from permissionless innovation. He concludes by discussing three practical solutions to overcome opposition to technological progress.

Ryan Calo adopts a more pragmatic approach in his essay on technological innovation. He argues that the distinction between precaution about technology and permissionless innovation is a false dichotomy. Instead, he argues that the proper approach to technology policy is to experiment and then use law and public policy to ensure the benefits of technology do not come with high costs. In support of his position, Calo notes that those who argue for permissionless innovation have a hard time pointing to actual cases where precautions about new technology impeded progress. More normatively, permissionless innovation provides no benchmark as to when law and policy may have a role to play in supporting experimentation and cataloging problems that may require innovation.

Recreational Alcohol and Drugs

Jeffrey Miron and Angela Dills make the case that while the recreational use of alcohol, drugs, and tobacco has both personal and social harms, these outcomes are often related to underlying issues faced by individuals. Suppression of these substances, without treatment of the underlying conditions, often leads to unintended consequences. The heavy regulation of these substances often leads to illegal markets characterized by violence, corruption, and a reduction in quality control. These features of illegal markets frequently have a disparate impact on marginalized communities. The move toward legal markets that are taxed and regulated creates both tax revenue and is better than outright prohibition. While the authors do not favor complete deregulation, they note how current regulations often make product innovation difficult, to the consumer's detriment.

Armineh Zohrabian also notes that alcohol and drugs cause great harm to both individuals and society. She details the economic arguments for regulating them but notes that it is not straightforward to change risky health behaviors. The law of unintended consequences is likely to come into play with any single-dimensional policy, such as outright prohibition. Instead, she argues that regulation should proceed strictly on a cost–benefit basis informed by rigorous evaluations and distributional concerns.

Conclusion

While there clearly exist some areas of agreement explaining the status quo in these markets, a reading of the essays clarifies that there are real substantive disagreements regarding what should be done in the future. These disagreements hinge on differences in focus, differences in reading of the literature, differences in normative commitments, and differences in the weight put on today versus tomorrow.

We hope that readers will explore the tensions in these essays in their own scholarship. What is the right path forward in each of these markets? Whom are we privileging when we move toward more open markets? What role does government play in mitigating harm to individuals today to ensure future benefits? These are but a handful of questions we hope this volume will inspire.

We would be remiss if we did not acknowledge a number of people who assisted with this project. The John Templeton Foundation and the Institute for Humane Studies provided funding for this project. We want to thank Jonathan Fortier for his help in catalyzing our thoughts on this project and Maria Rogacheva for her patience as COVID played havoc with our deadlines. Thank you to all the authors for your willingness to be part of this project. We hope you are happy with the result.

Part I

Land Use

2

The Case for Dynamic Cities

Brian J. Asquith and Margaret C. Bock

Things change. And what if, tomorrow, cities woke, and went walking? If Tokyo engulfed your town? If Vienna came striding over the hill toward you? If the city you inhabit today just upped and left, and you woke tomorrow wrapped in a thin blanket on an empty plain, where Detroit once stood, or Sydney, or Moscow?

Don't ever take a city for granted.

Neil Gaiman, *SIMCITY*

We thank Tim Bartik, Josh Hall, and Brad Hershbein for suggestions and insights. Any errors are our own.

B. J. Asquith (✉)
W.E. Upjohn Institute for Employment Research, Kalamazoo, MI, USA
e-mail: asquith@upjohn.org

M. C. Bock
Goucher College, Baltimore, MD, USA
e-mail: Margaret.Bock@goucher.edu

A. L. Kassens and J. C. Hall (eds.), *Challenges in Classical Liberalism*, Palgrave Studies in Classical Liberalism,
https://doi.org/10.1007/978-3-031-32890-9_2

Introduction

Cities are constantly caught between two interlocking challenges: addressing past decisions that hinder the present while simultaneously anticipating future needs. The case for dynamism is simply that cities cannot pilot a successful path forward without the willingness to disrupt a deleterious or calcified status quo. In this chapter, we make the case for why policymakers must be prepared to embrace change, even as we acknowledge that past experiments have sometimes been harmful to poor, vulnerable, or minority populations. We do so by highlighting two important past policies presently ailing many US cities: infrastructure and zoning decisions that often disproportionately hurt the poor and racial minorities as well as the hangover from the building boom of the postwar period. We also identify two future trends that will reshape cities in the coming decades: global and national population aging and the rise of remote working. We conclude our chapter with a review of policies that could address the problems we raise. The common thread uniting our recommendations is that some of the best solutions are found when cities and private citizens are freed to pursue growth and innovation.

Past Decisions and Current Problems

One reason that current policymakers may be more reluctant to embrace dynamic policies is that past policymakers were often quite happy to make radical changes, often to the detriment of oppressed groups or poor people. We are sympathetic to this thermostatic reaction ("If they were too hasty, we should course-correct by being more cautious,") and the first section of our chapter chronicles some of these consequential past policies that lie at the root of many of today's urban problems. Nonetheless, we will argue further below that this thermostatic reaction is wrong: even accounting for haste, the only answer to past dynamic mistakes are current dynamic policies, else the past becomes a straight-jacket on the future.

Urban Planning Policies of the Past While this chapter seeks to make a forceful case for dynamism, we begin by acknowledging that past infrastructure and planning decisions have often had persistent effects that influence current urban issues. From zoning to infrastructure construction, the consequences of these policy decisions are often far-reaching and constrain current policymakers.

Federal neighborhood classifications are a classic example of a past urban planning mistake that weighs on the present. This started in the 1930s, when those seeking a new home loan would go through the Federal Housing Administration (FHA). The FHA did not handle existing loans; it only created new ones that were required to be "economically sound" by the federal government. In order to mitigate the risk to collateral values presented by racial transition, the FHA would not insure mortgages in neighborhoods potentially subject to change (Fishback et al. 2021). The FHA used data sources created by New Deal statistical projects to identify neighborhoods where they would be less likely to lend to minority groups.[1]

Another example is the construction of the interstate highway system. Deciding where and when to build a highway through a central city involves considering a host of factors: will buildings have to be torn down? Will individuals have to be relocated? How will this highway impact travel times for suburban commuters? What about the commute and travel patterns of inner-city dwellers? Yet, once the pavement is laid, the policy path in the United States tends to treat that pavement as a permanent part of the urban landscape.

These decisions reshaped their cities right down to the present. Brinkman and Lin (2019) explore the construction of the Interstate Highway System and the political channels that influenced the placement of its segments. They find that actual interstate construction deviated quite a bit from planned construction routes in central cities when compared to suburban interstate segments. The authors argue that

[1] Additionally, recent research has shown the persistent, harmful effects of the arbitrary boundaries drawn on the 1930's Home Owners Loan Corporation (HOLC) "redlining" maps. The HOLC was a temporary program created to handle existing home loans. Not only were factors such as home ownership and home values stunted in neighborhoods deemed more risky by the HOLC in the 1930's, but it has been shown that racial segregation by neighborhood grade was found across the maps' drawn boundaries. Areas graded D, or most risky, became more heavily African American than nearby C-graded areas over the course of the twentieth century (Aaronson et al. 2021).

policymakers did not expect white city dwellers to be so opposed to the potential negative externalities of the highways. Minority neighborhoods thus bore, and continue to bear, the brunt of the negative secondary effects of interstate highway construction.[2]

The consequence of both mid-20th Century policies is that central cities have many physically divided neighborhoods that are often highly racially and ethnically segregated. Specifically, these policies helped facilitate white flight and suburbanization (Baum-Snow 2007; Patterson 2020). As economic opportunities and a large share of the tax base left the inner city for the suburbs, minority groups were generally left behind on many fronts. These troubled neighborhoods now have concentrated poverty, higher commute times, and the other environmental harms that come from living near busy highways like air pollution, crime, and increased risk of traffic-related pedestrian death (see, e.g., Anderson [2020] and Herrnstadt et al. [2021], and the references cited therein).[3]

Excesses of the Postwar Housing Boom Cities throughout the United States are confronting myriad housing challenges, with much of the academic literature and public debate focused on sky-high housing prices in thriving metropolitan areas like San Francisco, Los Angeles, and Boston (e.g., Bunten 2017; Asquith et al. 2021; Hsieh and Moretti 2019). The dynamic policy case for these cities—permit more housing, streamline environmental re-views, upzoning—has been made in many venues. In this chapter, we seek to call attention to another acute challenge that has received less popular and academic attention: what should cities do with the hangover from the postwar housing boom?

---

[2] Mohl (2004) discusses the urban history of freeway revolts. In the city of Baltimore, for example, city planners initially hired Robert Moses to draw a plan for where highways should be located. The Moses plan projected the displacement of some 19,000 people in the central city, mostly in slums. Moses was quoted stating the benefits of this plan to cut through poorer neighborhoods as "the more of them that are wiped out the healthier Baltimore will be in the long run." The Moses plan drew widespread opposition, primarily from people in the targeted neighborhoods but also from respected Baltimoreans.

[3] Using recent American Community Survey data, Patterson (2020) notes important current trends: 20% of Black households do not have access to an automobile, 24% of public transit riders are Black, the second largest group of riders (even though their share of the US population is 12%), 24% of Blacks live near highly trafficked roads, and 18% of traffic-related pedestrian deaths are Black.

The discrepancies between the nature of the postwar housing stock and the needs of today's economy are stark (Parolek 2020).[4] The postwar period saw a large, sustained housing boom catering to the working- and middle-classes across the entire country, partially in response to provisions in the 1944 GI Bill that allowed returning WWII and Korean War veterans to obtain mortgages with zero down payments and interest rates capped at 4% (Chambers et al. 2014). These policy innovations helped spur a massive building boom in the central cities' outer neighborhoods, as well as in the former farmlands and small towns in their peripheries, turning them into today's inner-ring suburbs (Jackson 1985). The Baby Boom and strong postwar wage growth for young adults made even small houses on small lots enormously appealing (Chambers et al. 2014). In consequence, the average MSA in 2019 had 25.6% of its housing stock built in just that 20-year 1940–1960 period (encompassing WWII and the immediate postwar period). Some MSAs like Detroit, Flint, and Los Angeles have more like 40% of their housing stock from that period.[5]

Today, these houses sell at a discount, particularly in markets where the housing supply has been highly price elastic (Rolheiser 2020).[6] Rolheiser (2020) gives several reasons beyond age why postwar housing is increasingly disfavored. The first is that the average single family home in 1950 was 1,065 square feet, but this same figure had risen to 2,721 by 2015 (see cites within Rolheiser 2020). Second, these homes rarely have any capacity for home offices or other features that would be desired by many higher-earning white-collar workers. Third, most of the population growth in the next 20 years is going to come from

[4] Houses built prior to WWII but after the turn of the last century tended to cater to a rising class of relatively affluent automobile owners, while building housing for working-class people (such as duplexes and triplexes) tapered off (Harris 2013). These houses tend to be somewhat easier targets for redevelopment, because they were built quite close to city centers as the infant paved-road network made it impractical to build too far out. There were some exceptions during this time period, as the 1920's also saw a large number of small, single-family detached houses built for the rising manufacturing workforce in certain cities, such as Detroit (Farley and Danzinger 2000; Martelle 2014), or new boomtowns, such as Greater Miami (Knowlton 2020).

[5] Source: Authors' calculations from the 2019 American Community 1 Year Survey (Table B25034).

[6] We note that these vintage effects favoring pre-1945 housing and discounting postwar housing appear in other countries, such as the Netherlands (Rolheiser et al. 2020).

groups who have few reasons to buy a small-ish, single-family detached home in a suburban area: older households; single-individual households; and households without children (Spader 2019). These homes are too far from city centers to compete for homebuyers desiring dense, walkable neighborhoods, but are also on lots too small to compete with the wide open spaces of the exurbs. Lastly, updating these houses for modern tastes is complicated by the fact that they are overwhelmingly in neighborhoods and cities zoned exclusively for single-family housing (Badger and Bui 2019; Micklow and Warner 2014). These factors make postwar housing an unappealing target for upscale redevelopment, while being also unappealing to downscale homebuyers worried about the budgetary implications of buying an aging home. It is thus little surprise that suburbs with high concentrations of postwar housing have seen rising poverty rates and population losses, particularly those in the postindustrial Midwest (Renn 2017).

Current Trends and Future Outcomes

Restructuring from past mistakes involves not just retooling with current needs in mind, but ideally with future ones as well. There are myriad challenges cities in the United States and elsewhere will face in our tumultuous 21st Century, such as global warming, mass migration, and technological change, but we want to focus on two here that only very recently have received much attention: global population aging and remote working.

Remote Working and Urban Policy A modest but permanent shift toward remote working, particularly among higher earners (Barrero et al. 2021; Dingel and Neiman 2020), will weaken many cities' ability to raise tax revenue through traditional channels, like property and income taxes. Understanding the nature of this challenge requires looking no further than the celebrated Tiebout (1956) model. Tiebout argues that if consumer-voters are fully mobile across localities, then the socially optimal level of public goods provision can actually be obtained thanks to self-sorting by individuals according to their preferences and competition between localities. If occasionally life imitates art, then remote working brings the life of cities one step closer to the simulated world of Tiebout's model.

Cities will need to be dynamic to embrace the reality of this increased competition for residents. First, cities will collect less commercial property taxes than in the past. Even if workers still have to come in to the office at least a couple of times of month, companies will be more reluctant to pay for the kind of physical office space that would sustain having thousands of people in the same building at the same time if that only occurs irregularly.[7]

Second, while cities ideally would simply recoup lost commercial property tax revenues by taxing residential home offices, there are several reasons why it may be impractical. Many states have both property tax caps and homesteading exemptions for homeowners, which effectively limits what cities and school districts can raise from residential property taxes (Twait and Langley 2018). Further, intensified Tiebout competition for high-earning remote workers will make it harder for cities to try to raise land taxes. Those residents most likely to work from home will be even more sensitive to property and income tax rates than they were in the past, now that they no longer have to factor in daily commuting time into their location decisions. We have already seen some of this pattern emerge during the initial remote work shock of the COVID-19 Pandemic, where many residents and businesses decamped from their cities' Central Business District for lower-density suburban ZIP codes (Ramani and Bloom 2021). While we expect some reaggregation to occur after the pandemic ends, several influential commentators (e.g., Glaeser and Cutler 2021; Florida and Ozimek 2021; Fox 2021) expect attracting (or not repelling) remote workers to be a top-tier concern.

Population Aging Pre-industrial cities were "death sinks" affected by many crises, from the increased spread of disease to nutrition concerns. However, as individuals in cities became richer, new evidence notes that the positive income effects of industrial urbanization may have

[7] While we believe that remote working will be higher after the COVID-19 pandemic than before, we note that while office vacancy rates and utilization declined with the onset of the pandemic, there is yet no evidence as of this writing (in Fall 2021) that commercial rents have declined, perhaps because landlords are reluctant to change their rates in either direction until there is more economic clarity (Chung and Dill 2021).

outweighed its negative health effects (Gindelsky and Jedwab 2021). As schooling increased and infant mortality fell, "industrious" residents of large cities likely began decreasing their fertility, focusing on quality over quantity of children.

Fast-forwarding to the present, population growth has seen steady declines across the globe. Individuals are intending to have fewer children than their immediate predecessors, which may translate into a decline in cohort completed parity (Hartnett and Gemmill 2020). Globally, people over 65 are the fastest growing segment of the population and outnumbered children under 5 for the first time in 2019 (Jarzebski et al. 2021). This fact creates a mismatch: many city amenities in "hot cities" are geared more for young, hip adults, leaving them poorly positioned for a world where people 65 and older are expected to be the largest growing demographic.

There are several reasons why fertility has declined. One important reason in the US is that many of the cities with the greatest number of job opportunities for young people also have the highest living costs and consequently the lowest childbearing rates. In San Francisco, for example, only 13% of the population is under 18, compared to 23% nationally (Fuller 2017). Other reasons include that younger individuals were forming their childbearing desires during the Great Recession period that was difficult for childbearing (Kearney et al. 2021),[8] as younger cohorts faced larger financial constraints, such as higher student debt with poorer job prospects, compared with previous generations.

While there are a variety of forces acting to suppress birth rates, the key takeaway is clear: if birth rates continue to stagnate or fall, the number of prospective in-migrants from rural hinterlands, small cities, and countries abroad is expected to fall throughout this coming century, barring a remarkable reversal in birthrates outside of Sub-Saharan Africa. Thus, the challenge facing cities is that they will have to cater to the needs of a growing number of aging residents while simultaneously attempting to

[8] Dettling and Kearney (2014) find that increased housing prices lead to fewer children born. In their analysis, housing prices exert a larger effect on birth rates than unemployment rates.

attract young in-migrants, who will still be needed for economic growth and prosperity.[9]

Policy Responses: Dynamic Is the Answer

If you are a mayor of a city confronting one or more of these challenges—that is to say, practically every mayor in the United States—how do you begin to act? In the past, cities often reinvented themselves either in the aftermath of disasters (e.g., the 1872 Boston Fire, Hornbeck and Keniston 2017) or by running rampant over the rights of the poor, like Baron Haussmann's redevelopment of Paris or Robert Moses' mid-century redevelopment efforts in New York City. We as a society have not yet invented the socio-political technology (if such a thing even exists) that will allow urban policymakers to both redevelop and redesign as needed while also respecting property rights (or without the pretext of a major emergency). This absence is likely playing a role in the frustrations voiced by several cultural and economic commentators about the US' increasingly stagnant economic and physical landscape (e.g., Cowen 2011; Douthat 2020; Andreessen 2020).

Fortunately, there are policies at hand that ameliorate several of these issues simultaneously that do strike precisely this balance. We now highlight a couple of such policies, but a common thread through all of our selected solutions is that mayors, policymakers, and (yes) citizens need to embrace the wisdom of the adage: "If we want everything to stay as it is, everything has to change."

Return to Annexations and Mergers Many cities around the world are struggling with sustainable depopulation strategies (Detroit [Owens et al. 2020], Baltimore, large parts of Germany, Japan, etc.). In response to declining urban populations, cities in the United States have taken a

[9] Of course, general population decline is not the only demographic threat. Highlighting the US experience, the 2020 Census data showed between 2010 and 2020 domestic migration shifts to smaller metros and non-metropolitan counties as jobs and housing began to disperse outward in the aftermath of the Great Recession. This trend may further solidify in the COVID-19 era thanks to the aforementioned remote working shift (Frey 2020).

variety of planning responses. We believe that some of the most important barriers to smart planning are psychological. LaFrombois et al. (2019) summarize these city plans as everything from ignoring population decline to actively incorporating population trends in future plans. For example, despite the fact that Toledo's population has been declining since 1970, the city's 2010 strategic plan stated a population goal of 400,000 (2010 population was 287,208) while having no data to support or justify this goal. As of the 2020 census, Toledo's population stands at 270,871, implying ten years of essentially unproductive spending by the city.[10] Instead of relying on overly optimistic growth forecasts with relative population stagnation likely over the near future, cities may need to rediscover an old solution: annexations.

In the nineteenth and early twentieth centuries, annexations and mergers were the primary means for cities to grow. In fact, Chicago, Philadelphia, and other cities all aggressively annexed surrounding towns, including land that had not even been surveyed yet Jackson (1985). Annexations became less popular throughout the early twentieth century, and essentially ground to a halt in the postwar period, as white-flighting suburbanites used their political muscle to have state legislatures pass laws making it much harder for cities to follow them out to the suburbs via annexations.[11]

With these suburbs now facing demographic and fiscal decline, there are now many good reasons for states to reconsider their laws hindering municipal mergers and annexations. Many of these inner rings, white-flight suburbs suffer from problems compounded by having a high

[10] That is not to say that population decline is irreversible. For example, Washington, DC recovered from a mid-century population slump, in part through active civic engagement and policy planning. In the mid-1990s, business and civic leaders planned and pushed for both a new downtown sports and entertainment arena and the establishment of a downtown business improvement district stretching from the White House to the Capitol Building. Using city-owned land, tax increment financing, tax abatements, arts grants, and zoning changes, the goal was to produce a "living downtown" to complement office buildings with more housing, culture, and entertainment. However, many cities have been trying similar strategies without Washington's success, meaning there is no policy panacea for the decline.

[11] For example, Wisconsin started in the 1950s making it much easier for outlying areas to incorporate (which makes it harder for them to be annexed) and have its courts to interpret the law to make it harder for municipality-initiated annexations to occur. The result is that almost all Wisconsin cities' avenues for growth into unincorporated territory have been closed off (Zeinemann, 2007).

concentration of postwar housing: declining residential and commercial property values, aging housing, and property taxes higher than their anchor cities. A 2017 report by the Manhattan Institute argues that municipal merger and annexation offer a chance to avoid an inequitable situation where poverty becomes concentrated in a band of suburbs on central cities' outskirts while wealth becomes concentrated either near the urban core or in the exurbs—an outcome that the rise of remote working seems even more likely to midwife (Renn 2017). Many of these suburbs face a future of encroaching poverty and fiscal distress. Thus, while their citizens may resist a merger even when the mayor and city council support it—as has already happened in Ecorse, Michigan, and East Cleveland, Ohio—it probably represents the best path forward for the communities themselves.[12]

Mergers have significant benefits for the central cities as well. One is that if growth is now less likely to come from "natural" population forces,[13] then annexation is one way to help maintain a city's population size. Another benefit is that expanding the tax base to include a wider variety of housing can be strategic, because development and redevelopment waves tend to occur over very long cycles interspersed with long periods of sustained low prices (Glaeser and Gyourko 2005; Rosenthal 2008). For example, Indianapolis, which has a consolidated city-county government, was able to maintain fiscal stability over the 1980s and 1990s when the city core was disfavored and the suburbs were prosperous, as well as recently when the core has become wealthier and its de facto inner-ring suburbs have seen rising poverty rates (Renn 2017). Having the age, quality, and design of housing vary over a large area

[12] In both cities, efforts by elected officials to pursue a merger with Detroit and Cleveland (respectively) caused a citizen backlash, resulting in recall campaigns. Readers should bear in mind that these cities are now majority African American, who purposefully sought to *leave* the center cities for the suburbs. The politics of these mergers should thus not be taken for granted by researchers or policymakers, even in the case of extreme fiscal distress.

[13] By "natural," we mean migration, net births, or immigration. All of these have either been in decline for some time or are forecasted to decline as sources for population growth (for migration, see Molloy et al. [2017]; for births, see Kearney et al. [2021]; and for immigration, see Tavernise and Gebeloff [2021]).

helps ensure that at least some part of the municipality will still have highly desired housing on an ongoing basis.[14]

Lastly, more land (and population) means a greater say over how infrastructure is built and maintained in the future. Currently, many mass transportation services have to operate over several different municipalities, each with its own seat at the table. For example, the Boston-area Massachusetts Bay Transportation Authority serves 78 different towns and cities in Massachusetts and Rhode Island, meaning that Boston (the primary employment hub) has a relatively diluted voting share. In some cities like Baltimore and New York, final decisions about public transit funding and expansion are controlled by the state. A consolidated municipal government could thus have more political sway, leaving it better situated to make sure all of its constituent's needs are met, particularly if they are low-income or minority.

We note here that while we believe that larger, more powerful cities could theoretically be more effective custodians of the interests of low-income and minority residents, we also acknowledge (as in this chapter's first section) that this has historically often not been the case. It is imperative that public participation and public trust are fostered either by copying successful policies from other cities or by coming to terms with how past policies and actions encouraged or dampened public approval and the quality of life of local residents (Kahn and McComas 2021). To whit, cities need to do a better job of working with communities, making residents believe that they have a voice, and ensuring that public goods are community based and oriented.

Missing Middle Housing While we think that the empirical literature strongly backs developing large, multi-unit rental housing to address the worst housing shortages in the Coastal United States (e.g., Asquith et al. 2021; Bunten 2017; Hsieh and Moretti 2019; Li 2021; Pennington 2021), we also want to draw attention to what to do with increasingly undesired postwar housing and the "missing middle" housing problem (Parolek 2020). The roadblocks to reinventing or repurposing much

[14] Cities should of course aim not to get overzealous in their annexation attempts. Memphis recently began de-annexing some outlying neighborhoods that were simply not generating enough tax revenues to cover their costs. These neighborhoods tended to be exurban or semi-rural in character, thus much less dense than your average inner-ring suburb.

of this housing are substantial. One major problem is these houses are often found in the neighborhoods where "citizen voice" rings out the most loudly. Specifically, postwar housing is disproportionately found in the little municipalities ringing central cities that are heavily owner-occupied, and are thus heavily incentivized to protect these areas from any changes which might threaten their property values, often militating against densification or rezoning.[15]

The first step is identifying who now comprises the market for these neighborhoods. In our view, these neighborhoods will be a mix of retirees or near-retirees and the working poor and lower middle class: for example, people like the COVID-19 pandemic's much-lauded essential workers. Broadly speaking, these are people who cannot work from home, but make enough money to pursue homeownership for their families. This will be in part a consequence of increasingly aggressive sorting along Tiebout lines, with the wealthy, the young, and the upper-middle class continuing to occupy the city centers[16]; another chunk of people able to work from home will concentrate in the exurbs, as technology slackens the locational tether of the daily commute; and the very poor will probably continue to be disproportionally distributed in rural areas or in certain inner-city neighborhoods.

Thus, this really becomes two questions: how can central cities and their inner-ring suburbs encourage private redevelopment of this housing to accommodate (largely) working- and lower-middle-class non-remote workers? And, given the rising numbers of people retiring in place, what do cities need to do to be able to serve a growing population of older people?[17]

---

[15] As Mast (2020) shows with ward versus at-large representation, councillors representing small geographical units are much less likely to support new housing development.

[16] We suspect that COVID-19 will not dent young, affluent, unmarried people's desire to live in "trendy" parts of large cities. Educational sorting and agglomeration economies continue to ensure that these locations remain the best places for dating for young, college-educated people. While dating can occur remotely, most people (for obvious reasons) will find this undesirable for longer than short stretches.

[17] We expect both groups to grow, spurred jointly by population aging, which will strongly increase the demand for professions like home health aides and nurses (Goodhart and Pradhan 2020).

Putting pressure on single-family housing zoning is the best way to address the shortage of "missing middle" housing that can best serve these groups (Wegmann 2020). While most cities' ability to redevelop housing directly is limited, giving developers a freer hand can make a big difference here even on a parcel-by-parcel basis.[18] Accessory dwelling units (ADU) and duplexes can appeal toward those young working-class and lower-middle-class people whose wages have been stagnant and are still reliant on a daily commute, but want a path toward living in a conventional suburb while they slowly accumulate the money for a down payment. Many duplexes have little backyards children can play in, allowing a young family to start their small children in a local school system while they look for a home. Duplexes can also appeal to older people looking to downsize, but who (for whatever reason) neither want to live in the center city nor out in the exurbs or rural areas. For example, a 60-year old in somewhat poor health may find a duplex close-ish to the center city appealing. They may need to downsize some years before they finish their working careers,[19] and can live on the first floor of a duplex without the inconveniences of stairs or lawn maintenance. Similarly, this same 60-year old could move into their son or daughter's ADU to help them with childcare, while similarly fulfilling their desire to downsize (Micklow and Warner 2014). Fortunately, efforts are already underway in many states and localities to encourage greater density, such as Minneapolis' and Oregon's recent bans on single-family housing; Massachusetts' new law forcing towns to permit multi-family housing near commuter rail stations; and California's new law allowing up to three additional housing units to be built on any plot zoned for single-family housing. For those localities who hold out against densification, the federal or state government can exert further pressure: in exchange for fiscal help to cover property tax shortfalls or grants to local home-owners to cover some of the costs of updating aging homes, the localities have to make changes to their zoning codes to permit "gently" denser

[18] While most developers prefer to operate on big, undeveloped plots of land, great innovations are occurring with manufactured homes and 3D printing to make small-scale development quickly, cheaply, and well, e.g., Kamin (2021).

[19] Asquith (2021) shows that renting has risen steadily among older workers since the Great Recession, particularly among those without a college education.

housing. Gentle densification will (presumably) not excite as much opposition as putting in large new apartment buildings, but will still help put these suburbs on a more sustainable fiscal and demographic path.[20] This leverage can also extend toward improving local transportation options, such as having requirements that these cities cannot oppose efforts to extend commuter rail, subway, or bus lines from the center city into their neighborhoods, which will help ease some of the inequities of the past in newly diversifying suburbs. The result would (hopefully) be that these inner-ring suburbs could be (literally) rejuvenated by new residents who will enjoy expanded housing options reasonably close to the city at a lower carbon impact than exurban development.

Fostering Urban Amenities and Valuing Non-Mobile Businesses Beyond housing and mergers, what else can cities do to maintain their appeal? Here, too, we argue that a dynamic approach that is willing to disrupt the status quo is going to be best suited for orienting a city toward a successful future. For example, one solution to newly underutilized commercial office space could be converting offices into apartments or condos.[21] This greater density can magnify cities' key advantage: the ability to provide large, complex public goods (Glaeser 2000). This same logic could even be applied to decaying parts of the single-family housing stock, where cities may have a freer hand than suburbs to upzone or encourage redevelopment to have home offices.

Cities will also have to consider making a break with a past mindset of pursuing tech companies and the "creative" class, because many of these residents and companies are going to have a much smaller physical footprint going forward.[22] Namely, it will be harder to rationalize throwing millions of dollars of tax breaks at an Amazon HQ3 or a Googleplex2. In contrast, it may increase the value of attracting a major manufacturer or

[20] This is in part because in most states the effective property tax rate on an apartment building of any size is higher than a single-family home, due to "homestead" exemptions.

[21] In fact, this is simply an extension of a trend begun in the 1980's when many abandoned urban factories were converted to loft apartments (Hornick and O'Keefe 1984).

[22] For example, the (Bartik 2018) results on the impact of local incentives are heavily dependent on the assumption that 100% of the directly created jobs will appear in the local area—even relatively small reductions in the number of jobs that might be done remotely greatly diminish the value proposition of most incentive policies.

entertainment industry (like an NFL team), whose value is much more tied to the location in question.

Cities also need to figure out how to square the circle of keeping taxes relatively low while offering more amenities to attract new residents. Amenities or industries that increase appeal and city revenues simultaneously are probably the desired sweet spot. For example, if a permanent increase in remote working leads to less road utilization and housing demand, then cities can experiment with amenities like pedestrian malls and urban farming. Pedestrian malls in particular are famously attractive to residents, cheap for cities to implement, and increase the property values of nearby buildings (Amos 2019).[23] More speculatively, another solution that views amenities as both an attraction and as a source of revenue could be something like a publicly funded maker space. People could walk in, register, a program in CAD anything that they want to be produced in an advanced manufacturing setting, and then walk home with the prototype. The maker space, like private ones, could offer classes on welding, sewing, metal stamping, etc. This would be a location-specific amenity that would be valued by entrepreneurs and hobbyists who would want to live nearby. By the same token, it could also be a tax opportunity, because the city could then claim a small fraction of the royalties generated by any patents or businesses that emerge from its maker space. To keep claims of originality and ownership straight, each CAD design could be registered on a city-operated blockchain. There are of course some significant technical, financial, and legal challenges that would have to be overcome for the municipal assessors office to establish a stake in the profits or royalties from projects that would emerge from the maker space, and a city would initially not earn any of these tax revenues for quite some time. That said, with capital and labor more mobile than ever before, and labor on track to become scarcer as well, municipalities will need to find creative solutions to resolve some of the problems created by a smaller, more flighty tax base.

Ultimately, it is in the interest of national and state policymakers to encourage these experiments in local amenity creation and tax collection.

---

[23] They can also be successfully implemented in fairly small cities. The first city to build one was Kalamazoo, Michigan, whose current population is about 76,000.

While another intriguing possibility is to dangle incentives for remote workers to relocate, currently pursued by places like Tulsa (Tulsa Remote) and West Virginia (Ascend WV), there are still inherent limits to having municipalities chase a limited pool of relatively mobile remote workers. While some of this Tiebout-like competition will probably lead to better public goods provision than in its absence, classic Tiebout competition with property taxes can actually be socially *suboptimal* (Calabrese et al. 2012), a point policymakers should bear in mind.

Final Thoughts

Whether we are looking back or looking forward, it is easy to list the problems cities face. We ourselves begin by observing the consequences of past urban policies. Exclusionary loaning practices and highway construction in center cities have led to disproportionately negative effects on minorities in inner city neighborhoods. The boom of postwar housing construction has left present-day city residents with a mismatch between the housing stock as it exists and the housing they prefer. Issues like the rise of remote workers and population aging highlight the challenges cities will find lying ahead.

Giving cities the ability to experiment, be bold, and be flexible in addressing past, current, and future issues is of utmost importance if we want them (and their residents) to thrive. We suggest several policies that will allow cities to do just that. A push for cities to embrace annexations and mergers could simultaneously alleviate concerns about urban depopulation as well as provide housing-type diversification and make more inclusive transportation choices feasible. Specially, focusing on rewriting current zoning laws or incentivizing construction of the "missing middle" housing stock could allow cities to attract new residents and provide current residents with more housing options. Finally, encouraging cities to lean into their respective amenity comparative advantages, as well as thinking about realistic but innovative new amenities, could be a potential cure for population aging and the flightiness of remote workers.

Ultimately, we view these policy responses as being united thematically by giving cities a freer hand to grow, build, and experiment. We also argue that it is important that policymakers continue to leave room for private actors to innovate and build as well. The Greene Street Project of Easterly et al. (2016) ably demonstrates the limits of policy and the importance of private actors. The project maps out the 400-year long evolution of one block of Greene Street in Manhattan's SoHo neighborhood. Given that the block is currently highly affluent, it is somewhat of a surprise that the block was much more working class for most of its history, including hosting brothels and factories. The reader inexorably draws the lesson from the Greene Street Project that policymakers who may have been tempted at any given point in its history to freeze it in time would likely have derailed its socioeconomic ascent and done their city a disservice.

At the end of the day, cities will always have problems to solve. The problems themselves may fade into the past, or they may change and become more acute. The only reasonable response is for cities themselves to retain a willingness to disrupt the status quo, even (or especially) when it is backed by powerful constituents, find ways to harness the vital energies of their residents, and maintain a balance between present decisiveness and future flexibility.

References

Aaronson D, Hartley DA, Mazumder B (2021) The effects of the 1930s HOLC 'Redlining' maps. American Economic Journal: Economic Policy, Forthcoming.

Amos D (2019) Understanding the legacy of pedestrian malls. Journal of the American Planning Association 86:11–24.

Anderson ML (2020) As the wind blows: The effects of long-term exposure to air pollution on mortality. Journal of the European Economic Association 18:1886–1927.

Andreessen M (2020) It's time to build. Marc Andreessen's Blog.

Asquith BJ (2021) Why are older workers moving less while working longer? Working Paper.

Asquith BJ, Mast E, Reed D (2021) Local effects of large new apartment buildings in low-income areas. The Review of Economics and Statistics, Forthcoming.

Badger E, Bui Q (2019) Cities start to question an American ideal: A house with a yard on every lot. The New York Times.

Barrero JM, Bloom N, Davis SJ (2021) Why working from home will stick. Working Paper 28731, National Bureau of Economic Research.

Bartik TJ (2018) Who benefits from economic development incentives? How incentive effects on local incomes and the income distribution vary with different assumptions about incentive policy and the local economy. Technical report.

Baum-Snow N (2007) Did highways cause suburbanization? The Quarterly Journal of Economics 122(2):775–805.

Brinkman J, Lin J (2019) Freeway Revolts! Working Papers 19-29, Federal Reserve Bank of Philadelphia.

Bunten DM (2017) Is the rent too high? Aggregate implications of local land-use regulation (2017-064).

Calabrese SM, Epple DN, Romano RE (2012) Inefficiencies from metropolitan political and fiscal decentralization: Failures of Tiebout competition. Review of Economic Studies 79(3):1081–1111.

Chambers M, Garriga C, Schlagenhauf DE (2014) Did housing policies cause the postwar boom in home ownership?, pp 351–385.

Chung J, Dill J (2021) Has the COVID-19 pandemic affected demand for office space? Federal Reserve Bank of Atlanta's Macroblog.

Cowen T (2011) The great stagnation: How America ate all the low-hanging fruit of modern history, got sick, and will (eventually) feel better. Dutton Adult.

Dettling LJ, Kearney MS (2014) House prices and birth rates: The impact of the real estate market on the decision to have a baby. Journal of Public Economics 110:82–100.

Dingel JI and Neiman B (2020) How many jobs can be done at home? Journal of Public Economics 189:104235–104242.

Douthat R (2020) The decadent society: How we became victims of our own success. Simon and Schuster.

Easterly W, Freschi L, Pennings S (2016) A long history of a short block: Four centuries of development surprises on a single stretch of a New York City street. Working Paper 97, Development Research Institute.

Farley R, Danzinger S (2000) Detroit Divided. Russell Sage Foundation, New York.

Fishback PV, Rose J, Snowden KA, Storrs T (2021) New evidence on redlining by federal housing programs in the 1930s. Technical report, National Bureau of Economic Research.

Florida R, Ozimek A (2021) How remote work is reshaping America's urban geography. Wall Street Journal. Accessed: September 2021.

Fox J (2021) Superstar cities are (probably) immune from WFH. Bloomberg. Accessed: September 2021.

Frey WH (2020) Even before coronavirus, census shows U.S. cities' growth was stagnating. Brookings. Accessed: September 2021.

Fuller T (2017) San francisco asks: Where have all the children gone? The New York Times. Accessed: October 2021.

Gindelsky M, Jedwab R (2021) Killer cities and industrious cities? New data and evidence on 250 years of urban growth. Working paper.

Glaeser EL (2000) Demand for density? The functions of the city in the 21st Century. Brookings Papers on Economic Activity. Accessed: September 2021.

Glaeser EL, Cutler D (2021) Survival of the city: Living and thriving in an age of isolation. Penguin Press.

Glaeser EL, Gyourko J (2005) Urban decline and durable housing. Journal of Political Economy 113:345–375.

Goodhart C, Pradhan M (2020) The great demographic reversal: Ageing societies, waning inequality, and an inflation revival. Palgrave Macmillan.

Harris R (2013) The rise of filtering down: The American housing market transformed, 1915–1929. Social Science History 37.

Hartnett C, Gemmill A (2020) Recent trends in U.S. childbearing intentions. Demography 57:2035–2045.

Herrnstadt E, Heyes A, Muehlegger E, Saberian S (2021) Air pollution and criminal activity: Microgeographic evidence from Chicago. American Economic Journal: Applied Economics 13:70–100.

Hornbeck R, Keniston D (2017) Creative destruction: Barriers to urban growth and the Great Boston Fire of 1872. American Economic Review 107:1365–1398.

Hornick S, O'Keefe S (1984) Reusing industrial loft buildings for housing: Experiences of New York City in revitalization and misuse. Washington University Joural of Urban & Contemporray Law 27:157–212.

Hsieh C-T, Moretti E (2019) Housing constraints and spatial misallocation. American Economic Journal: Macroeconomics 11(2):1–39.

Jackson KT (1985) Crabgrass Frontier: The Suburbanization of the United States. Oxford University Press.

Jarzebski MP, Elmqvist T, Gasparatos A, Fukushi K, Eckersten S, Haase D, Goodness J, Khoshkar S, Saito O, Takeuchi K, et al (2021) Ageing and population shrinking: Implications for sustainability in the urban century. npj Urban Sustainability 1(1):1–11.

Kahn ME, McComas M (2021) Unlocking the potential of post-industrial cities. Johns Hopkins University Press.

Kamin D (2021) How an 11-foot-tall 3-D printer is helping to create a community. The New York Times. Accessed: September 2021.

Kearney MS, Levine PB, Pardue LW (2021) The puzzle of falling US birth rates since the Great Recession. Working Paper 29286, National Bureau of Economic Research.

Knowlton C (2020) Bubble in the sun: The Florida boom of the 1920's and how it brought on the great depression. Simon and Schuster.

LaFrombois MEH, Park Y, Yurcaba D (2019) How U.S. shrinking cities plan for change: Comparing population projections and planning strategies in depopulating U.S. cities. Journal of Planning Education and Research 0(0):1–13.

Li X (2021) Do new housing units in your backyard raise your rents? Journal of Economic Geography.

Martelle S (2014) Detroit: A Biography. Chicago Review Press, Chicago.

Mast E (2020) Warding off development: Local control, housing supply, and NIMBYs. Upjohn Institute Working Paper #20-330.

Micklow AC, Warner ME (2014) Not your mother's suburb: Remaking communities for a more diverse population. Urban Lawyer 46:729–751.

Mohl RA (2004) Stop the road: Freeway revolts in American cities. Journal of Urban History 30(5):674–706.

Molloy R, Smith CL, Wozniak A (2017) Job changing and the decline in long-distance migration in the United States. Demography 54:631–653.

Owens I R, Rossi-Hansberg E, Sarte P-D (2020) Rethinking Detroit. American Economic Journal: Economic Policy 12(2):258–305.

Parolek DG (2020) Missing Middle Housing. Island Press.

Patterson RF (2020) New routes to equity: The future of transportation in the Black community. Report, Congressional Black Caucus Foundation.

Pennington K (2021) Does building new housing cause displacement? The supply and demand effects of construction in San Francisco. Technical report.

Ramani A, Bloom N (2021) The donut effect of COVID-19 on cities. Working Paper 28876, National Bureau of Economic Research.

Renn AM (2017) Mergers may rescue declining suburbs. Policy brief, Manhattan Institute.
Rolheiser L (2020) Old, small and unwanted: Post-war housing and neighbourhood socioeconomic status. Urban Studies.
Rolheiser L, van Dijk D, van de Minne A (2020) Housing vintage and price dynamics. Regional Science and Urban Economics 84:103569.
Rosenthal SS (2008) Old homes, externalities, and poor neighborhoods. A model of urban decline and renewal. Journal of Urban Economics 63(3):816–840.
Spader, J. (2019). Tenure projections of homeowner and renter households for 2018–2038. Technical report.
Tavernise S, Gebeloff R (2021) U.S. population over last decade grew at slowest rate since 1930s. The New York Times. Accessed: October 2021.
Tiebout CM (1956) A pure theory of local expenditures. Journal of Political Economy 64:416–424.
Twait A, Langley AH (2018) 50-state property tax comparison study. Policy brief, Lincoln Land Institute.
Wegmann J (2020) Death to single-family zoning… and new life to the missing middle. Journal of the American Planning Association 86:113–119.
Zeinemann RD (2007) Overlooked linkages between municipal incorporation and annexation laws: An in-depth look at Wisconsin's experience. The Urban Lawyer 39:257–317.

3

What's Wrong with American Land Use: Market Failures, Bad Policies, or Politics?

Jenny Schuetz

In 2013, the city of Irwindale, California, filed a lawsuit against Huy Fong Foods, the producer of Sriracha hot sauce. Some residents had complained about the smell of roasting chiles wafting from the factory into their neighborhoods. The complaints created an unenviable position for city council members: while some voters were unhappy about the odor, the company employed 70 year-round workers and more during peak bottling season, creating substantial revenues for the city (Lovett 2014). The case illustrates a key fact of urban development: the structures and economic activity that occupy a piece of land can have a variety of different impacts—both positive and negative—on people who live or work nearby.[1] That is, land use almost always involves externalities.

[1] Five years later, the city and company ceased mutual legal hostilities, and production continues today (San Gabriel Valley Tribune 2018).

J. Schuetz (✉)
Brookings Institution, Washington, DC, USA
e-mail: jschuetz@brookings.edu

A. L. Kassens and J. C. Hall (eds.), *Challenges in Classical Liberalism*, Palgrave Studies in Classical Liberalism,
https://doi.org/10.1007/978-3-031-32890-9_3

Because the impacts are often complex, involve multiple parties, and can occur at a range of spatial scales, designing public policies that encourage developers and property owners to internalize the costs or benefits is no simple task.

In this essay, I discuss how current land use governance in the U.S. attempts to mitigate spillovers and several limitations of existing policies. The U.S. has assigned governance of land use to local governments, which rely heavily on input from existing homeowners in regulating urban development. Over the past several decades, land use governance has become increasingly complex and discretionary, contributing to higher housing costs and limited supply, especially in high-opportunity locations. The governance system focuses mostly on preventing hyper-local negative externalities and limiting city-level fiscal costs, while largely ignoring regional labor market and climate impacts. The political dominance of land use governance by affluent, mostly white homeowners exacerbates racial and economic segregation and limits economic mobility for low- and moderate-income households.

How Does Land Use Regulation in the U.S. Work?

The market for urban development—broadly encompassing land, residential and commercial buildings, and urban infrastructure—has several unusual features that distinguish it from many other goods and services. The U.S. has chosen to assign regulatory power over land use to local governments within a legal framework created by state governments, leading to wide variation across places in how land markets function (or don't function). A property owner who wishes to build, demolish, or substantially alter a structure on land that she owns must generally receive permission from the local government in which the land is located.[2] The federal government has relatively little direct influence over

[2] New construction and demolition are almost always regulated in some way by city or county governments, while requirements to alter existing structures vary more widely. For instance, Washington, D.C. requires property owners to receive permits and pay fees in order to

land use decisions; even the construction of federally subsidized housing is subject to local regulations.

Cities and counties use a number of different policy tools to regulate land use, beginning with zoning laws. Zoning enumerates what types of structures or activities (e.g., single-family detached homes, daycare centers, golf courses) are permitted on all land parcels within the jurisdiction (Desegregate CT 2021; Schuetz 2019). Zoning laws also establish dimensional requirements for each structure type, such as minimum lot size, maximum building height, or minimum number of off-street parking spaces. And they define the process by which the local government grants permission to develop—or redevelop—land. One approach is to allow structures or uses "by right," also referred to as "ministerial approval," meaning that development proposals can be reviewed and approved by administrative staff (usually in the locality's planning or building department), as long as the proposal conforms to specified dimensional requirements.

Alternatively, the local government may require additional review for building types referred to as "conditional uses" or "special uses" (Dain 2019; Schuetz 2008, 2009). The process required to receive a conditional use permit varies widely across localities—and even across neighborhoods within a locality—but typically the developer or property owner must hold public meetings where residents can voice their opinions over the proposal. Conditional use permits sometimes require (super) majority votes from elected or appointed officials, such as city councils, county supervisors, or Zoning Boards (Quigley and Raphael 2005). On the face of it, requiring conditional use permits might not be a substantial obstacle to development. Officials in growth-friendly jurisdictions may approve proposals with little additional time or cost than that required for by-right development. But creating an overlay process introduces more uncertainty into the outcome of a given proposal—effectively increasing the riskiness of development.

Besides zoning laws, urban development is subject to numerous other regulations: building codes, environmental laws, historic preservation,

replace exterior windows and doors—an alteration that does not require government permits in Birmingham, AL.

and fiscal tools such as impact fees (HUD 2021). Most of these regulations are also adopted and administered by local governments, although state governments play an important role in defining the tools available to localities. For instance, reliance on impact fees is higher in states where legislatures have restricted localities' ability to levy (or increase) property and/or sales taxes (Haveman and Sexton 2008).

Since the 1970s, land use governance in the U.S. has become increasingly discretionary rather than rules-based (Dain 2019; Dougherty 2020; Schuetz 2008). The process for changing laws (updating Comprehensive Plans and zoning codes) and for developing individual land parcels often explicitly requires community engagement—effectively giving existing residents veto power over changes to their neighborhood. Manville and Osman (2017) describe the current approach as "pretextual zoning": local governments adopt rules that are more restrictive than they actually want, in order to set up negotiations with developers for financial contributions. For instance, zoning might require developers to build three structured parking spaces for each new two-bedroom apartment, which could increase construction costs by $150,000 per unit, but offer to reduce parking requirements if the developer agrees to set aside 10% of the apartments for low-income residents, or provide a cash contribution toward renovating neighborhood schools. Strict written regulations allow local governments to shift the financial burden of improving public services onto developers and, by extension, onto consumers of newly built housing, without having to raise taxes on existing residents.

While zoning and other regulations apply to both residential and nonresidential uses, this essay (like most of the existing literature) focuses primarily on how land use governance affects residential development. Even in major cities, the majority of land is designated for residential use. As discussed below, the availability and cost of housing has direct implications on household well-being, and prior research has demonstrated that current systems of land use governance have created harmful distortions in housing market outcomes.

Urban Development Generates Spillovers That Are Unevenly Distributed Across Space

Changes in land use can create costs and benefits for surrounding communities. Some impacts tend to be most concentrated on spatially nearest neighbors, although broader fiscal and environmental impacts can occur at the jurisdiction and regional scale. Disaggregating the types of costs and benefits associated with urban development yields useful insights into the political economy of zoning: what unwanted activities are communities trying to prevent through land use regulation, and which households stand to gain or lose from restrictive zoning.

The traditional economic rationale for zoning (and related laws like building codes) is to mitigate direct impacts of unpleasant land uses on immediately adjacent neighbors (New York City 1916; Shertzer et al. 2022). As the Huy Fong Foods example illustrates, industrial activities can pollute the air, water, or land. High-rise buildings block sunlight for shorter buildings. Adding more homes, offices, and shops to existing communities invites more traffic congestion and generates more demand for parking. Poorly constructed or maintained properties are visually unappealing. In the view of Progressive Era reformers who advocated for more oversight of housing development, while low-income households may be willing to live in overcrowded, shoddily built fire-traps, such buildings pose health and safety threats to the surrounding community as well as residents themselves.

On the flip side, well-maintained residential and commercial properties create positive spillovers for their neighbors. Jane Jacobs (1961) famously posited that socially active neighborhoods with diverse land uses serve as "eyes on the street" to deter crime and provide collective oversight of children. A beautifully landscaped garden benefits neighbors who contribute nothing to its maintenance—an externality that underpins the formation of homeowners' associations and commercial business improvement districts (Ellen et al. 2007; Cheung and Meltzer 2014).

Positive and negative externalities from nearby land uses affect their neighbors in direct quality-of-life interactions and are capitalized into property values. Amenities like community gardens can increase nearby home prices (Voicu and Been 2008), while undesirable activities like foreclosures drive down prices (Gerardi et al. 2015; Hartley 2014; Mian et al. 2015; Schuetz et al. 2008). Home equity is the largest single financial asset for middle-income households (Fig. 3.1), which makes homeowners financially as well as personally invested in potential changes to their neighborhoods (Fischel 2005).

Renter households are also impacted by nearby land uses, although the impacts are more complicated than on homeowners. An increase in nearby amenities is unambiguously good for homeowners: it improves their quality of life and increases asset values. Renter households may experience consumption value from the opening of a new park or coffeeshop, but it may also translate into higher monthly rent payments. This tension can show up in public reactions to development proposals, especially in moderate- or lower-income communities: renters may oppose projects that appear to upgrade local amenities, because of concerns that rents would rise faster than the income of existing residents (Hankinson 2018).

The fiscal impacts of urban development can potentially affect the entire political jurisdiction (city or county) in which a land parcel is located. For local governments, an essential question in governing land

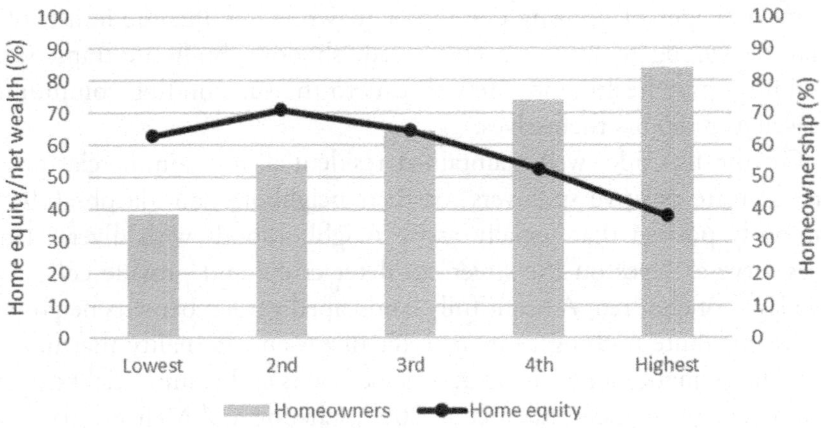

Fig. 3.1 Home equity is the largest financial asset for middle-income households. Homeownership rates and housing equity by income quintile (*Source* Author's calculations using data from Survey of Income and Program Participation 2015)

use is how new developments will impact the consumption of locally funded public services, relative to tax revenues generated. Net fiscal impacts can be complicated to predict, because they vary by the size and type of development project, as well as local and state tax policies. New residential developments that attract in-migration of households with children will increase the demand for schools—one of the largest expenses for local governments. Some localities overtly use age-restricted zoning to limit in-migration of households with children (Zegras et al. 2012). Other substantial expenditure categories for local governments include public safety (police, fire, emergency services), parks and recreational facilities, health services, roads and transportation. Commercial developments such as offices and retail may not directly increase demand for schools, but could increase usage of roads and public transportation systems. Entertainment venues, such as bars, nightclubs, and sports arenas may require increased public safety expenditures.

Revenues generated by new development also vary by type of development, as well as the set of fiscal tools available to local governments. Property taxes make up nearly half of local government direct revenues, excluding inter-governmental transfers (Fig. 3.2). While property taxes are typically assessed on both residential and commercial properties, in some states, local governments may set different millage rates by property type, thus altering the fiscal incentives for allowing development. Local sales taxes and related tools such as hospitality taxes (applied to restaurant meals and hotels) may also make commercial development more financially appealing than housing to local governments. The type of fiscal tools available to local governments varies across states. Forty-four states and the District of Columbia have imposed some limits on local governments' taxing abilities, such as caps on property tax rates or limits on annual increases to taxes (Lincoln Institute 2020).

Land use regulations offer local governments an alternative way to manage the fiscal impacts of development, sometimes referred to as "fiscal zoning" (Fischel 2013). Governments can use tools such as large minimum lot sizes and apartment bans to limit development of lower-valued homes, which are perceived to impose net fiscal losses (Furth and Gray 2019). Fiscal zoning generally precludes new development

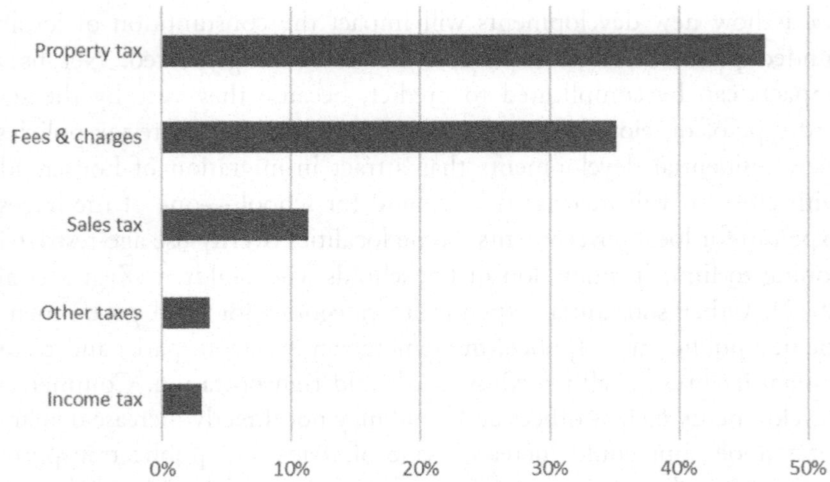

Fig. 3.2 Local governments rely heavily on property taxes. Percent of own-source local government revenue (2017) (*Source* Author's calculations using data from Urban-Brookings Tax Policy Center. Excludes transfers from state and federal governments)

of housing affordable to low- and moderate-income households, especially renters, so over time fiscally zoned communities become less economically and racially diverse.

The third category of externalities associated with urban development, environmental impacts, have the broadest potential geographic scope. Where new homes, offices, shops, and factories are built—or not built—within metro areas has substantial impacts on regional and national carbon footprints (Glaeser and Kahn 2010; Kahn 2007). Since the 1950s, housing growth has been consistently higher in suburban and exurban counties than in the urban core (Raphael and Stoll 2010). Suburban dwellers have larger household carbon footprints than their urban counterparts, largely because of differences in housing consumption and transportation (Jones and Kammen 2014). The dominant housing type in suburbs is a single-family detached house, which consumes more energy than an apartment in a multifamily building. Post-World War II suburbs were designed around two climate unfriendly features: low-density residential neighborhoods that are difficult to serve efficiently with public transit, and strict separation between housing and commercial activities. Households in suburban areas thus rely primarily on solo driving for commuting, shopping, entertainment, and other daily activities, and travel longer distances on average than urban households. At the regional level, accommodating population and job growth through infill development—increasing density close to city centers and public transportation—creates less environmental harm than the typical U.S. model of low-density suburban development.

Overly Strict Land Use Regulation Has Some Serious Downsides

Figuring out how to effectively mitigate the negative externalities associated with urban development without creating additional market distortions may be possible in theory, but in practice, land use regulations across much of the U.S. fall well short of this goal. In many locations, land use governance focuses on preventing hyperlocal negative externalities—like building apartments next to single-family homes—while ignoring regional environmental impacts and economic mobility. Excessively restrictive land use regulations create three (somewhat related) problems. First, in metro areas with strong demand for housing but tight constraints on housing development, regulations lead to inadequate supply and artificially high housing costs, which makes it hard for employers to attract and retain workers. Second, limiting housing supply near job centers and public transit pushes growth toward the urban fringe, leading to longer commutes and environmentally harmful development patterns. Third, restrictive zoning in affluent, mostly white communities with high-quality public services limits economic mobility for low- and moderate-income households, while reinforcing economic and racial segregation.

One of the most common ways that land use regulations distort housing markets is by limiting density, or the number of homes that can be built on a given land parcel. Most directly, localities use zoning to prohibit any structure other than single-family detached homes—a structure type that requires more land per housing unit. Even in large cities, more than three-quarters of land is zoned exclusively for single-family detached houses, a designation that is rarely changed (Badger and Bui 2019; Ellickson 2020). Other dimensional restrictions intended to limit density include minimum lot sizes, caps on building height, maximum floor-to-area ratios, and minimum setbacks (Glaeser et al. 2006; Murray and Schuetz 2019). While single-family detached homes can generally be built as of right, many communities require developers to obtain conditional use permits for multifamily buildings (Dain 2019; Schuetz 2008; Schuetz 2009).

Whether zoning effectively limits housing density relative to unregulated markets, and what kinds of rules would constitute binding constraints, depends on underlying land values, construction costs, and the expected rents or prices of new housing. Developers seek to build high-density housing—small quantities of land per housing unit—in locations where land is expensive. Vertical construction requires more expensive construction materials (steel and concrete versus wood) and labor, while allowing developers to reduce the amount of land used. High-rise apartments are likely to maximize developer profits in downtown San Francisco and Manhattan, but make no financial sense in rural Texas.

Urban economists and other housing scholars have for decades grappled with the best way to measuring zoning stringency, in order to estimate the impacts of zoning on housing outcomes such as prices and production levels. Gyourko and Molloy (2014) offer a comprehensive review of methods used to measure regulatory restrictiveness and summarize findings from an extensive empirical literature. Because of the complexity and labor-intensive nature of collecting data on zoning, studies vary widely in specific metrics, geographic areas studied, and empirical approaches. Nonetheless, research has produced a strong consensus about which parts of the U.S. have been substantially constrained by regulations. Large West Coast metros including the San Francisco Bay Area, Southern California, Seattle, and Portland rank high on most indices of regulatory stringency, as well as the Boston, New York, and Washington, D.C. metros (Hsieh and Moretti 2019; Glaeser and Gyourko 2018; Gyourko et al. 2008). While a strong labor market (the main driver of housing demand) is a necessary prerequisite for regulatory constraints to bind, there are clear examples of metros with strong housing demand but relatively elastic housing supply. Notably, Sunbelt metros from Atlanta to Houston to Phoenix have absorbed large population and job growth without much increase in housing costs, because their flexible regulations have allowed supply to expand.

At the national and regional scale, regulations that limit housing growth and increase costs translate into substantial macroeconomic impacts. Hsieh and Moretti (2019) estimate that restrictive land use regulations slowed GDP growth in the U.S. by about 36% between 1964 and 2009. Firms in high-cost regions have difficulty hiring and retaining workers, restricting potential growth and innovation, while some workers wind up with lower-paid jobs in less productive regions.

While research that highlights the macroeconomic costs of regulation helps draw attention to the problem of high-cost regions, it is important to recognize that regulations vary widely across local jurisdictions within regions, and even across neighborhoods within a single city or county. Not all localities in constrained regions like the Bay Area and Boston are equally resistant to growth. Land use governance in metro areas like Atlanta, Baltimore, Houston, and St. Louis may not impact regional labor markets or reduce U.S. aggregate growth, but the practices of individual jurisdictions can contribute to other problems, particularly limited economic mobility and climate change.

Opposition to housing growth in general, and high-density housing in particular, is most frequent among affluent, predominantly white communities (Einstein 2021; Murray and Schuetz 2019; Rothstein 2017; Trounstine 2018). For instance, within the Washington, D.C. metro area, wealthy jurisdictions like Falls Church city and Arlington County, Virginia, had much slower housing growth between 2000 and 2017 than middle-income counties like Prince William, Virginia, and Frederick, Maryland (Begley et al. 2019). The same pattern is visible looking across neighborhoods within jurisdictions. Wealthy neighborhoods in the District of Columbia, including Georgetown, Capitol Hill, and Kalorama, have built almost no additional housing following the Great Recession, while the bulk of new development was concentrated in middle-income neighborhoods with more flexible zoning (Schuetz

2020). Nor is this pattern unique to high-cost regions: wealthy, predominantly white suburbs like Highland Park (near Dallas) and Bloomfield Hills (near Detroit) wield restrictive zoning to limit new development, especially of multifamily rental housing (Schuetz 2022).

Restrictive zoning in wealthy areas reinforces economic and racial segregation and limits economic mobility. If low-wage workers cannot afford to rent homes in affluent neighborhoods, their children typically are not eligible to attend the high-quality public schools in those areas.

Research from the Opportunity Insights team (Chetty et al. 2014, 2016) shows that where people live is strongly correlated with intergenerational mobility: children who grow up in places with lower residential segregation and less income inequality tend to do better as adults than their parents. Children who move to low-poverty neighborhoods when they are young have higher incomes as adults—an outcome that benefits the entire country. Adults also benefit from the opportunity to move to low-poverty neighborhoods, experiencing better mental health outcomes from living in a safer and less stressful environment (Ludwig et al. 2013).

Across the U.S., Black and Latino households have substantially lower incomes and wealth than non-Hispanic white households and are much more likely to rent their homes (Bhutta et al. 2020). (The income gap between Asian and white households is less consistent, varying by geography.) Zoning restrictions on multifamily housing in affluent neighborhoods may not be intended to restrict access to Black and Latino families, but they certainly have that effect.

Hyperlocal Land Use Governance Leads to Inefficient Regional Outcomes

The scale at which land use governance operates has become increasingly mismatched with the goals of the mitigating externalities arising from urban development. A system designed around empowering existing residents to block hyperlocal nuisances—the Jane Jacobs model of citizen engagement—is not well suited to meeting the housing, transportation, and public service needs of regional labor markets. Each homeowner, neighborhood, and local city council has financial incentives to block less desirable land uses, such as moderately priced apartments, Big Box stores, and wastewater treatment facilities. But a region that lacks those components of physical and economic infrastructure will struggle to support households and businesses.

The growing popularity of impact fees illustrates the spatial mismatch between local (e.g., city or county-specific) incentives and regional needs. Since the 1960s, local governments increasingly rely on impact fees assessed against new development to cover the costs of locally provided public services, such as water and sewer systems, roads, sidewalks, schools, and public safety (Been 2005). In theory, impact fees are an efficient way to pay for such investments, because they force developers and consumers of newly built housing to internalize the costs of growth on existing residents (Brueckner 1997). But formal models of impact fees often assume that policymakers who design and implement impact fees operate at the geographic scale corresponding to a regional labor and housing market (e.g., a metropolitan area). In reality, large metro areas often consist of more than 100 incorporated places and/or counties, each of which writes its own zoning code and sets its own impact fees. If jurisdictions in the urban core—say, small residential suburbs adjacent to Boston—choose policies that limit housing growth near large job centers and commuter rail stations, while jurisdictions on the urban fringe have permissive land use regulation, subsequent development patterns will yield more commuters traveling longer distances and creating more aggregate traffic. For impact fees to produce efficient regional growth patterns, policies would need to be shifted to regional governments or would require better coordination between localities.

Political science suggests another limitation of delegating land use to local governments. Older, wealthy, white homeowners are disproportionately represented among elected officials and in the ostensibly democratic public engagement process (Einstein et al. 2019). Even in large cities with majority-renter populations, a super-majority of mayors and city council members are homeowners. Moreover, existing residents in any community are, by definition, people who can afford to live in that community. Many of the households that would benefit from expanding and diversifying housing supply in high-opportunity communities do not live in those communities now, and so have no voice in proposed developments or policy changes.

Conclusion and Future Policy Directions

Land use and urban development can create several categories of spillover effects on surrounding areas at varying spatial scales. Immediately adjacent neighbors worry about nuisances that impact their quality of life and drive down property values. Local governments try to assess the net fiscal impact of new residential and commercial developments. Regional population and job growth patterns impact greenhouse gas emissions, thereby contributing to climate change. The widespread presence of externalities suggests a role for public policy to improve the efficiency of urban land markets. However, current land use governance systems in the U.S. focus mostly on the smallest scale externalities, while exacerbating larger environmental, economic, and social problems.

Local, state, and federal policymakers have recently shown increasing interest in reforming land use regulations. In 2018, Minneapolis became the first major city to legalize small multifamily buildings in all residential parts of the city, effectively ending single-family exclusive zoning (Grabar 2018). The state of Oregon adopted similar reforms the following year. California, Connecticut, and Massachusetts have all passed statewide zoning reforms of varying scale and ambition within the past year (Schuetz 2022). During the 2020 campaign, nearly all Democratic presidential candidates had housing platforms mentioning the need for regulatory reform. This level of national political attention to the harms created by excessively strict zoning is unprecedented. But major reforms face widespread opposition from one of the largest and most powerful interest groups in the U.S.—home voters.

Two caveats are important to avoid overselling the benefits of better land use policy. First, housing availability and affordability in high-demand places will take time to show substantial improvement, even if large-scale zoning reform happened tomorrow. Supply-constrained metro areas have underbuilt housing for several decades, and new construction takes time, even under a more streamlined process.

Second, zoning reform alone will not solve housing affordability for low-income households. The poorest 20% of U.S. renters spend over half of their income on housing even in parts of the country where regulations are flexible and housing is abundant (Larrimore and Schuetz 2017). Affordability for the poorest households is driven primarily by low incomes: they earn too little to cover the operating costs of market-rate housing without direct subsidies (Mallach 2019). Making it easier to build rental housing in high-opportunity neighborhoods could expand the reach of existing programs, such as housing vouchers, but the gap between income and rent will still require subsidy. Zoning reform is a necessary but not sufficient condition for improved housing stability for low-income Americans.

References

Badger E, Bui Q (2019) Cities start to question an American ideal: A house with a yard on every lot. New York Times, 18 June.

Been V (2005) Impact fees and housing affordability. Cityscape: J Pol Dev Res 8:139–185.

Begley J, Brooks L, McCabe B, Schuetz J (2019) State of the capitol region's housing 2019. GWU Center for Washington Area Studies, Washington DC.

Bhutta N, Chang AC, Dettling LJ, Hsu JW (2020) Disparities in wealth by race and ethnicity in the 2019 Survey of Consumer Finances. Board of Governors of the Federal Reserve System, FEDS Notes 2020-09-28.

Brueckner J (1997) Infrastructure financing and urban development: The economics of impact fees. J Pub Econ 66:383–407.

Chetty R, Hendren N, Kline P, Saez E (2014) Where is the land of opportunity? The geography of inter-generational mobility in the United States. Q J Econ 129:1553–1623.

Chetty R, Hendren N, Katz L (2016) The effects of exposure to better neighborhoods on children: New evidence from the Moving to Opportunity experiment. Amer Econ Rev 106:855–902.

Cheung R, Meltzer R (2014) How are homeowners associations capitalized into property values? Reg Sci Urban Econ 46: 93–102.
Dain A (2019) The state of zoning for multifamily housing in Greater Boston. Massachusetts Housing Partnership, Boston.
Desegregate CT (2021) Connecticut zoning atlas.
Dougherty C (2020) Golden gates: Fighting for housing in America. Penguin Press, New York.
Einstein KL (2021) The privileged few: How exclusionary zoning amplifies the advantaged and blocks new housing—and what we can do about it. Urban Aff Rev 57:252–268.
Einstein KL, Palmer M, Glick DM (2019) Who participates in local government? Evidence from meeting minutes. Perspect Polit 17:28–46.
Ellen IG, Schwartz AE, Voicu I, Brooks L (2007) The impact of business improvement districts on property values: Evidence from New York City. Brookings-Wharton Papers on Urban Affairs: 1–39.
Ellickson R (2020) The zoning straitjacket: The freezing of American neighborhoods of single-family houses. Indiana Law J 96:395–428.
Fischel WA (2005) The homevoter hypothesis: How home values influence local government taxation, school finance, and land-use policies. Harvard University Press, Cambridge.
Fischel WA (2013) Fiscal zoning and economists' views of the property tax. Lincoln Institute of Land Policy, Working Paper.
Furth S, Gray MN (2019) Do minimum-lot-size regulations limit housing supply in Texas? Mercatus Center, Washington DC.
Gerardi K, Rosenblatt E, Willen P, Yao V (2015) Foreclosure externalities: New evidence. J Urban Econ 87:42–56.
Glaeser E, Gyourko J (2018) The economic implications of housing supply. J Econ Perspect 32:3–30.
Glaeser EL, Kahn ME (2010) The greenness of cities: Carbon dioxide emissions and urban development. J Urban Econ 67:404–418.
Glaeser EL, Schuetz J, Ward B (2006) Regulation and the rise of housing prices in Greater Boston. Rappaport Institute, Working Paper.
Grabar H (2018) Minneapolis confronts its history of housing segregation. Slate, 7 December.
Gyourko J, Molloy R (2014) Regulation and housing supply. National Bureau of Economic Research, Working Paper 20536.
Gyourko J, Saiz A, Summers A (2008) A new measure of the local regulatory environment for housing markets: The Wharton Residential Land Use Regulatory Index. Urban Stud 45:693–729.

Hankinson M (2018) When do renters behave like homeowners? High rent, price anxiety, and NIMBYism. Amer Polit Sci Rev 112:473–493.
Hartley D (2014) The effect of foreclosures on nearby property prices: Supply or disamenity? Reg Sci Urban Econ 49:108–117.
Haveman M, Sexton T (2008) Property tax assessment limits: Lessons from 30 years of experience. Lincoln Institute of Land Policy, Cambridge.
Hsieh CT, Moretti E (2019) Housing constraints and spatial misallocation. Amer Econ J-Macro 11:1–39.
Jacobs J (1961) The death and life of great American cities. Vintage Books, New York.
Jones C, Kammen D (2014) Spatial distribution of U.S. household carbon footprints undermines greenhouse gas benefits of urban population density. Envir Sci Tech 48:895–902.
Kahn M (2007) Green cities: Urban growth and the environment. Brookings Institution Press, Washington DC.
Larrimore J, Schuetz J (2017) Assessing the severity of rent burdens on low-income families. Board of Governors of the Federal Reserve System, FEDS Notes, Washington DC.
Lincoln Institute of Land Policy (2020) State-by-state property tax at a glance. Lincoln Institute for Land Policy, Cambridge.
Lovett I (2014) Sriracha factory irritates some California noses but entices politicians. New York Times, 14 May.
Ludwig J, Duncan GJ, Gennetian LA, Katz LF, Kessler RC, Kling JR, Sanbonmatsu L (2013) Long-term neighborhood effects on low-income families: Evidence from Moving to Opportunity. Amer Econ Rev 103:226–231.
Mallach A (2019) Rents will only go so low no matter how much we build. Shelterforce, 13 December.
Manville M, Osman T (2017) Motivations for growth revolts: Discretion and pretext as sources of development conflict. City Community 16:66–85.
Mian A, Sufi A, Trebbi F (2015) Foreclosures, house prices, and the real economy. J Financ 70: 2587–2634.
Murray C, Schuetz J (2019) Is California's housing market broken? The relationship between zoning, rents, and multifamily development. UC Berkeley Terner Center for Housing Innovation, Working Paper.
New York City (1916) Zoning ordinance.
Quigley J, Raphael S (2005) Regulation and the high cost of housing in California. Amer Econ Rev 95:323–328.

Raphael S, Michael S (2010) Job Sprawl and the Suburbanization of Poverty. Washington DC: Brookings Institution research brief. https://www.reimaginerpe.org/files/0330_job_sprawl_stoll_raphael-1.pdf
Rothstein R (2017) The Color of Law: A Forgotten History of How Our Government Segregated America. New York: Liveright Publishing.
San Gabriel Valley Tribune (2018) Sriracha, Irwindale drop dueling lawsuits over stinky plant. San Gabriel Valley Tribune, 7 September.
Schuetz J (2008) Guarding the town walls: Mechanisms and motives for restricting multifamily housing in Massachusetts. Real Estate Econ 36:555–586.
Schuetz J (2009) No renters in my suburban backyard: Land use regulation and rental housing. J Policy Anal Manag 28:296–320.
Schuetz J (2019) Is zoning a useful tool or a regulatory barrier? Brookings Institution, Washington DC.
Schuetz J (2020) Teardowns, popups, and renovations: How does housing supply change? J Reg Sci 60:459–480.
Schuetz J (2022) Fixer upper: How to repair America's broken housing systems. Brookings Institution Press, Washington DC.
Schuetz J, Been V, Ellen IG (2008) Neighborhood effects of concentrated mortgage foreclosures. J Hous Econ 17:306–391.
Shertzer A, Twinam T, Walsh RP (2022) Zoning and segregation in urban economic history. Reg Sci Urban Econ 94:103652.
Trounstine J (2018) Segregation by design. Cambridge University Press, New York.
U.S. Department of Housing and Urban Development (2021) Eliminating regulatory barriers to affordable housing: Federal, state, local, and tribal opportunities. U.S. Department of Housing and Urban Development, Office of Policy Development and Research, Washington DC.
Voicu I, Been V (2008) The effect of community gardens on neighboring property values. Real Estate Econ 36:241–283.
Zegras C, Lee JS, Ben-Joseph E (2012) By community or design? Age-restricted neighbourhoods, physical design and baby boomers' local travel behaviour in suburban Boston. Urban Stud 49:2169–2198.

Part II

Education

4

Funding Students Instead of Systems: The Case for School Choice

Patrick J. Wolf and Corey A. DeAngelis

The concept of creative destruction is central to policy debates over private school choice programs. "Private school choice" is an umbrella term for any initiative that allows families to take their children's taxpayer-funded education dollars to the approved education provider of their choosing. Choice programs include taxpayer-funded school vouchers, tax-credit-funded K-12 scholarships, and Education Savings Accounts (ESAs) funded with taxpayer dollars or via tax-credit donations. As of 2020, 30 U.S. states plus the District of Columbia and Puerto Rico were home to 67 private school choice programs.

P. J. Wolf (✉)
University of Arkansas, Fayetteville, AR, USA
e-mail: pwolf@uark.edu

C. A. DeAngelis
American Federation for Children, San Antonio, TX, USA
e-mail: cdeangelis@federationforchildren.org

A. L. Kassens and J. C. Hall (eds.), *Challenges in Classical Liberalism*, Palgrave Studies in Classical Liberalism,
https://doi.org/10.1007/978-3-031-32890-9_4

The famous theory of Joseph Schumpeter (1942) that competition drives inferior providers to bankruptcy informs the claims of both supporters and opponents of funding K-12 students directly. Supporters claim that competition from school choice pressures otherwise monopolistic government-run schools to improve their educational service or risk being destroyed by customers "voting with their feet" to be educated elsewhere. The threat of destruction, they argue, tends to generate a positive response from public schools that creates a "rising tide (of student achievement) that lifts all boats" (Hoxby 2001).

Opponents of funding students directly also rest their case at least partly on creative destruction. They characterize the government-run school system as so fragile that the loss of students to school choice mechanisms will bleed the system of necessary resources of funding and highly motivated students, thereby destroying the government-run institutions (Nelson 2017; Oropeza 2021). It is an odd defense of the public school system that it must be isolated from competition lest so many students flee the schools that they would have to close. And why would simply giving families a choice "defund" and "destroy" the government-run schools, anyway? By making this argument, defenders of the educational status quo reveal that they understand families are unhappy with the services provided by the government-run schools.

The most advantaged families already have "school choice" in the sense that they have the resources to afford to live near the best so-called "public" schools and to pay out-of-pocket for private school tuition and fees. Blocking the funding from following the child disproportionately prevents the least advantaged families from having exit options. Funding students directly empowers more disadvantaged families to access educational opportunities. In this sense, school choice is an equalizer.

Although the theories of action of both school choice supporters and opponents rely upon creative destruction to buttress their claims, those competing claims produce starkly different hypotheses regarding the degree of organizational destruction that will occur in a choice-rich environment and how "creative" that destruction will be for students. Choice supporters generally argue that the destruction that competition will wreak on the public school system will be modest and that the results of any institutional destruction will be positive. Choice opponents tend to claim that the destruction from private school choice will be apocalyptic in terms of both degree and kind. These competing claims regarding school choice and creative destruction present testable hypotheses.

As we discuss in the remainder of this chapter, the empirical evidence overwhelmingly supports the predictions of school choice supporters that competition from funding students directly and empowering families produces little destruction but at least some positive change in the government-run school system that benefits students and society.

Since competition from school choice is beneficent, we recommend more of it. To facilitate greater creative destruction from school choice, we support an overhaul of the funding of public education so that dollars are directed to students, based on their relative need, and not to education systems, regardless of student enrollments or needs. Put simply, we should fund students, not systems.

School Choice and Creative Destruction: Competing Theories of Action

Private schools have served as a major provider of K-12 education almost always and everywhere. Prior to the late nineteenth century, virtually all education around the world was delivered through private or home schools (Coulson 1999). Such was true in the United States until after the Civil War, when the fledgling public school system first launched by Horace Mann in Massachusetts became a general model for most U.S. states (Glenn 1988). In 1922, the state of Oregon, with support from the Ku Klux Klan, passed a law banning private schooling (Bunting 2021). The law was challenged all the way to the Supreme Court which, in *Pierce v. Society of Sisters* (1925), ruled against Oregon (and the Klan), famously stating: "The child is not the mere creature of the state." Private schooling would continue to be available throughout the United States in the twentieth century and would grow to claim over 15% of the K-12 market in the 1960s (Murnane et al. 2018).

Government financial support for private schooling has a deep history in the United States. In 1869, Vermont established a "town-tuitioning" program that continues to this day. Maine followed suit in 1873. Since most areas of these northeastern states lack public schools serving certain grades—especially high school and junior high—parents in communities without a government-run school can use a taxpayer-funded voucher to enroll their child in a private school of their choosing (Hammons 2002). Both states permitted the vouchers to be used at religious private schools until the 1980s, when they decided that their actions over the previous 100 years had somehow violated the Establishment Clause of the U.S. Constitution.

The reality, however, is that funding students directly at the K-12 level does not violate the Establishment Clause for the same reason Pell Grants—which can be used at private religious universities—do not violate the Establishment Clause: the primary beneficiaries of these programs are the students as opposed to the institutions. Educational organizations—whether public or private, religious or secular-only receive dollars based on the free decisions of individuals, not through the coercive power of the state, a position confirmed by the U.S. Supreme Court in *Zelman v. Simmons-Harris* (2002).

Even since *Zelman*, Vermont and Maine have limited their town-tuitioning vouchers to "nonsectarian" private schools, a restriction recently invalidated by the U.S. Supreme Court in *Carson v. Makin* (2022). The court had earlier ruled in *Espinoza v. Montana* (2020) that the application of Montana's "no-aid" provision, which is similar to Maine and Vermont's voucher restriction, violated the Free Exercise Clause of the U.S. Constitution by discriminating against religious schools and families. In his majority opinion, Chief Justice John Roberts wrote that "A State need not subsidize private education. But once a State decides to do so, it cannot disqualify some private schools solely because they are religious" (p. 10).

The first private school choice program in an urban area of the United States was launched in 1990 in Milwaukee, Wisconsin (Witte and Wolf 2017). The Milwaukee Parental Choice Program (MPCP) initially limited the vouchers to secular private schools, and only 341 students participated in its inaugural year (Wolf 2008: p. 3). The state expanded the program to religious private schools in 1996, a decision that was judged to comport with the Wisconsin State Constitution in

1998, and the program has grown to enroll 28,583 students in 131 participating schools in the fall of 2020 (EdChoice 2021: p. 78).

The MPCP is the fifth largest of the 67 private school choice programs in the United States. The Florida Tax-Credit Scholarship Program leads the list with 100,028 students enrolled in 2020, followed by the Pennsylvania Educational Improvement Tax-Credit Program with 45,882 students, the Indiana Choice Scholarship Program with 36,707, and the Arizona Original Individual Income Tax-Credit Scholarship Program with 36,579 (EdChoice 2021). Over 600,000 students were supported by one of the 67 private school choice programs in the United States in 2020 (EdChoice 2021: p. 8). Most countries of Northern Europe and the British Commonwealth operate private school choice programs in which the government uses taxpayer funding to pay private schools to educate students (Berner 2017; Macedo and Wolf 2004). Private school choice is a global phenomenon.

The Role of Creative Destruction for School Choice Advocates

Creative destruction is a key element in the theory of action for supporters of private school choice. Absent choice, the public school system is a government-run monopoly with a guaranteed customer base and thus an assured revenue stream. The monopolistic nature of the public school system is enhanced by the fact that K-12 education is compulsory to age 16. Absent school choice, the only alternatives to the public school monopoly are self-financed private schooling or homeschooling. Both of those options demand extensive family resources. It is no accident that government-run public schools enrolled 82% of school-age children as recently as 2016.

Government monopolies are "closed systems" that possess all the resources they need to sustain themselves in the future (Miles and Snow 1978). They do not have to respond to the needs of their customers. If Walmart ran the only grocery stores in the country, then Walmart would not show the concern for customer satisfaction they are forced to heed by operating in a competitive environment.

School choice programs provide exit options to students in government-run schools. Since eligible families can take their children's taxpayer-funded education dollars elsewhere, public schools in communities where choice programs are launched suddenly are faced with the threat of creative destruction if they fail to satisfy customer needs.

Most supporters of school choice predict that government-run schools will tend to respond to competitive pressure from choice in constructive ways (Betts 2005; DeAngelis and Holmes Erickson 2018; Friedman 1955; Greene 2002; Hoxby 2001). Thus, (1) the creative destruction that stems from market competition in K-12 education will be modest and (2) the outcomes for students who remain in the government-run schools will improve when choice programs are initiated or expanded. Creative destruction will do its beneficial work as a threat to government-run schools much more so than as a reality, choice supporters predict.

The Role of Creative Destruction for School Choice Opponents

Institutional destruction also is central to the theory of action for opponents of choice. They claim that the government-run school system is so fragile that it can only endure as a protected monopoly. If more students are allowed to choose an alternative to their residentially assigned public school, they claim, the system will collapse. Although that statement might seem alarmist, legislators and policy analysts regularly make apocalyptic public statements regarding the consequences of market-based competition through choice mechanisms (Bedrick and Tarnowski 2021). Representative David Tollett, during floor debate over an Arkansas proposal to provide tax-credit scholarships to 0.1% of the schoolchildren in the state, said:

This bill represents the last aspect of public education that has not been sold out to private interests. I'm asking you to […] vote this bill down. If not, vote yes and put us out of our misery, put the final nail in the coffin of public education. (Bedrick and Tarnowski 2021: p. 18)

In nearby Kentucky, Senator Reginald Thomas stated in a floor debate on Kentucky's ESA pilot program, "'We once again see public education with its neck inside a guillotine, getting ready to have his head cut off'" (Bedrick and Tarnowski 2021: p. 18). Steven Nelson (2017) claimed in the *Huffington Post*, "voucher programs are certain to end public education as we know it."

School choice supporters and opponents agree that choice programs expose government-run schools to the challenge of competition for customers. Choice supporters have confidence that public schools will rise to that challenge, producing a more creative change in their existing institutions and little destruction. Choice opponents claim that public schools are incapable of responding creatively to competition and therefore will be destroyed by it.

Evidence of Public School Funding Loss Due to Choice

A key reason why choice opponents argue that government-run schools are too fragile to handle competition from school choice is the claim that choice programs will defund the public school system (Faw and Jabbar 2016). School choice opponents predict that students will flee the government-run schools in droves, taking their education funding with them, thereby denying the public schools the resources they need to educate the few remaining students effectively (Levin 2001).

This common prediction of school choice opponents is divorced from reality. First, school choice programs primarily serve as an escape valve for students who are not thriving in the government-run school sector. Even as student enrollments in private school choice programs have grown dramatically in the past decade, the private school sector as a whole has merely maintained its market share. Second, the dollars attached to public school students do not all travel with them to their private school of choice. The funds that are driven by per-pupil formulas tend to stay in the government-run school system for several years after a student exercises school choice, a phenomenon called "phantom funding" (Fullerton and Roza 2013).

The funds that are not grounded in the per-pupil formulas remain in the public system in perpetuity. Thus, student exits enabled by school choice lead to higher, not lower, per-pupil funding in the government-run public school system. Finally, public school districts can and do adjust to enrollment losses in ways that improve their efficiency in the medium to long term.

Do Massive Numbers of Students Flee Government-Run Schools When Offered Choice?

Public school enrollment losses to private school choice programs have been modest at the micro level and null at the macro level. Typically, the first year of a school choice program sees 2–5% of eligible students participate, a proportion largely consistent with annual fluctuations in public school enrollments at the district level (Wolf et al. 2005). Programs that are narrowly targeted to highly disadvantaged students, and that are aggressively regulated by the government, such as the BOOST Program in Maryland and the original Milwaukee Parental Choice Program, hardly grow after their launch year. Programs with more expansive eligibility, such as the Florida Tax-Credit Scholarship and the Indiana Choice Scholarship Program, tend to add a few thousand students a year in states with school-age populations that number in the millions.

School choice programs do not instigate the mass exodus of students from government-run schools that choice opponents predict. But, even if they did, is the point of K-12 education funding to educate children or to prop up institutions regardless of how well they perform? Low-income families shouldn't be forced to spend their children's taxpayer-funded education dollars at residentially assigned government-run schools just because of the theoretical possibility of a mass exodus. Education funding is meant for educating children—not for protecting a particular institution, public or private.

In the aggregate, the expansion of private school choice in the United States has merely stabilized private school enrollments that otherwise have been declining. In Fig. 4.1, the darker sections of the bars represent self-financed private school enrollments since 2001. Those enrollments dropped by around 300,000 immediately after the dot.com bubble burst and by over 600,000 during and shortly after The Great Recession. Absent choice programs, the private school market share would have declined from 10% in 2001 to 8.5% in 2013, a 15% drop. As demonstrated by the lighter sections of the bars, private school enrollments enabled by school choice programs have helped the private school sector recover about half of the customers it lost due to the two financial crises of the early 2000s. By 2017, private school market share was back up to about 9.4%, with 10% of those enrollments comprising students in school choice programs.

Funding students directly has merely lessened the magnitude of the seemingly unrelenting decline in the proportion of the K-12 population educated in private schools. Based on the aggregate enrollment counts and trends, *it is not the public school sector that is in danger of Armageddon due to school choice, it is the private school sector that is threatened with near extinction in spite of school choice*. This reality has been largely overlooked amidst the heated debate over choice. Just imagine if you were trying to sell cars if the government was going around giving expensive ones away for "free." In that sense, it's surprising that the private school market share has remained relatively steady while competing with "free" government-run schools that now cost over $15,000 per student per year.

Does Choice "Drain Resources from the Public Schools"?

Students in government-run schools also have not suffered a loss of educational resources due to school choice. Bedrick and Tarnowski (2021) examine the inflation-adjusted per-pupil funding levels for students in public schools in the five states where private school choice

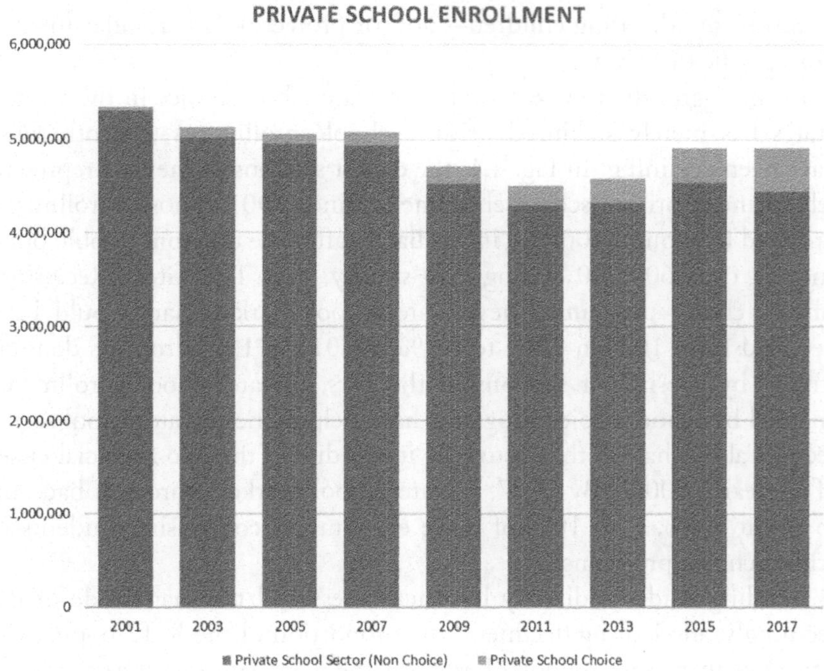

Fig. 4.1 Private school enrollment by tuition-paying or private school choice, 2001–2017 (*Sources* U.S. Department of Education, NCES, *Private School Universe Survey*, 1989–1990 through 2005–2006; 2007–2008; 2009–2010; 2011–2012; 2013–2014; 2015–2016; 2017–2018; Table 14. EdChoice, *The ABCs of School Choice*, 2020 Edition, pp. 7–8)

programs hold their largest market share: Arizona, Florida, Indiana, Ohio, and Wisconsin. In all five "choice rich" states, from 2002 to 2019, real per-pupil funding in public schools increased: by 1.2% in Arizona, 1.5% in Indiana, 5.1% in Wisconsin, 6.3% in Florida, and a whopping 12.7% in Ohio (Bedrick and Tarnowski 2021: p. 8). Private school choice programs do not stop states from spending on K-12 public education in excess of the inflation rate.

Phantom funding is a key reason why per-pupil revenue goes up when school choice programs are launched or expanded (Fullerton and Roza 2013). Large amounts of public school revenue come from grants to school districts that are not tied to student enrollment. When students leave public school districts due to choice programs, those funds remain in the district to be spread across fewer students. Even the foundation funding tied to public school enrollments is based on student counts one or two years in the past. Thus, when a student leaves a government-run school district to participate in a private school choice program, the state pays the district to educate a "phantom" child who is no longer there. Revenue from phantom funding then gets rolled into the per-pupil funding for the students who remain in the district. As students leave government-run school districts via school choice, per-pupil funding goes up mechanistically.

Can Public Schools Adjust to Enrollment-Driven Financial Losses?

The formula funding of phantom students disappears after 2–4 years. At that point public schools *have* lost some revenue due to choice-enabled enrollment declines. When government-run school districts lose substantial enrollments to robust private school choice programs, they demonstrate the ability to "right-size" through a process of creative destruction that produces efficiency gains. The best evidence of the right-sizing of government-run school districts comes from the public charter school literature.

Charter schools are publicly funded entities that are independently operated and usually permitted to enroll students regardless of where they live. They are public schools of choice. Christian Buerger and Robert Bifulco (2016) have established that charter school operation and expansion generates competitive pressure on government-run school districts to operate their schools efficiently—to "right-size" them. After conducting a dynamic fiscal and enrollment analysis of charter school expansion in New York State, they conclude, "We find that charter schools increase the cost of providing education in the short term and increase efficiency in the medium term. Estimated efficiency increases in the medium term are slightly larger than estimated cost increases" (Buerger and Bifulco 2016: p. 1). Enrollment losses to charter schools yield fiscal benefits for public school districts as early as the medium term, when local school districts demonstrate the clear capacity to adjust their operations in response the loss of students. Buerger and Bifulco estimate the right-sizing occurs 5–8 years after the first charters open.

Mark Weber (2018) finds results remarkably similar to Buerger and Bifulco by studying the launch and expansion of public charter schools in New Jersey. Weber reports clear efficiency gains in the affected public school districts after 5–8 years, when charter enrollments reached 11–24% of the K-12 market. When government-run schools lose enrollments to choice programs, real per-pupil funding tends to increase even as per-pupil costs decline. Public schools have more money to spend on a less expensive educational service. No wonder competition rarely destroys them!

Evidence of the Competitive Effects of Choice

When government-run public schools face competition from school choice, they not only get more efficient, they get more effective. Jay Greene and colleagues examined the association between a state's degree of education freedom and statewide student outcomes on the National Assessment of Education Program (NAEP) in two studies, 20 years apart. In both evaluations, the researchers constructed a composite measure of school competition in the state from private school choice programs, homeschooling, charter schooling, and ease of choice among government-run public schools.

In Greene's first education freedom study, a solo effort in 2002, he rated Arizona the state with the most education freedom, followed by New Jersey, Delaware, and Florida. Given the consistent statistical association between levels of education freedom and NAEP scores, Greene (2002) concluded that the average state could increase its proportion of students who are proficient on the NAEP math test by 4.1% for every extra point of school competition in the state as measured by the Education Freedom Index.

Nearly 20 years later, Greene assembled a larger team of researchers to revisit the association between education freedom and student NAEP outcomes (Wolf et al. 2021). Arizona remained the freest state, educationally, followed by Indiana, Minnesota, and Wisconsin. The researchers confirmed Greene's findings from 2002: states with more competition due to various forms of school choice were associated with larger student achievement gains on the NAEP. These macro studies provide proof of the concept that choice-induced competition pressures government-run schools to deliver better outcomes for students.

Micro studies of competitive effects provide even more convincing evidence that expanded private school choice makes the K-12 education sector more dynamic, to the benefit of students. We know of 28 rigorous empirical evaluations of the effects of private school choice launch or expansion on the achievement of students who remain in affected government-run schools (Table 4.1). Remarkably, 30 different researchers have contributed to this deep and rich policy literature.

Also remarkable is the consistency of their findings. Twenty-six of the 28 studies report that choice-induced competition produced achievement gains for the students remaining in government-run schools. One study, of Florida, reports statistically significant negative effects of the competitive threat of private school choice on student test scores but only in some of the statistical models and only in reading, not in math (Bowen and Trivitt 2014). One study of competition from the launch of the private school choice program in Washington, D.C., finds no competitive effects in the early years of the program, when government-run public schools in the district were protected from any financial losses due to student exits to private schools (Greene and Winters 2007). This study of the proverbial "dog that didn't bark," reinforces the point that, if monopolistic public schools are shielded from the consequences of enrollment losses, competition from school choice cannot instigate its usual positive process of creative destruction.

The most direct evidence of creative destruction from a private school choice program comes from a descriptive report on the Milwaukee Parental Choice Program. Thirty-six private schools in the choice program and 49 government-run schools in the city closed during the study period of 2006–2011. With individual student-level data, the researchers tracked the moves of students from closed schools in both sectors to persisting schools. They conclude based on that evidence,

Table 4.1 Competitive effects of private school choice programs in the United States

Study (N = 28)	Program type	Study year	Summary of findings
Florida (11)			
Bowen and Trivitt	Voucher	2014	Null to negative
Chakrabarti	Voucher	2013	Positive
Rouse, Hannaway, and Goldhaber	Voucher	2013	Positive
Forster	Voucher	2008a	Positive
Figlio and Rouse	Voucher	2006	Positive
West and Peterson	Voucher	2006	Positive
Greene and Winters	Voucher	2004	Positive
Greene	Voucher	2001	Positive
Greene and Winters	Disability voucher	2008	Positive
Figlio, Hart, and Karbownik	Tax-credit scholarship	2021	Positive
Figlio and Hart	Tax-credit scholarship	2014	Positive
Milwaukee (6)			
Mader	Voucher	2010	Positive
Greene and Marsh	Voucher	2004	Positive
Chakrabarti	Voucher	2008	Null to positive
Carnoy et al	Voucher	2007	Positive
Hoxby	Voucher	2003	Positive
Greene and Forster	Voucher	2002	Null to positive
Ohio (3)			
Figlio and Karbownik	Voucher	2016	Positive
Carr	Voucher	2011	Positive
Forster	Voucher	2008b	Null to positive
San Antonio, Texas (2)			
Gray, Merrifield, and Adzima	Voucher	2016	Null to positive
Greene and Forster	Voucher	2002	Positive
District of Columbia (1)			
Greene and Winters	Voucher	2007	Null
Indiana (2)			

(continued)

Table 4.1 (continued)

Study (*N* = 28)	Program type	Study year	Summary of findings
Canbolat	Voucher	2021	Positive to negative
Egalite	Voucher	2014	Null to positive
Louisiana (1)			
Egalite and Mills	Voucher	2021	Positive
Maine (1)			
Hammons	Town-tuitioning	2002	Positive
Vermont (1)			
Hammons	Town-tuitioning	2002	Positive

"worse schools are being closed and students are moving into better schools as a result. The improvement appears to be especially pronounced in the public sector" (McShane et al. 2012: p. 18). That's a lot of creative destruction, which is a feature of school choice, not a bug.

Put simply: underperforming private schools shut down. Underperforming government-run schools get more money, especially in the short term. This is because families can more easily vote with their feet away from underperforming private schools than underperforming public schools. Absent school choice mechanisms, children from low-income families are trapped in failing government-run schools for 13 years without exit options. Inject choice into such a system and nurture it over many years, as policymakers did in Milwaukee, and underperforming schools in both the public and private sectors are creatively destroyed.

This maxim played out clearly during the COVID-19 pandemic. Private schools had a strong incentive to keep their doors open for in-person instruction. Government-run schools, however, had an incentive to remain closed for extended periods because they could use reopening as another bargaining chip for more taxpayer resources. As a result, nearly 11 million students in government-run schools have voluntarily changed schools, expressed a desire to switch but an inability to do so, or disappeared entirely from any school rolls (Spurrier et al. 2021).

Conclusion: Fund Students Instead of Systems

COVID-19 did not break the public school system. In some ways it was already broken. The response to the pandemic simply shined a spotlight on the rigidity and lack of responsiveness that typifies K-12 public education in the absence of substantial competition from school choice. Thankfully, families are waking up to the fact that funding bureaucratic institutions makes little sense when we can fund students directly instead.

It is bad enough that many institutions receive children's taxpayer-funded education dollars despite failing to provide them with an adequate education year after year. It is altogether worse for those same institutions to receive children's education dollars regardless of whether they even open their doors to educate them.

Private schools fought to reopen from the beginning of the pandemic. Meanwhile, teachers' unions fought to keep public schools closed for over a year. The main difference was one of the incentives. Private school leaders understood they needed to provide their customers with meaningful educational services if they wanted to stay afloat. The teachers' unions, however, understood that keeping their schools closed would put them in a better position to bargain for even more taxpayer money without any real risk of losing revenue streams.

Private schools had a powerful bottom-up incentive to cater to the needs of families. Teachers' unions had a perverse top-down incentive to bolster their monopolistic institutions by forestalling school reopenings.

The main problem with our country's K-12 education system was exposed: a massive power imbalance between the government-run public school monopoly and individual families. In our view, the best way to fix that power imbalance is to empower families with options by funding students directly.

We already fund students directly when it comes to Pell Grants, the GI Bill for higher education, and existing government pre-K programs such as Head Start. With each of these programs, the funding follows the student to the public or private, religious or non-religious, education provider of their choosing. We fund individuals directly when it comes to other taxpayer-funded initiatives such as food stamps and Medicaid.

We do not force low-income families to spend their food stamp dollars at residentially assigned government-run grocery stores. Instead, families are allowed to choose to take the funding to Walmart, Trader Joe's, Safeway, or just about any other provider of groceries. We should apply the same logic to K-12 education and fund students, not systems.

The latest data from the U.S. Census Bureau indicates that public schools spent $15,656 per student in 2019. Meanwhile, the latest data from Private School Review shows that the average private school tuition was only about $11,844 per student during the 2021–2022 school year. Families should be able to take their children's education dollars to the education provider of their choosing. After all, education funding is supposed to be meant for educating children, not for insulating a particular type of institution from the workings of creative destruction.

Many of the people who support funding students directly when it comes to higher education and pre-K oppose it during the in-between years of K-12 education. Why the logical inconsistency? It is simple when you consider power dynamics. Choice is the norm with higher education, pre-K, and just about any other industry in the United States. But choice threatens an entrenched special interest that would otherwise receive children's education dollars regardless of families' preferences. And that special interest fights as hard as possible to keep that funding and power (Moe 2011).

School choice initiatives return the money to the hands of the intended beneficiaries of the funding—the children and their families. Choice only results in the loss of funds for public schools if families are unsatisfied with the education those schools are providing. The best schools welcome competition. Expressing fear about allowing families to choose their child's school signals a lack of confidence in the education sector you are defending.

Public schools tend to benefit financially when they lose students to school choice competition. They are only partially funded based on enrollment counts, meaning they can keep substantial amounts of funding for students who remain after some of their peers leave for private schools. Imagine if Walmart were able to keep large portions of your grocery funding each week even after your family started shopping at Trader Joe's. That would be a fantastic deal for Walmart! Public schools should be happy they get to keep any money at all for students they no longer educate.

Public schools also up their game in response to competition. Twenty-six of 28 studies and the latest peer-reviewed meta-analysis on the topic (Jabbar et al. 2022) find that private school choice competition generally leads to better outcomes in public schools. For example, the latest study on the subject, published in May 2021, found that increased competition from expanding the Florida Tax-Credit Scholarship Program improved academic and behavioral outcomes in nearby public schools (Figlio et al. 2021).

The silver lining of 2020 is that families have seen the light. The latest nationwide survey from RealClear Opinion Research found a 10-percentage point jump in support for school choice in one year—from 64% support in April 2020 to 74% support in June 2021. Nineteen states expanded or enacted private school choice programs in 2021. The teachers' unions, by ignoring the data and fighting to keep schools closed for over a year, have inadvertently done more to advance the concept of school choice than anyone could have ever imagined. Many families are never going to forget how powerless they felt regarding K-12 education in 2020. They are going to fight to be in a position where they never have to feel that way again. Thus, we expect to see more school choice in the future, and more of the creative destruction that it delivers, to the benefit of all students.

References

Bedrick J, Tarnowski E (2021) Who's afraid of school choice? Examining the validity and intensity of predictions by school choice opponents. EdChoice, Indianapolis.

Berner AR (2017) Pluralism and American public education: No one way to school. Palgrave Macmillan, New York.

Betts JR (2005) The economic theory of school choice. In: Betts JR, Loveless T (eds) Getting choice right: Ensuring equity and efficiency in education policy. Brookings Institution Press, Washington DC.

Bowen DH, Trivitt JR (2014) Stigma without sanctions: The (lack of) impact of private school vouchers on student achievement. Educ Pol An Arch 22:1–19.
Buerger C, Bifulco R (2016). The effect of charter schools on district costs and efficiency: The case of New York State. Education Research Alliance for New Orleans, New Orleans.
Bunting R (2021) Pierce v. Society of Sisters (1925). Oregon Encyclopedia.
Canbolat Y (2021) The long-term effect of competition on public school achievement: Evidence from the Indiana choice scholarship program. Educ Pol An Arch 29:1–25.
Carnoy MF, Adamson A, Chudgar T, Luschei F, Witte JF (2007) Vouchers and public school performance: A case study of the Milwaukee Parental Choice Program. Economic Policy Institute, Washington DC.
Carr M (2011) The impact of Ohio's EdChoice on traditional public school performance. Cato J 31:257–284.
Carson v. Makin. 2022. 142 S. Ct. 1987.
Chakrabarti R (2008) Can increasing private school participation and monetary loss in a voucher program affect public school performance? Evidence from Milwaukee. J Pub Econ 92:1371–1393.
Chakrabarti R (2013) Vouchers, public school response, and the role of incentives: Evidence from Florida. Econ Inq 51:500–526.
Coulson A (1999) Market education: The unknown history. Routledge, New York.
DeAngelis CA, Erickson HH (2018) What leads to successful school choice programs? A review of the theories and evidence. Cato J 38:247–263.
EdChoice (2021) The ABCs of school choice. EdChoice, Indianapolis.
Egalite AJ (2014) Competitive impacts of means-tested vouchers on public school performance: Evidence from Louisiana and Indiana. Program on Education Policy and Governance, Harvard University, Cambridge.
Egalite AJ, Mills JN (2021) Competitive impacts of means-tested vouchers on public school performance: Evidence from Louisiana. Educ Fin Pol 16:66–91.
Espinoza v. Montana. 2020. US Docket 18-1195. Retrieved from https://www.supremecourt.gov/opinions/19pdf/18-1195_g314.pdf.
Faw L, Jabbar H (2016) Poor choices: The sociopolitical context of 'grand theft education.' Urban Educ 55:3–37.
Figlio DN, Hart CMD (2014) Competitive effects of means-tested school vouchers. Amer Econ J-App Econ 6:133–156.

Figlio DN, Hart CMD, Karbownik K (2021) Effects of scaling up private school choice programs on public school students. CESifo Working Paper No. 9056.

Figlio DN, Karbownik, K (2016) Evaluation of Ohio's EdChoice scholarship program. Thomas B. Fordham Institute, Washington DC.

Figlio DN, Rouse CE (2006) Do accountability and voucher threats improve low-performing schools? J Pub Econ 92:239–255.

Forster G (2008a) Lost opportunity: An empirical analysis of how vouchers affected Florida public schools. Friedman Foundation for Educational Choice, Indianapolis.

Forster G (2008b) Promising start: An empirical analysis of how EdChoice vouchers affect Ohio public schools. Friedman Foundation for Educational Choice, Indianapolis.

Friedman M (1955) The role of government in education. In: Solo RA (ed) Economics and the public interest. Rutgers University Press, New Brunswick, pp 123–144.

Fullerton J, Roza M (2013) Funding phantom students. Educ Next 13:8–16.

Glenn CL (1988) The myth of the common school. University of Massachusetts Press, Amherst.

Gray NL, Merrifield JD, Adzima KA (2016) A private universal voucher program's effects on traditional public schools. J Econ Fin 40:319–344.

Greene, JP (2001) An evaluation of the Florida A-Plus accountability and school choice program. Manhattan Institute for Policy Research, New York.

Greene JP (2002) 2001 education freedom index. Manhattan Institute for Policy Research, New York.

Greene JP, Forster G (2002) Rising to the challenge: The effect of school choice on public schools in Milwaukee and San Antonio. Manhattan Institute for Policy Research, New York.

Greene JP, Marsh RH (2004) The effect of Milwaukee's parental choice program on student achievement in Milwaukee Public Schools. School Choice Demonstration Project, University of Arkansas, Fayetteville.

Greene JP, Winters MA (2004) Competition passes the test. Educ Next 4:66–71.

Greene JP, Winters MA (2007) An evaluation of the effect of DC's voucher program on public school achievement and racial integration after one year. Catholic Educ: J Inq Pract 11:83–101.

Greene JP, Winters MA (2008) The effect of special education vouchers on public school achievement: Evidence from Florida's McKay scholarship program. Manhattan Institute for Policy Research, New York.

Hammons CW (2002) The effects of town tuitioning in Vermont and Maine. Milton and Rose D. Friedman Foundation, Indianapolis.
Hoxby CM (2001) The rising tide. Educ Next 1:69.
Hoxby CM (2003) School choice and school productivity. In: Hoxby CM (ed) The economics of school choice. University of Chicago Press, Chicago.
Jabbar H, Fong CJ, Germain E, Li D, Sanchez J, Sun WL, Devall M (2022) The competitive effects of school choice on student achievement: A systematic review. Educ Pol 36: 247–281.
Levin H (2001) Bear market: The recent entry of for-profit schools into the K–12 arena is an intriguing trend. Educ Matters 1:6–15.
Macedo S, Wolf PJ (2004) Introduction: School choice, civic values, and problems of policy comparison. In: Wolf PF, Macedo S, Ferrero DJ, Venegoni C (eds) Educating citizens: International perspectives on civic values and school choice. Brookings Institution Press, Washington DC, pp 1–27.
Mader NS (2010) School choice, competition, and academic quality: Essays on the Milwaukee parental choice program. Dissertation, University of Wisconsin Madison.
McShane MQ, Kisida B, Jensen LI, Wolf PJ (2012) Milwaukee parental choice program: Descriptive report on participating schools, 2010–11. University of Arkansas, SCDP Milwaukee Evaluation Report #33.
Miles RE, Snow CC (1978) Organizational strategy, structure, and process. McGraw Hill, New York.
Moe, TM (2011) Special Interest: Teachers Unions and America's Public Schools. Brookings, Washington, DC.
Murnane RJ, Reardon SF, Mbekeani PP, Lamb A (2018) Who goes to private school? Educ Next 18:58–66.
Nelson S (2017) Vouchers will destroy public education. Huffington Post, 7 March.
Oropeza K (2021) The New Florida voucher bills are a 'death knell' for public education. Progressive Magazine, 10 March.
Pierce v. Society of Sisters (1925) 268 US 510.
Rouse CE, Hannaway J, Goldhaber D (2013) Feeling the Florida heat: How low performing schools respond to voucher and accountability pressure. Amer Econ J-Econ Pol 5:251–281.
Schumpeter JA (1942) Capitalism, socialism and democracy. Harper & Brothers, New York.
Spurrier A, Squire J, Rotherham AJ (2021) The overlooked. Bellwether Education Partners, August.

Weber M (2018) The effects of charter school proliferation on public district school spending: Evidence from New Jersey. Rutgers, The State University of New Jersey, working paper.
West MR, Peterson PE (2006) The efficacy of choice threats within school accountability systems. Econ J 116:48–62.
Witte JF, Wolf PJ (2017) The Wisconsin role in the school choice movement. Economics Research Network, Department of Education Reform, College of Education and Health Professions, University of Arkansas, EDRE Working Paper No. 2017–12.
Wolf PJ (2008) The comprehensive longitudinal evaluation of the Milwaukee Parental Choice Program: Summary of baseline reports. University of Arkansas, Fayetteville.
Wolf PJ, Greene JP, Ladner M, Paul JD (2021) Education freedom and student achievement: Is more school choice associated with higher state-level performance on the NAEP? University of Arkansas, Fayetteville.
Wolf P, Gutmann B, Eissa N, Puma M, Silverberg M (2005) Evaluation of the DC opportunity scholarship program: First year report on participation (ED-01-CO-0082/0016). U.S. Department of Education, Institute of Education Sciences, National Center for Education Evaluation and Regional Assistance: Washington DC.
Zelman v. Simmons-Harris (2002) US Docket 00-1751. Retrieved from https://www.oyez.org/cases/2001/00-1751.

5

The Trouble with Outsourcing School Management

Samuel E. Abrams

In his 1859 classic defense of individual freedom, *On Liberty*, John Stuart Mill laid what could be called the foundation for the modern-day school choice movement. The government in Britain had yet to play a role in education. That would soon come with the Elementary Education Act of 1870, mandating the education of all children aged five to thirteen in state schools. Matriculation would require weekly fees, though the state would cover costs for parents too poor to pay; parents could opt to send their children to private (termed "voluntary") schools, but no aid from the state would be available to that end (Dalgleish 1870). Mill nevertheless anticipated this role of government in education and vehemently rejected it, calling instead for the freedom of all parents to choose schools for their own children, with those in need getting necessary assistance from the state.

S. E. Abrams (✉)
Teachers College, Columbia University, New York, NY, USA
e-mail: sa307@tc.columbia.edu

A. L. Kassens and J. C. Hall (eds.), *Challenges in Classical Liberalism*, Palgrave Studies in Classical Liberalism,
https://doi.org/10.1007/978-3-031-32890-9_5

"That the whole or any large part of the education of the people should be in State hands, I go as far as anyone in deprecating," Mill (1859 [1989]: p. 106) wrote. "All that has been said of the importance of the individuality of character, and diversity in opinions and modes of conduct, involves, as of the same unspeakable importance, diversity of education. A general State education is a mere contrivance for moulding people to be exactly like one another: and as the mould in which it casts them is that which pleases the predominant power in the government, whether this be a monarch, a priesthood, an aristocracy, or the majority of the existing generation, ... it establishes a despotism over the mind, leading by natural tendency to one over the body."

While Mill wrote "that the State should require and compel the education, up to a certain standard, of every human being who is born a citizen," he contended that the state "should leave to parents to obtain the education where and how they pleased, and content itself with helping to pay the school fees of the poorer classes of children, and defraying the entire school expenses of those who have no one else to pay for them" (1859 [1989]: pp. 105–106). Annual exams administered by the state for students in all grades, Mill wrote, would hold parents accountable for securing the education of their children (1859 [1989]: pp. 106–107).

School choice in many countries today comports in large part with what Mill recommended. The big difference is that government funding now covers all basic expenses, regardless of parental income, for students attending public schools and much if not all basic expenses, regardless of parental income, for students attending private schools or some variation on them in countries with school choice programs. Vouchers in the Netherlands, introduced in 1917, cover all tuition at private schools (Walford 2001); government grants in France cover about 90% of tuition at so-called contract (*sous contrat*) schools, introduced in 1959 (French National Assembly and Senate 1959; Butrymowicz 2018a, b); vouchers in Chile, introduced in 1981, cover all tuition at most private schools[1];

[1] The degree to which vouchers cover tuition at private schools in Chile has evolved over time. From 1981 to 1993, private schools accepting vouchers could not charge additional fees. In acknowledgment of fiscal pressures, the government altered its policy, deferring to Milton Friedman's prescription, described below, allowing schools to charge additional fees. By 2015,

vouchers and tuition tax-credit scholarships in the United States, introduced in 1990 and 1997, respectively, cover all or most tuition for low- and middle-income families at many private schools while charter schools, introduced in 1992, are fully funded by the government (Abrams 2019, 2020; Welner 2008); vouchers cover all tuition at free schools (*friskolor*) in Sweden, introduced in 1992 (Abrams 2016) and academies or free schools in Mill's Britain, introduced in 2002 and 2010, respectively, are fully funded by the government (Ladd and Fiske 2016).

Yet for all of Mill's clairvoyance, his theory of school choice has run into substantial problems in practice. The same holds for elaborations on his ideas by successors on the left as well as the right, as much research into social division, incomplete contracting, and civic disengagement should have foretold.

Echoes of Mill

In updating Mill's argument a century later, Milton Friedman built on Mill's belief in the pluralistic value of educational choice and made his own case for both the positive effect of competition among schools and the desegregating impact of schooling options for students living in troubled neighborhoods (Friedman 1955). In the name of pluralism, Friedman wrote in "The Role of Government in Education," published in 1955 as a chapter in a festschrift honoring a mentor, "[T]he denationalization of education would widen the range of choice available to parents." Let government funds in the form of vouchers, Friedman continued, "be made available to parents regardless where they send their children—provided only that it be to schools that satisfy specified minimum standards—and a wide variety of schools will spring up to meet the demand" (Friedman 1955: p. 129). To give schools more

conceding that such differentiation had caused significant socioeconomic segregation at private schools, the government vowed to phase out this policy, forbidding all private schools accepting vouchers to charge additional fees. However, throughout this time, about 7% of the country's schools, charging far more than the value of the vouchers, have elected not to participate at all in the voucher system. For more on the Chilean system, see Elacqua (2012), Grandin (2015), Castro-Hidalgo and Gómez-Álvarez (2016), and Murnane et al. (2017).

autonomy, Friedman granted them control over admissions as well as freedom to set tuition (Friedman 1955: pp. 127, 131). Should parents wish to send their children to schools charging more than the specified value of the voucher, they would have to pay the difference. To amplify choice, Friedman urged the inclusion of commercially operated schools (Friedman 1955: p. 127).

Such empowerment of parents as consumers of education for their children, Friedman wrote, would force schools through competition to improve instruction and, with that goal, boost teacher pay to attract and retain talent (Friedman 1955: pp. 129–131). At the same time, such empowerment of parents, Friedman wrote, would allow children to break through residential barriers to attend more integrated schools (Friedman 1955: p. 130). Friedman subsequently fleshed out his integrationist rationale for vouchers in columns in *Newsweek* in 1967 and 1972, contending that vouchers at once gave inner-city black students a way out of underperforming schools and placed pressure on such schools to get better (Friedman 1967; 1972).

Friedman, in fact, had significant company on the left in making this case for vouchers. The sociologist David Rogers (1968: pp. 486–487) invoked Friedman's argument in his deep analysis of the New York City Board of Education, *110 Livingston Street*, published in 1968, as a legitimate response to the bureaucratic pathology defining urban school systems. Rogers described the New York City school system, in particular, as "typical of what social scientists call a 'sick' bureaucracy—a term for organizations whose traditions, structure, and operations subvert their stated missions and prevent any flexible accommodation to changing client demands" (Rogers 1968: p. 267).

The psychologist Kenneth Clark, a civil rights icon whose research into children's perspectives on race played a decisive role in the fight for school desegregation in the 1950s, wrote in the *Harvard Educational Review* in 1968: "The rigidity of present patterns of public school organization—and the concomitant stagnation in the quality of education and academic performance of children—may not be amenable to any attempts at change working through and within the present system" (Clark 1968: p. 108).

In advocating "parallel systems of public schools" as the answer to this crisis, Clark articulated in rudimentary form the concept of charter schools is a generation ahead of their establishment. Such "parallel systems," Clark envisioned, would be "organized and operated on a quasi-private level, and with quality control and professional accountability maintained and determined by Federal and State educational standards and supervision" (Clark 1968: p. 113). Moreover, in sync with Friedman, Clark lauded the virtues of competition: "American industrial and material wealth was made possible through industrial competition. America's educational health may be made possible through educational competition" (Clark 1968: p. 113).

Allying with Rogers and Clark in 1968 on the left was the sociologist Christopher Jencks, who expressed similar frustration with the status quo in a *New York Times Magazine* article entitled "Private Schools for Black Children." Jencks derided inner-city schools as "little more than custodial institutions for keeping children off the street" and appealed for a system of vouchers, though one barring commercially operated schools from participation and favoring poor families by calibrating the value of vouchers according to need (Jencks 1968: pp. 19–21, 30). In an essay soon afterward in *The New Republic*, Jencks echoed Friedman in describing vouchers as a means of integration. With vouchers, Jencks wrote, "no child could be excluded from any participating school simply because his family was not rich enough or white enough to buy a house near the school" (Jencks 1970: pp. 19–21).

At the same time, the education historian Ted Sizer (1969), a fellow advocate for the rights of poor children, likewise called for income-adjusted vouchers, redeemable at both sectarian and nonsectarian private schools, in an article in *The Saturday Review* entitled "Education in the Ghetto: The Case for a Free Market." A decade later, the legal scholars John Coons and Stephen Sugarman (1978) made a similar argument in crafting a plan for income-adjusted vouchers and tried to get it on the California ballot for a referendum vote in 1979, but their petition failed to collect the number of signatures required (Catterall 1984: pp. 435–440).

Picking up where Clark left off, but from the right, the political scientists John Chubb and Terry Moe (1990: pp. 219–224) called for a parallel system of publicly funded but privately run schools in *Politics, Markets, and America's Schools*, published in 1990. These schools, "chartered by the state," would have control over curricula as well as admissions. Defining autonomy as the most important characteristic of effective schools and "direct democratic control" as its greatest obstacle, Chubb and Moe termed school choice a cure-all (Chubb and Moe 1990: pp. 183–184, 217, 225). "Without being too literal about it," they wrote, "we think reformers would do well to entertain the notion that choice *is* a panacea. This is our way of saying that choice is not like the other reforms and should not be combined with them as part of a reformist strategy for improving America's schools. Choice is a self-contained reform with its own rationale and justification. It has the capacity *all by itself* to bring about the kind of transformation that, for years, reformers have been seeking to engineer in myriad other ways" (Chubb and Moe 1990: p. 217).

In calling for "scholarships" that would go directly from district "choice offices" to participating schools selected by parents—rather than vouchers that would go to parents as a means of payment for tuition at private schools—Chubb and Moe distanced themselves from Friedman and defined a key facet of the mechanics basic to charter schools (Chubb and Moe 1990: p. 220).

An unlikely addition to this chorus a decade later was Robert Reich, President Bill Clinton's former secretary of labor. In an op-ed in *The Wall Street Journal* in 2000 entitled "The Case for 'Progressive' Vouchers," Reich sided in the thick of the presidential election with George W. Bush against Al Gore in endorsing vouchers for poor students attending failing schools. "The only way to begin to decouple poor kids from lousy schools," Reich wrote, "is to give poor kids additional resources, along with vouchers enabling them and their parents to choose how to use them" (Reich 2000: p. A26).

In contrast to Friedman, Reich, like Jencks and Sizer, proposed that the value of vouchers not be fixed but rather inversely related to family income. Yet with Friedman and in nearly identical language, Reich proposed that the vouchers could be employed "at any school that meets certain minimum standards," whether public or private, though Reich opted to set aside, for the time being, "the tricky First Amendment issue of public money for religious schools" (Reich 2000: p. A26).

Problems

With such vigorous bipartisan support for outsourcing the management of schools, one might wonder what could possibly go wrong. A lot could go wrong and has. As Friedman himself conceded in his seminal essay in 1955, the argument had been made "that private schools would tend to exacerbate class distinctions." Friedman elaborated: "Given greater freedom about where to send their children, parents of a kind would flock together and so prevent a healthy intermingling of children from decidedly different backgrounds." Friedman granted that this argument was "valid in principle" but expressed doubt "that the stated results would follow" (Friedman 1955: pp. 129–130).

However, precisely such parental behavior has led to social division, even in countries where schools accepting vouchers cannot set tuition above the value of the voucher or where open-enrollment programs allow parents to choose charter or conventional public schools. Moreover, much as Friedman conceded that similar parents might migrate together, Reich acknowledged that sorting would happen according to levels of student academic achievement and conduct as well as parental commitment.

Reich addressed this matter bluntly in his *Wall Street Journal* op-ed. "The biggest drawback to vouchers is that kids who are most troublesome, or whose parents couldn't care less or are overwhelmed with other problems, would almost certainly end up bunched together in the worst schools," he wrote. "Such schools would become even worse than they were before. After all, the increasing concentration of poor kids in America's poor schools has already compounded the problems these kids and those schools must deal with. Assuming that the kids who leave these schools take public money with them, the worst schools would end up with fewer resources per difficult child" (Reich 2000: p. A26).

While Reich accepted the cost of these negative externalities, they may have exceeded his expectations. The costs of concentrating underperforming students in default neighborhood public schools have indeed been steep. To anyone who has been a teacher, this should come as no surprise. And the problem is not linear. Teaching a class with eight difficult students out of, say, 30 is not twice as hard as teaching a class with four such students. It can be exponentially more difficult because of the daunting task of containing a chain reaction of bad behavior. Drawing on nine years of data from 22 elementary schools in a Florida school district, the economists Scott Carrell and Mark Hoekstra (2010: p. 212), in fact, documented in a 2010 article entitled "Externalities in the Classroom" that "adding one more troubled boy peer to a classroom of 20 students … increases the number of disciplinary infractions boys commit by 40 percent."[2]

This combination of flight and ensuing difficulties has manifested itself in several countries with strong school choice programs. Following the introduction of open enrollment in New Zealand in 1991, scholars found a significant movement of students from the majority population of European descent, known as Pakeha, away from schools with the highest proportion of the minority Maori and Pacific Island students. Given the substantial overlap of minority and low-income status, this pattern of migration corresponded, as well, to flight from schools with a higher proportion of poor students (Lauder and Hughes 1999; Fiske and Ladd 2000; Thrupp 2006).[3]

With this pattern of migration, many of the country's schools on the losing end of such activity spiraled into what one television network termed "forgotten schools" in a documentary by that name (Fiske and Ladd 2000: pp. 255–257). "New Zealand's application of the principle of competition to the delivery of compulsory education," Edward Fiske and Helen Ladd wrote in their book *When Schools Compete: A Cautionary Tale*, "created a situation in which the most popular schools position themselves to serve primarily academically motivated students from

---

[2] As someone who was a high school teacher for 18 years, I know this challenge of classroom management well.

[3] See also Butrymowicz (2018a, b).

families with high socioeconomic status. They attract the best teachers and concentrate on teaching a relatively narrow range of academic subjects well. By contrast, a significant number of schools at the other end of the popularity spectrum must deal with increasing concentrations of difficult-to-teach students: those with learning or behavioral problems, those for whom English is a second language, or those living in poverty or in dysfunctional families" (Fiske and Ladd 2000: p. 10).

Scholars have documented similar segregation and related consequences on account of school choice in the Netherlands, the United States, and Sweden (Karsten 1994; Ladd et al. 2009; Vlachos 2011; Abrams 2016; Brandén and Magnus Bygren 2022; Ladd and Singleton 2020). In the United States, there has been significant white flight to charter schools (Ladd and Turaeva 2020; Denice et al. 2021). In addition, there has been a growing trend of white communities seceding outright from school districts to create their own miniature districts (Superville 2017; Sparks 2019). In a telling illustration of the impact of school choice in Sweden, Bengt Westerberg, deputy prime minister in the government of Carl Bildt in the early 1990s and an advo-cate along with Bildt of school vouchers at that time, reversed himself two decades later. Westerberg, who had been the leader of the Liberal People's Party from 1983 to 1995, explained in a 2012 interview that he had anticipated neither the role of private equity in buying up school companies and then trimming and flipping them within a few years for great financial gain nor the significant migration of native Swedish students from public to independent schools (*friskolor*). Westerberg said he found both developments disturbing and recounted a recent visit to his high school alma mater, located in Södertälje, a midsized city outside of Stockholm with a large immigrant community from the Middle East. In touring the school, he observed that nearly all of the students were of Middle Eastern origin. When he asked the principal about the native Swedish students in Södertälje, the principal said, "They almost all now go to *friskolor*" (Abrams 2016).

In countries where schools accepting vouchers can set tuition above the value of the voucher—in keeping with Friedman's recommendation—such division has been particularly pronounced. In a critique of

Friedman's proposal in *The Urban Review* in 1968, Henry Levin identified precisely this problem (Levin 1968: p. 34). For this scenario, Chile serves as a salient example. In 1980, the year prior to the establishment of vouchers in Chile, 78% of students attended public schools; 15%, private schools with modest government subsidies; and 7%, unsubsidized elite private schools. By 2006, the percentages were 51, 43, and 6, respectively (Elacqua 2012).

In their initial incarnation, from 1981 to 1993, vouchers in Chile could not be topped up by parents willing to pay for more expensive schooling. However, in response to fiscal pressures, the government relented to conform with Friedman's prescription. By 2007, just over half of students using vouchers attended schools requiring top-up fees (Elacqua 2012; Murnane et al. 2017). "The net effect," Richard Murnane and colleagues reported in a 2017 analysis published by the National Bureau of Economic Research, "was that school segregation by socioeconomic status increased substantially in the first two decades of the voucher system" (Murnane et al. 2017: p. 4). Moreover, Chilean students underperformed their counterparts on international exams and exhibited significant differences correlating with family income (Murnane et al. 2017).

Such underperformance as well as divergence in results was especially evident from the country's first participation in the OECD's administration of the Program for International Student Assessment (PISA), a triennial exam in reading, math, and science given to a sample of approximately 5000 15-year olds in all OECD member nations and many affiliated nations. The OECD started administering this exam in 2000. Chile first participated in 2006. The results from 2006 for Chile were not only far below the OECD mean but also displayed substantial between-school variation.

These outcomes led the Chilean government in 2008 to enact the Preferential School Subsidy Law, which allocated vouchers worth 50% more to students from families in the bottom two quintiles in earnings and required participating schools to waive additional fees for these students (Murnane et al. 2017). Focusing on achievement in math, Murnane and colleagues documented that over the next five years, "student test scores increased markedly and income-based gaps in those scores declined by one-third" (Murnane et al. 2017). Armed with such data, the government of Michelle Bachelet in 2015 turned the clock back to 1993 to bar schools accepting vouchers from charging additional fees. In addition, Bachelet's government at the same time took steps to phase out for-profit operation of private schools as well as selective admission policies (Grandin 2015).

That schools should be run as commercial enterprises is itself highly problematic and has been cause for much pushback in Chile, Sweden, and the United States (Castro-Hidalgo and Gómez-Álvarez 2016; Abrams 2016). The fundamental trouble with Friedman's claims that schools be operated like businesses is that there simply isn't sufficient transparency for proper contract enforcement in a domain as complex as education (Levin 1968: p. 34). In the language of principal–agent theory, there is too much potential for moral hazard in this context, with school operators well positioned to cut corners in the name of profit.

In an essay in *The New York Times Magazine* in 1973 entitled "Selling School Like Groceries: The Voucher Idea," Friedman (1973) fleshed out his argument that vouchers be redeemable at schools run by for-profit operators. Comparing schools to grocery stores, Freidman contended that much as competition among commercially managed grocery stores has meant much better service than could ever be imagined with government-run grocery stores, competition among schools facilitated by vouchers should achieve a similar outcome. Yet schools are not grocery stores. Whereas schools may be assessed by adults only from a necessary distance, grocery stores may be fully judged by adults according to cost, service, inventory, organization, cleanliness, and atmosphere. Decades of economic literature on information asymmetry make this problem clear. Ronald Coase, Kenneth Arrow, Oliver Williamson, and Henry Hansmann all addressed this matter in detail.

Coase and Williamson concluded, in sum, that producing, rather than purchasing, certain goods and services involving complex processes was necessary when contracts cannot be written with sufficient specificity (Coase 1937; Williamson 1971). "In more numerous respects than are commonly appreciated," Williamson wrote in a 1971 article in *The American Economic Review*, "the substitution of internal organization for market exchange is attractive less on account of technological economies associated with production but because of what may be referred to broadly as 'transactional failures' in the operation of markets for intermediate goods" (Williamson 1971: p. 112). Because of the opacity of the educational process, schools run by outside operators are precisely the kind of institutions that can suffer from such transactional failures. To Arrow and Hansmann, market failure necessarily results when the provider knows so much more about a service than the recipient or when the payer and recipient are separate parties (Arrow 1963; Hansmann 1980).[4] Whether the situation is a doctor treating a patient, as Arrow described, or a philanthropic organization connecting a donor and a beneficiary, as Hansmann described, the commercial model fails because of information asymmetry. The same holds for schools.

The market fulfills its mission in schools for discrete goods—like textbooks and computers—or services—like transportation and software maintenance. But in the case of schooling itself, the immediate consumer is a child, who can know only so much about how subjects should be taught. The parent, legislator, and taxpayer have little to go on. They're separated from the recipient, much as Hansmann detailed. And testing as a control on the quality of education is rife with problems: setting aside that teachers can give students more time on tests, provide assistance during tests, or alter answer sheets afterward, entire schools can teach to the test at the direction of administrators and in the process sacrifice critical aspects of responsible pedagogy.

Such pressure exists across all schools in this era of high-stakes testing, but it is that much more acute in the case of commercially operated schools given that contract renewals hinge so much on boosting test scores. In the United States, one experiment after another with for-profit school management has ended in disappointment if not scandal. The country's first experiment with for-profit school management involved Oklahoma-based Dorsett Educational Systems, hired in 1970 by the Office of Economic Opportunity to provide remediation services. Dorsett was soon after exposed for test-tampering to boost scores (Abrams 2016: pp. 7–8). Minnesota-based Educational Alternatives, Inc., hired to run nine schools in Baltimore in the early 1990s, was

---

[4] See also Chou (2002).

likewise exposed for test-tampering as well as financial chicanery (Abrams 2016: pp. 62–67). New York-based Edison Schools, Inc., hired a decade later to run three schools in Baltimore and many more in cities across the country, was exposed for erring in nearly the same ways as EAI (Abrams 2016: pp. 70–95).

In addition, in Philadelphia, where Edison ran as many as 22 schools in the early aughts, the company was exposed for shelving its writing and science curricula to focus on reading and math given that contract renewals with the Philadelphia School Reform Commission were determined largely by test results in the latter two subjects. "Reading and math scores became the company's currency," explained one company executive in 2009 (Abrams 2016: pp. 156–165). When the Boston Consulting Group was summoned in 2012 by the Philadelphia School Reform Commission to review its decade of outsourcing school management and to chart a path forward, BCG recommended that the city continue contracting with charter schools but stipulated, in italics, that no for-profit organizations be involved (Abrams 2016: pp. 167–168). The New York State Legislature had likewise amended its education law in 2010 to read, underlined, and in boldface, that applications from for-profit operators to run charter schools would no longer be reviewed (Abrams 2016: p. 169). Consistent with these stipulations, Wall Street forecasts in the 1990s that 10–20% of U.S. schools would be commercially operated by 2010 fell far short. By 2010, the percentage was 0.8% (Abrams 2016: pp. 37, 164–165).

While for-profit school management has grown significantly since vouchers were introduced in Sweden in 1992, the sector has faced similar issues. The economist Jonas Vlachos exposed in a 2011 study that the country's free-market school reforms had led to substantial grade inflation at commercially operated schools. Vlachos (2011) documented that students from lower-secondary independent schools posted significantly lower grades at upper-secondary municipal schools than they had earned at the lower-secondary level while their peers who had attended lower-secondary municipal schools exhibited no such shift. To Vlachos (2011), the implication was clear: independent schools inflated grades both to convey effectiveness to parents and to keep students enrolled as satisfied customers (Abrams 2016: p. 273). More damning was a documentary broadcast the same year by UR, the Swedish Educational Broadcasting Company, describing school management companies as fueled by greed. Entitled *Vinstmaskinerna* ("Profit Machines"), the documentary chronicled bloated executive compensation as well as vacuous curricula, grade inflation, and falsification of student attendance to retain per-pupil government payments (Abrams 2016: pp. 275–276).

Turning school management over to for-profit operators ultimately represents a worrisome retreat from public engagement. Given the bureaucratic pathology of many urban school systems derided by Rogers, Clark, Sizer, Jencks, and Reich as well as Friedman and Chubb and Moe, the impulse to outsource school management is no doubt understandable. But it is a form of surrender, and that is especially true in the case of turning over schools to commercial operators. There is, after all, no exit from bad public education. Much like national defense or clean air and water, education should be considered a public good, something that can't benefit anyone without benefiting everyone. "Actually, of course, a private citizen can 'get out' from public education by sending his children to private school," wrote the economist Albert O. Hirschman two generations ago in *Exit, Voice, and Loyalty*, "but at the same time he *cannot* get out, in the sense that his and his children's life will be affected by the quality of public education" (Hirschman 1970: p. 102).

To Hirschman, the implications of Friedman's message were obvious. Many empowered parents would withdraw from the public system and take with them their voices to bring about improvement. In challenging Friedman, Hirschman appealed for public engagement: "[T]he decision to voice one's views and efforts to make them prevail are contemptuously referred to by Friedman as a resort to 'cumbrous political channels.' But what else is the political, and indeed the democratic, process than the digging, the use, and hopefully the slow improvement of these very channels?" (Hirschman 1970: p. 17).[5]

In communities where doctors, bankers, lawyers, and engineers send their children to public schools, the public schools typically thrive for the very reason that parents raise their voices to demand smaller classes,

[5] For more on such exit and its ramifications, see Henig (1994) and Levin (1998).

modern science labs, rich electives, and better teacher pay. In communities where professionals exit the public schools and pay the so-called "private school tax" or move to suburbs with well-funded school systems, the public schools typically suffer because there isn't the parental voice necessary to demand such improvements.

Solutions

Mill was right to worry about indoctrination in a monolithic state system of education, but Mill, like Friedman and many in his wake, did not foresee significant problems with government funding of privately run schools, with segregation, moral hazard, and erosion of civic engagement chief among them. Regulation can curb such untoward effects, though certainly not eliminate them. Such regulation would involve, among other measures, eliminating top-up fees beyond the value of vouchers, as the Chilean government concluded in 2015, and increasing the value of vouchers to provide students access to private schools currently out of reach, as the study by Murnane and colleagues suggested; prohibiting for-profit organizations from running schools, as the Chilean government also concluded in 2015, as have several state legislatures across the United States before and since (Heilig 2018); and bolstering public school systems to keep parents of means from exiting them. Regulation can likewise curb the indoctrination in state schools that Mill feared, and it has largely succeeded in doing so by keeping religion out of schools, for example, and barring creationism, in particular, from being taught in science classes.[6]

What should nevertheless be clear is that school choice is no panacea, contrary to the claim made by Chubb and Moe (1990: p. 217). Much as there is no true exit from bad public education, given all the negative ramifications for the society of bad public schools, there is no way to choose our way out of bad public education. A 2018 *Wall Street Journal* analysis of vouchers in Milwaukee, in fact, documented that the vast majority of students using vouchers who posted better

[6] *Edwards v. Aguillard*, 482 U.S. 578 (1987).

results on state exams attended schools with hard caps on the number of voucher students admitted. "As the percentage of voucher students rises," the *Journal* reported, "the returns diminish until the point when there is little difference between the performance of public and private institutions" (Hobbs 2018: p. A1).

In his dissent in *Zelman v. Simmons-Harris*, the 2002 Supreme Court decision permitting parents to use vouchers at religious schools in Cleveland, Justice John Paul Stevens captured the scale of our education challenge. Vouchers themselves, Stevens wrote, cannot redress or compensate for "the disastrous conditions [in Cleveland] that prevented over 90% of the student body from meeting basic proficiency standards." Such failure, he wrote, necessitated "massive improvements unrelated to the voucher program."[7]

While Stevens did not elaborate on what such improvements would involve, exploring this matter can put us on the path to true solutions. To start, as the economist James Heckman, among others, has repeatedly contended, no spending of public dollars generates a greater rate of return than investment in high-quality preschool (Heckman 2006; Heckman et al. 2010, 2013; Heckman and Raut 2016; Heckman and Karapakula 2019). Longitudinal data tracking participants in high-quality preschool programs going back to the 1960s document lower levels of grade retention, special education designation, juvenile delinquency, teenage pregnancy, and high school dropout. The benefits extend into adulthood, with lower levels of incarceration and unemployment, among other metrics.

The data from one study in Michigan initiated in 1962 now even allow for findings about the children as well as siblings of participants in the treatment group, experiencing two years of high-quality preschool, compared to those in the control group, who did not. "The children of treated participants have fewer school suspensions, higher levels of education and employment, and lower levels of participation in crime, compared with the children of untreated participants," Heckman and Ganesh Karapukala wrote in a 2019 working paper published by the National Bureau of Economic Research. "Impacts are especially

[7] *Zelman v. Simmons-Harris*, 536 U.S. 639 (2002).

pronounced for the children of male participants. These treatment effects are associated with improved childhood home environments. The intergenerational effects arise despite the fact that families of treated subjects live in similar or worse neighborhoods than the control families" (Heckman and Karapukala 2019).

Such high-quality preschool is expensive. By one estimate, it costs about three times as much as the government spends on Head Start, the national preschool program for low-income children launched in 1965 as part of President Lyndon Johnson's War on Poverty (Traub 2000). But to Heckman's point, it is expensive only in the short run. The same goes for shrinking class size, as evidenced by a massive study in Tennessee conducted from 1985 to 1989 involving students in kindergarten through third grade. This intervention likewise conferred lasting benefits (Mosteller 1995). Like high-quality preschool, reducing class size is expensive but only in the short run.

Boosting teacher pay is also expensive but only in the short run, as it attracts more qualified candidates to the profession and retains them. Low teacher turnover, in turn, improves learning outcomes, as it means more experienced teachers in the classroom, mentorship for younger teachers, and institutional stability (Ronfeldt et al. 2013). The teacher walkouts in 2018 in West Virginia, Oklahoma, Kentucky, and Arizona made clear that too many teachers struggle to make ends meet (Goldstein 2018a, b). Comparative data on teacher pay from the OECD, in this regard, is grim and telling: on average, U.S. teachers at the lower-secondary level (grades seven to nine) in 2016 earned 65% of what their college classmates made in contrast to an OECD mean of 91% (OECD 2018: Table D3.2A).

In looking abroad, we have, in effect, a natural experiment for comparing the impact of school choice, on the one hand, and, on the other, systemic reform that involves improving teacher pay and preparation as well as investing in smaller classes and richer curricula. Sweden, as noted, introduced a robust system of vouchers in 1992. By 2010, 12% of students in grades one through nine and 24% of students in grades 10 through 12 used vouchers. Of the 1230 private schools they attended, 930, or 76%, were operated by for-profit organizations (Abrams 2016: pp. 254–255). Upon becoming prime minister in 1991,

Carl Bildt declared that the revitalization of Sweden required substantial privatization of the country's services, schooling among them. "The time for the Nordic model has passed," he said. "It created societies that were too monopolized, too expensive, and didn't give people the freedom of choice that they wanted; societies that lacked flexibility and dynamism" (Abrams 2016: pp. 251–253).

Finland meanwhile had chosen a different path a generation earlier and stuck with it. A subject state under Sweden and then Russia until 1917, poor in natural resources, defeated by the Soviets in World War II and forced to give up 10% of its territory, resettle 450,000 citizens, and pay reparations until 1952, Finland had to invest in its human capital to join the modern world. "We had no choice," recalled Social Democratic Member of Parliament Matt Saarinen in a 2010 interview. "In Finland, we have our timber and we have our brains. That is all" (Abrams 2016: pp. 281–282). To that end, Finnish authorities from 1972 to 1979 phased out academic tracking of students through seventh grade, mandated that all new teachers from 1979 onward earn a master's degree before taking over a classroom (making it the only Nordic country to do so), boosted teacher pay in recognition of the additional required study, phased out tracking through ninth grade in 1985, and at the same time boosted teacher pay again and reduced class size in acknowledgment of the steeper challenge of leading classes of students with mixed aptitudes in the upper grades (Abrams 2016: pp. 280–281). Both to make school more enticing and to teach math and science in a practical manner, authorities mandated a rich array of classes in art, music, and crafts. In grades one through nine, students spend from four to eleven periods a week taking such classes (Abrams 2016: p. 298).

Much as the OECD's PISA served as a wake-up call for Chile, it validated the Finnish strategy. Over the seven administrations of the triennial exam in reading, math, and science from 2000 to 2018, Finnish 15-year olds have substantially outperformed their Swedish peers. This has been especially true in science, which appears to be a far more school-dependent subject than reading or math. Unless a student's parents are scientists, after all, it is highly unlikely that he or she is doing science experiments in the kitchen. Schools and science labs, in particular, are essential for science education. The Finns make labs the heart of their science curricula and they typically cap labs at 16 students, in keeping with a national rule that any course making use of machinery (from woodshop to culinary arts) be limited to that number in the name of safety. This focus on labs does not hold in Sweden (Abrams 2016: pp. 286–287).

The OECD mean score for science over the seven administrations of PISA from 2000 to 2018 was a 497, as it was for the United States. A year of learning corresponds to about 35 points; one standard deviation amounts to 100 points, meaning 497 places a country at the 50th percentile and a 597, at the 84th percentile. For these seven administrations of PISA, students in Sweden posted a mean score in science of 499 while students in Finland posted a mean score of 543.[8]

While Sweden is slightly more heterogeneous than Finland, the difference in this context is not meaningful. Where the OECD has posted data disaggregated according to the native and immigrant status of students for both countries, the differences for native students are sharp. For example, the OECD published such data for reading for the 2009 administration of PISA: native students in Sweden posted a mean score of 507 while native students in Finland posted a mean score of 538. The OECD published such data for math for the 2012 administration of PISA: native students in Sweden posted a mean score of 490 while native students in Finland posted a mean score of 523.[9]

To address the concern that we cannot know whether Finland's reforms in the 1970s and '80s have led to these superior PISA results given that PISA only goes back as far as 2000, the OECD yields a powerful answer. In 2013, the OECD published the results from a study of adult literacy and numeracy. The study called the Program for the International Assessment of Adult Competencies (PIAAC) and conducted in 24 countries, disaggregated data by five age cohorts. Finns aged 55 to 65, a cohort educated before Finland reformed its school system, underperformed their Swedish counterparts in both literacy and numeracy. However, Finns aged 25–34, a cohort educated following the implementation of the reforms, substantially outperformed their Swedish

[8] Data derived from OECD (2022).

[9] Data derived from OECD (2022).

counterparts in both subjects, in keeping with the PISA results (OECD 2013b: Tables A3.2 (L) and A.3.2(N)).[10]

To Einar Fransson, director of education for Nacka, a suburb of Stockholm, the Finns have it right. Fransson is a career educator. After serving as a secondary teacher of history for four years, he was the principal of a municipal school for 15 years, and then the principal for seven years of a school belonging to one of the country's leading for-profit networks, Kunskapsskolan. In 2010, he assumed his current role in Nacka, where 20% of students use vouchers to attend *friskolor*. Fransson said in a 2012 interview that he liked the choice and innovation brought by the introduction of vouchers but agreed with Vlachos about grade inflation and with Westerberg about segregation. Moreover, Fransson said the focus on vouchers obscured the true problems with schooling in Sweden: inadequate teacher preparation and pay. Both were longstanding issues in Sweden that never got addressed, he said (Abrams 2016: p. 274).

Teachers in Sweden at the lower-secondary level earned 82% as much as their college classmates in 2011, according to the OECD, while their Finnish counterparts earned 98% as much (OECD 2013a: Table D3.2).[11] This difference surely explains, in part, the difference in the appeal of teaching in the two countries. While admission into teacher education programs at Finnish universities is quite selective (Abrams 2016: pp. 294–298), Sweden has a hard time staffing its schools, so much so that the country had only 10 new university graduates in 2012 certified to teach chemistry and was forced the following year to launch a fast-track teacher certification program called Teach for Sweden, modeled on Teach for America (Abrams 2016: p. 286).

While Finland never followed Sweden in implementing vouchers, it does provide students ample opportunities for choice within its public

---

[10] eFor literacy for the 55-to-65 cohort, the OECD average was 255. The results for the Finns and Swedes were 260 and 262, respectively. For literacy for the 25-to-34 cohort, the OECD average was 284. The results for the Finns and Swedes were 309 and 290, respectively. For numeracy for the 55-to-65 cohort, the OECD average was 253. The results for the Finns and Swedes were 260 and 268, respectively. For numeracy for the 25-to-34 cohort, the OECD average was 279. The results for the Finns and Swedes were 303 and 288, respectively.

[11] By 2019, this difference had closed somewhat, with Swedish teachers at the lower-secondary level earning 89% as much as their college classmates while their Finnish counterparts made 97%. See OECD (2020: Table D3.2).

system. At the primary level, neighborhood schools are central to the Finnish pedagogical philosophy, allowing young children to walk to and from school and thus develop a sense of geography and community through everyday experience. But at the lower- and upper-secondary levels, students can and often do travel across town to schools defined by different themes. There is even a small sector of government-funded independent schools, accounting for about 3% of the nation's total (European Commission 2021). These independent schools must operate as nonprofits and conform with specific regulations, such as hiring only certified teachers and following a national curriculum. Religion nevertheless has a place at these independent schools, as it does at public schools, where students take classes about their own faith (Finnish Ministry of Education and Culture 2022). Mill and Friedman as well as Chubb and Moe and Swedish voucher advocates might still find such a system too rigid, but they would have a hard time challenging the outcomes.

If choice alone is the objective, vouchers and the like largely serve their purpose. But if true improvement of a country's system of education is the goal, choice alone falls far short. Achieving such improvement calls for investment in high-quality preschool; better teacher preparation and pay; smaller classes; and richer curricula, including a range of classes in art, music, and crafts both to make school more enticing and to teach math and science in a practical manner. This path is expensive, but not in the long run.

References

Abrams SE (2016) Education and the commercial mindset. Harvard University Press, Cambridge.

Abrams SE (2019) Exit, voice, and charter schools. *La Rev Jur de la Univ de Puerto Rico* 88:895–919.

Abrams SE (2020) Perspectives on school vouchers. In: Berends M, Primus A, Springer MG (eds) Handbook of research on school choice. Routledge, New York, pp 177–191.

Arrow KJ (1963) Uncertainty and the welfare economics of medical care. Am Econ Rev 53:941–973.
Brandén M, Bygren M (2022) The opportunity structure of segregation: School choice and school segregation in Sweden. Acta Sociol 65:420–438.
Butrymowicz S (2018a) What would actually happen if we gave all parents the chance to pick their children's schools? *The Hechinger Report*, 18 February.
Butrymowicz S (2018b) This country spends billions on private schools—And has a terrible learning gap between poor and wealthy. *The Hechinger Report*, 1 March.
Carell SE, Hoekstra ML (2010) Externalities in the classroom: How children exposed to domestic violence affect everyone's kids. Am Econ J-Appl Econ 2: 211–228.
Castro-Hidalgo A, Gómez-Álvarez L (2016) Chile: A long-term neoliberal experiment and its impact on the quality and equity of education. In: Adamson F, Åstrand B, Darling-Hammond L (eds) Global education reform: How privatization and public investment influence education outcomes. Routledge, New York, pp 16–49.
Catterall JS (1984) Politics and aid to private schools. Educ Eval Pol An 6: 435–440.
Chou S (2002) Asymmetric information, ownership and quality of care: An empirical analysis of nursing homes. J Health Econ 21: 293–311.
Chubb J, Moe T (1990) Politics, markets, and America's schools. Brookings, Washington, DC.
Clark KB (1968) Alternative public school systems. Harvard Educ Rev 38: 100–113.
Coase R (1937) The nature of the firm. Economica 4: 386–405.
Coons JE, Sugarman SD (1978) Education by choice: The case for family control. University of California Press, Berkeley.
Dalgleish WS (1870) A plain reading of the Elementary Education Act. John Marshall & Co., London.
Denice P, DeArmond M, Carr M (2021) When schools open: Student mobility and racial sorting across new charter schools in Kansas City, Missouri. J Urban Aff 43: 1468–1491.
Edwards v. Aguillard, 482 U.S. 578 (1987).
Elacqua G (2012) The impact of school choice and public policy on segregation: Evidence from Chile. Int J Educ Dev 32: 444–453.
European Commission (2021) Eurydice, Finland, organisation of private education. European Commission, Brussels.

Finnish Ministry of Education and Culture (2022). Basic Education Act (628/1998). Finnish Ministry of Education and Culture, Helsinki.

Fiske EB, Ladd, HF (2000) When schools compete: A cautionary tale. Brookings, Washington, DC.

French National Assembly and Senate. Loi numero 59-1557 du 31 décembre 1959 sur les rapports entre l'Etat et les établissements d'enseignement privés. Accessed at https://www.legifrance.gouv.fr/jorf/id/JORFTEXT000000693420.

Friedman M (1955) The role of government in education. In: Solo R (ed) Economics and the public interest. Rutgers University Press, New Brunswick, pp 123–144.

Friedman M (1967) The negro in America. Newsweek, 11 December.

Friedman M (1972) Busing: The real issue. Newsweek, 14 August.

Friedman M (1973) Selling school like groceries: The voucher idea. New York Times Magazine, 23 September.

Goldstein D (2018a) Protests spread, as teachers press for better pay and more funding. New York Times, 4 April.

Goldstein D (2018b) Arizona teachers end walkout as Governor signs bill approving raises. New York Times, 4 May.

Grandin G (2015) Taxes, schools, voting rights, and abortion: Chile shows the way. The Nation, 23 February.

Hansmann HB (1980) The role of nonprofit enterprise. Yale L J 89:835–901.

Heckman JJ (2006) Skill formation and the economics of investing in disadvantage children. Science 312:1900–1902.

Heckman JJ, Karapakula G (2019) Intergenerational and intragenerational externalities of the Perry Preschool Project. National Bureau of Economic Research, Working Paper 25889.

Heckman JJ, Raut LK (2016) Intergenerational long-term effects of preschool-structural estimates from a discrete dynamic programming model. J Econom 191:164–175.

Heckman JJ, Moon SH, Pinto R, Savelyev P, Yavitz A (2010) The rate of return to the HighScope Perry Preschool Program. J Pub Econ 94:114–128.

Heckman JJ, Pinto R, Savelyev P (2013) Understanding the mechanisms through which an influential early childhood program boosted adult outcomes. Am Econ Rev 103:2052–2086.

Heilig JV (2018) California just banned for-profit charter schools. Why? Progressive Magazine, 7 September.

Henig JR (1994) Rethinking school choice: Limits of the market metaphor. Princeton University Press, Princeton.

Hirschman AO (1970) Exit, voice, and loyalty: Responses to decline in firms, organizations, and states. Harvard University Press, Cambridge.
Hobbs TD (2018) Do vouchers work? Look to Milwaukee. Wall Street Journal, 29 January.
Jencks C (1968) Private schools for black children. New York Times Magazine, 3 November.
Jencks C (1970) Giving parents money to pay for schooling: Education vouchers. New Republic, 4 July.
Karsten S (1994) Policy on ethnic segregation in a system of choice: The case of the Netherlands. J Educ Pol 9:211–225.
Ladd HF, Fiske, EB (2016) England confronts the limits of school autonomy. National Center for the Study of Privatization in Education, Working Paper 232.
Ladd HF, Singleton JD (2020) The fiscal externalities of charter schools: Evidence from North Carolina. Educ Financ Policy 15:191–208.
Ladd HF, Turaeva M (2020) Parental preferences for charter schools in North Carolina: Implications for racial segregation and isolation. National Center for the Study of Privatization in Education, T Working Paper 243.
Ladd HF, Fiske EB, Ruijs N (2009) Parental choice in the Netherlands: Growing concerns about segregation. National Center for the Study of Privatization in Education, Working Paper 232.
Lauder H, Hughes D (eds) (1999) Trading in futures: Why markets in education don't work. Open University Press, Buckingham.
Levin HM (1968) The failure of the public schools and the free market remedy. Urban Review 2: 32-37.
Levin HM (1998) Educational vouchers: Effectiveness, choice, and costs. J Pol Anal Manag 17: 373–392.
Mill JS ([1859]1989) On liberty. Cambridge University Press, Cambridge.
Mosteller F (1995) The Tennessee study of class size in the early school grades. Future Child 5:113–127.
Murnane RJ, Waldman MR, Willett JB, Bos MS, Vegas E (2017) The consequences of educational voucher reform in Chile. National Bureau of Economic Research, Working Paper 23550.
OECD (2013a) Education at a glance 2013a. OECD, Paris.
OECD (2013b) OECD skills outlook 2013b: First results from the survey of adult skills. OECD, Paris.
OECD (2018) Education at a Glance. OECD, Paris.
OECD (2020) Education at a glance 2020. OECD, Paris.
OECD (2022) Programme for international student assessment. OECD, Paris.

Reich, R (2000) The case for 'progressive' vouchers. Wall Street Journal, 6 September.

Rogers D (1968) 110 Livingston Street: Politics and bureaucracy in the New York City School System. Random House, New York.

Ronfeldt M, Loeb S, Wyckoff J (2013) How teacher turnover harms student achievement. Am Educ Res J 50:4–36.

Sizer TR (1969). Education in the ghetto: The case for a free market. Saturday Review, 11 January.

Sparks SD (2019) The splintering of wealthy areas from school districts is speeding up. Education Week, 16 April.

Superville D (2017) Schools become whiter and wealthier in communities that secede from districts. Education Week, 21 June.

Thrupp M (2006) School admissions and the segregation of school intakes in New Zealand cities. Urban Stud 44: 1393–1404.

Traub J (2000) What no school can do. New York Times Magazine, 16 January.

Vlachos J (2011) Friskolor i förändring. In Hartman L (ed) Konkurrensens konsekvenser: Vad händer med svensk vualfärd? SNS Förlag, Stockholm, pp 66–110.

Walford W (2001) Privatization in industrialized countries. In: Levin HM (ed) Privatizing education: Can the marketplace deliver choice, efficiency, equity and social cohesion? Westview Press, Boulder, pp 178–200.

Welner KG (2008) NeoVouchers: The emergence of tuition tax credits for private schooling. Rowman and Littlefield, New York.

Williamson OE (1971) The vertical integration of production: Market failure considerations. Am Econ Rev 61:112–123.

Zelman v. Simmons-Harris, 536 U.S. 639 (2002).

Part III

Trade Openness

6

Free Trade as a Key to Economic Development

Arvind Panagariya

Introduction

Thinking on the role of free trade in development has had a checkered history. Immediately after the Second World War, as former colonies began to emerge as independent countries, economists, policy analysts and policymakers were uniform of the view that economic development in these countries required protection to industry. Ironically, the same actors simultaneously held that postwar reconstruction in the war devastated industrialized economies required progressive freeing of international trade. This latter consensus eventually translated into the establishment of the liberal multilateral trading system under the auspices of the General Agreement on Tariffs and Trade (GATT) that came into effect on January 1, 1948.

A. Panagariya (✉)
Columbia University, New York, NY, USA
e-mail: ap2231@columbia.edu

A. L. Kassens and J. C. Hall (eds.), *Challenges in Classical Liberalism*, Palgrave Studies in Classical Liberalism,
https://doi.org/10.1007/978-3-031-32890-9_6

But when the so-called tiger economies of East Asia—Hong Kong, Singapore, Taiwan and South Korea—broke away from the postwar consensus on development and began turning to outward-oriented trade policies in the late 1950s and early 1960s and quickly became growth powerhouses, the old consensus crumbled. Economists such as Jagdish Bhagwati and Ian Little, who had blessed the import substitution industrialization (ISI) strategy of countries such as India, went on to become the staunchest advocates of free trade as the principal engine of growth and development (Panagariya 2019: pp. 10–12). Prominent among those leading the charge on this front additionally came to include Anne Kruger and Bela Balassa. Three major research projects—the first led by Little and sponsored by the Organization for Economic Cooperation and Development (OECD), the second led by Bhagwati and Krueger and sponsored by the National Bureau of Economic Research and the third led by Balassa and sponsored by the World Bank—led to a replacement of the pro-protection postwar consensus by pro-free-trade consensus (Little et al. 1970; Bhagwati 1978; Krueger 1978; Balassa 1982).

Reaction against this new consensus emerged soon, however. Influential studies first by political scientists Alice Amsden and Robert Wade and later by economists Dani Rodrik and Ha-Joon Chang reinterpreted the South Korean and Taiwanese "miracles" as having resulted from carefully calibrated protection and industrial policy rather than liberal trade policies (Amsden 1989; Wade 1990, 2004; Rodrik 1995, 1999; Chang 2007). Rodrik and Chang also contended that the fastest growth in developing countries took place during the 1960s and the early 1970s, which they identify as import-substitution phase in the history of developing economies. Rodrik went so far as to describe this phase as the "golden age" of development.

These propositions did not go unchallenged. Little offered arguments countering Wade while Bhagwati responded to many of the propositions by Wade, Amsden and Rodrik. More recently, in a book entitled *Free Trade and Prosperity*, I have offered the first full-scale defense of free trade with developing countries at its center. In the book, I analyze in detail each of the arguments made by the critics of free trade and expose the fallacies underlying them. Luckily, barring rare exceptions, developing countries themselves have come to reject the pro-protections school and progressively embraced freer trade with happy outcomes.

The Folly of Immediate Postwar Export Pessimism

Export pessimism in the early decades following the Second World War had its origins in the erroneous conceptualization of the economy as consisting of only two traded sectors: industry and agriculture (Krueger 1997). In this conception, developing countries were naturally seen as importers of industrial products and exporters of agricultural products. It was then argued, correctly, that the income and price elasticities of demand for agricultural products being low, exports by developing countries would fetch progressively lower export revenues. The low-income elasticity meant that with rising incomes, developed country demand would shift away from agricultural and toward industrial products. This would lead to an exogenous shift in the terms of trade against agricultural products and hence reduced revenues for a given volume of developing country exports. In a similar vein, the low-price elasticity meant that any export expansion by developing countries would endogenously give rise to such a large decline in their terms of trade that the export revenues would fall.

It followed from this analysis that the reliance on exports as the engine of growth would be self-defeating. Developing countries had no choice but to develop industry, which required protection against imports. This prescription went against the principle of comparative advantage, however. Taken individually, each developing country was small in the world markets so that any protection would bring with it the usual efficiency losses in production and consumption. To rescue the prescription of ISI from this conundrum, economists went on to invoke the hitherto unused infant-industry argument.

As Krueger later pointed out, the error in this line of reasoning lay in the conceptualization of the economy into only two tradable goods: agriculture and industry. Policymakers in countries such as South Korea and Taiwan recognized this error and thought of industrial sector as consisting of multiple goods of which some required labor as the principal input while others replied predominantly on capital. In this conception, developing countries had a comparative advantage in a range of labor-intensive products even if they had a comparative disadvantage in industry as a whole. They could thus export a set of labor-intensive products while being net importers of industrial goods. Exports of labor-intensive goods did not suffer from low-income and price elasticities and could be exported them in large volumes without fear of a deterioration in the terms of trade. That was precisely the strategy they pursued and surprised the economists and policymakers all around.

Trade Openness and Growth

At the most basic level, it is the principle of comparative advantage that forms the basis of the conventional recommendation of free trade. The principle relies on the existence of differences in the opportunity costs of production across countries. In a nutshell, it says that each country benefits by specializing in and exporting products in which its opportunity costs of production is the lowest. Economies of scale provide an alternative source of benefits via specialization in a handful of products.

While these "static" efficiency gains from international specialization are important, they are often insufficient to move the political needle in favor of free trade in developing countries. The paramount concern in these countries is with removal of widespread poverty and bringing prosperity to the masses. To the extent that faster growth helps cut poverty by creating jobs for the masses at steadily rising wages as well as generating more and more tax revenues for the government to finance anti-poverty programs, the principal issue becomes whether liberal trade policies can help stimulate faster growth.

Unfortunately, when it comes to free trade and growth, theory turns out to be a lot more ambiguous. Depending on their specific structure, endogenous growth models may produce a positive, zero or even negative effect of free trade on growth. Therefore, the question becomes principally empirical: Based on the past experience, is free trade or protection more conducive to faster growth?

At the outset, I must make clear that no serious advocate of free trade argues that free trade by itself is sufficient to produce faster growth. Any concrete effects of trade liberalization must first impact the volume of trade itself. But there is no guarantee that such a response would always occur. For example, if the outside world is autarkic, a country's own liberalization cannot go far. Likewise, if internal transportation links are weak or ports are dysfunctional, the mere freeing of trade through a reduction in tariffs or non-tariff barriers cannot go far. Even internal domestic policies such as centralized planning, investment licensing and rigid labor laws can considerably limit the response to trade liberalization. It is keeping these considerations in view that all serious advocates of free trade simultaneously advocate domestic policy reform, building of infrastructure and trade facilitation through improved quality of port services.

One further clarification concerns what is meant by the terms "free trade" and "protection." At least in the present empirical context, neither the former should be interpreted to mean a complete absence of barriers to trade nor the latter should be equated to a total ban on any trade flow. Instead, the term free trade is to be interpreted as a policy regime characterized by low trade barriers and high exports-to-GDP ratio. In a similar vein, trade liberalization is to be identified with declining trade barriers and rising exports-to-GDP ratio.[1] Terms protection and progressive import substitution can be defined symmetrically.

Turning to evidence then, a useful stating point for it is the proposition that developing countries as a group have grown the fastest during the years 1961–1973 by following the ISI strategy of development. Dani Rodrik first offered this proposition in a short book published in 1999. Ha-Joon Chang subsequently echoed him in his influential 2007 book. Are these authors right?

The answer to this critical question turns out to be a categorical no. There are three reasons demonstrating the falsehood of why this Rodrik-Chang proposition.

[1] Instead of exports-to-GDP ratio, we could also use imports-to-GDP ratio or trade-to-GDP ratio since the three ratios generally move together. I prefer the exports-to-GDP ratio mainly because imports can also be influenced by external aid and remittance inflows.

First and foremost, factually, developing countries as a group did not grow the fastest during 1960–1973. In Table 6.1, I divide the period from 1960 to 2013 into three periods in two different ways and present the average growth rates in developing and OECD countries in each period. It is immediately from these growth rates that developing countries witnessed the fastest growth during the decades following 1990. This was also the period during which they came to embrace progressively more open trade policies.

Rodrik may be forgiven for missing this point since he lacked data beyond 1997 at the time he published his book. But by 2007, when Chang published his book, the evidence was loud and clear. The average growth rate of developing countries works out to 3.3% during 1990–2005 and 3.4% during 1995–2005. Therefore, data factually falsify his claim.

In the post-1990 decades, country after country went on to liberalize its trade regime. Unlike the liberalization during the 1980s, which the International Monetary Fund and the World Bank had forced on the countries, this liberalization was predominantly at the initiative of the country governments themselves. As a result, it was sustained and supported by complementary pro-growth domestic policy reform. China and India, by far the two largest countries by population, reversed their longstanding autarkic trade policies, the former starting in the late 1970s and the latter in the early 1990s. They went on to reap the benefits both in terms of growth and poverty alleviation. Many other countries in Asia,

Table 6.1 Growth in developing and OECD countries

Period	Growth rate	
	Developing	High income OECD
1961–75	2.9	3.6
1976–94	2.1	2.3
1995–2013	4.2	1.4
1961–73	2.9	4.2
1974–90	1.9	2.3
1991–2013	4	1.4

Source Authors' calculations using World Development Indicators data

Africa and Latin America also opened up their economies and achieved high growth rates on a sustained basis.[2]

The second reason why the proposition by Rodrik fails to stand up to close scrutiny is that even during the 1960s and early 1970s, fast-growing economies achieved such growth on the back of rapid expansion of international trade. Had Rodrik considered some key details of individual countries, he would have hesitated to reach his key conclusion. The cases of four East Asian tiger economies, which grew at average annual rates of 8–10% during these years, are well known. But even in the less-known case of Brazil, declining tariffs, depreciating domestic currency and rising trade-to-GDP ratio had been crucial to fast growth during the period.

In my recent book *Free Trade and Prosperity*, I look at the relationship between per-capita GDP growth and exports in developing countries at a more granular level. I find that during 1961–1975, per-capita GDP grew rapidly, defined as a rate equaling or exceeding 3%, in 29 countries. Out of them, data on exports of goods and services are available for the initial as well as terminal year for 20 countries. It turns out that in 16 out of these 20 countries, the exports-to-GDP ratio rose between 1961 and 1975. This means that exports of these countries grew even faster than GDP. Out of the remaining four countries, in two of them, the exports-to-GDP ratio remained extremely high in 1975 despite declining relative to its value in 1961. In Singapore, it was 137.1% and in Malaysia 43% in 1975. These countries were thus highly open during the period. Only in the cases of Mexico and Costa Rica did the exports-to-GDP ratio begin small in 1961 and fell further by 1975.

The final reason to question the Rodrik-Chang proposition is that the external environment for growth in developing countries was far more favorable during 1960–1973 than in the post-1990 decades. The OECD countries grew significantly faster during the former than the latter period. Therefore, the faster developing country growth in the post-1990 years testifies to the internal growth momentum in these countries, originating in their own openness to global markets.

[2] See Panagariya (2019). In the book, I discuss in careful detail the cases of India and China in Chapters 12 and 13, respectively. Additionally, I provide the evidence of low or declining trade barriers to trade alongside fast growth in per-capita GDP in other developing counties in Chapter 14.

Correlation Versus Causation

When confronted with the evidence of a strong positive correlation between growth and openness, free-trade critics shift the goalpost and contend that correlation does not imply causation. While I return to the evidence on causation below, at least at a rhetorical level, one must ask the critics whether they can provide similar correlation-based evidence favoring their hypothesis of superiority of import substitution over outward orientation. After all, policymakers must choose between either liberal or protectionist trade policies and if growth exhibits a positive association with outward orientation but not import protection, does that not decide the case in favor of the former?

More to the point, suppose that we cannot establish causation conclusively but do know that GDP growth and the expansion of trade move together. Then, surely, it is wiser to adopt policies that help expand trade since it would be accompanied by growth as well. While domestic policy reform can also help expand trade, when it comes to trade policy, it is liberalization rather than protection that expands trade. Therefore, even the positive association between trade and growth is sufficient to rule out protection as the desirable policy.

Luckily, today, we are in a position to make a stronger claim since economists have been able to amass considerable evidence establishing causation. Before I turn to this evidence, it is necessary to remind that establishing causation requires the application of econometric techniques. The latter in turn require accurate definition and measurement of the relevant variables. It turns out, however, that aggregation of various trade policy instruments into a single indicator of the degree of protection is fraught with serious difficulties. We lack a satisfactory method to convert non-tariff barriers such as licensing or quotas into numerical indicators. Indeed, even the aggregation of tariffs on different products at different rates into a single indicator is not a straightforward matter. As a simple example, if one half of the imports are subject to a custom duty of 10% and the other half to 20%, their aggregation into a single rate of 15% would seem plausible. Yet, the effect of the two rates on imports in the first case would be quite different from that of a single 15% rate on all imports in the second.

It is because of these measurement problems that the most compelling evidence on causation has relied on relating growth or the level of per-capita income to trade flows. Because trade flows and GDP exhibit two-way causation, researchers have deployed the instrumental variables approach to separate that part of trade flows that is not sensitive to changes in GDP. In particular, in providing some of the earliest evidence of a causal relationship between per-capita income and trade flows, economists Jeffrey Frankel and David Romer and Frankel and Andrew Rose deploy the gravity model to first identify the part of the total trade that depends solely on bilateral distance between two countries. Armed with this part of trade as the independent variable, they go on to measure the impact of openness on per-capita GDP. They find that trade has a strong positive impact on per-capita income. For example, Frankel and Romer (1999) find that 1% point increase in the trade-to-GDP ratio raises per-capita income by 2% points on the average. The effect turns out to be statistically significant and robust to corrections for many sources of variation in per-capita income.

Subsequent to Frankel and Romer and Frankel and Rose (2002) papers, numerous articles studying the causal relationship between growth and openness have appeared. This research has been greatly facilitated by the fact that a large number of developing countries have opened their economies to trade in the last two to three decades. Economist Douglas Irwin has surveyed these studies in a recent paper. Without reproducing findings of specific studies here, it suffices to quote the bottom line that Irwin offers. To quote him, "A consistent finding is that trade reforms have a positive impact on economic growth, on average, although the effect is heterogeneous across countries. Overall, these research findings should temper some of the previous agnosticism about the empirical link between trade reform and economic performance" (Irwin 2019: Abstract).

Selective Protection and Industrial Targeting

Critics of free trade have offered nothing by way of positive relationship between high or rising protection on the one hand and rising per-capita incomes on the other. Indeed, deep down, they know that such a relationship, even at the level of association as opposed to causation, does not exist and have therefore never looked for it. Instead, their approach has been to poke holes in the evidence linking free trade to growth and declare victory for protectionism by default. In terms of offering any positive evidence for their hypothesis, the most they have done is to point to the presence of protection and industrial targeting in countries that have achieved high growth and then resort to post hoc ergo propter hoc (after this, therefore, because of it) fallacy. In trying to establish any causal link between protection and targeting on the one hand and growth on the other, they have been utterly unconvincing.

I may note at the outset that the success of a specific industry after it is protected or subsidized proves nothing about the efficacy of the policies for at least two reasons. First, protection and subsidies make the industry profitable and therefore its expansion upon receiving support is to be expected. To be convincing, the advocates of protection and industrial targeting must also show that the policies did not cause harm to other sectors in the economy. There are good reasons to suspect such harm: Increased profitability in the sector receiving protection would move resources into that sector and derive other more competitive sectors of them.

The second reason why the success of certain protected sectors is insufficient to accept the conclusion reached by pro-protection advocates is that these successes must be weighed against failures. The history of economic development is full of failures produced by protection and import substitution. Even in South Korea on which pro-protection advocates often rely to make their case had established a highly capital-intensive ball-bearing factory in the 1970s that turned into a white elephant and had to be eventually shut down.[3] But this rarely finds a mention from advocates of industrial policy such as Amsden, Wade, Rodrik and Chang alongside the documentation of "successful" cases.

The key country on whose experience pro-protection advocates hang their case for industrial targeting most often is South Korea. Accordingly, let me review this case in some detail. Table 6.2 presents the growth rates of GDP, per-capita GDP, exports and imports from 1954 to 2008 in the country. I have divided this entire period into five phases. The first phase, spanning 1954–1962, is identified with import substitution. Both trade and GDP grew at a relatively slow pace during this period.

The second phase, lasting from 1963 to 1973, was one of outward orientation. Selective industry promotion during this phase was limited to cement, fertilizer, and petroleum refining in the early 1960s and to steel and petrochemicals in the late 1960s and early 1970s. Outside of these innervations, the policy regime was neutral in the sense that incentives did not discriminate among sectors. Larry Westphal (1990: Table 1) calculates that when the economy-wide implications of all interventions are considered, there existed a slight bias in the policy regime in favor of exports relative to free trade. Overall sector-level neutrality of policy meant that export sectors emerged according to comparative advantage. One sector that emerged to the surprise of all was wigs and human hair whose exports grew from nil in 1963 to 10.1% of all exports by 1970.

Table 6.2 Average annual growth rates in Korea

Period	GDP	Per-capita GDP	Exports of constant-price goods and services	Imports of constant-price goods and services
1	2	3	4	5
1954–62	4.2	1.3	13.9	5.2
1963–73	9.1	8.5	32.1	21.4
1974–82	6.9	5.1	14.0	12.2
1983–95	8.7	7.6	12.6	13.5
1996–2008	4.4	3.8	12.4	8.5

[3] Anne Krueger mentions this case when commenting on the author's book *Free Trade and Prosperity* at a Cato Institute event on May 30, 2019. A video of the presentation is available from the Cato Institute.

When claiming success for industrial targeting, pro-protection advocates entirely ignore the years 1963–1973 and focus nearly exclusively on the following phase, 1974–1982. It was during this phase that South Korea engaged in a heavy and chemical industry (HCI) drive. But the growth rate during it actually fell to 6.9%. Moreover, toward the end of this phase, the economy faced serious macroeconomic instability with the result that the government had to abandon the HCI drive and return to a neutral policy regime. That in turn restored growth to 8.7% during 1983–1995.

Chang claims that industrial targeting was successful despite the drop in growth because industries promoted under the HCI drive became eventually successful. But as I have noted earlier, the claim is based on a post hoc fallacy. Having already experienced near double-digit annual growth in real wages and a substantial increase in the savings rate, South Korea was well on its way to becoming a labor-scarce and capital-abundant country. Therefore, even absent the HCI drive, capital-intensive sectors promoted under it were destined to emerge over time. All the HCI drive did was to advance that process by a few years. As such success of the targeted industries many years later hardly proves the positive case for targeting. What is required, instead, is the demonstration that the benefits of advancing the process exceeded its costs. None of the advocates of industrial targeting including Chang and Rodrik has adhered to this standard of proof.

Wade, another influential advocate of industrial targeting, gives a lengthy documentation of government interventions, big and small, by the Taiwanese government during the 1960s and 1970s to make the case that these interventions catalyzed and sustained its rapid growth. But he offers no coherent explanation of how the interventions led to the high growth. His account is full of repeated references to the government acting strategically but does not articulate a "strategic action" model of economic development that other countries could emulate. To make his case for the success of targeting, he offers the following bottom line:

> The fact of big leadership or big followership does not mean that government intervention has been effective in promoting economic growth; it only means that government intervention cannot be dismissed as having

> made a negligible difference to outcomes. But the balance of presumption must be that government industrial policies, including sectoral ones, helped more than they hindered. To argue otherwise is to suggest that economic performance would have been still more exceptional with less intervention, which is simply less plausible than the converse. (Wade 1990: pp. 305–306)

This statement is illustrative of the low bar that pro-protection advocates set for themselves while insisting on a much higher standard of proof from their pro-free-trade opponents. Such a tactic may mislead some innocent readers but not economists who came to the pro-free-trade view after realizing their earlier mistake of having defended import substitution, as is true of Little. The latter was quick to respond to Wade forcefully in these terms: "Since the less interventionist Hong Kong, Singapore, and Taiwan grew faster than Korea, it is unclear why Wade thinks it simply less plausible that less intervention would have been better, given also the widespread failure of government industrial policies elsewhere. I find it simply more plausible that Korea grew fast despite its industrial policies, than because of them" (Little 1994: p. 365).

Echoes of Wade's style of analysis can also be heard in the accounts of more recent experiences of China and India that Rodrik and Chang offer. Rodrik argues that the experience of China cannot be interpreted as supporting the position of pro-free-trade advocates since it remains subject to numerous government interventions. Chang goes a step further and argues that China and India succeeded precisely because they refused to wear a free-trade straitjacket that free-trade advocates recommend.

But if continued government interventions are behind the success of these countries, once rapid growth had been achieved, any further removal of the interventions and acceleration of trade liberalization should have hurt the growth prospects of the countries. But such is scarcely the case with either country. China had already achieved nearly 10% growth in the 1980s. If the remaining protection and government interventions are to be credited for this shift in the growth rate, their withdrawal should have led to a decline in the growth rate. But the reality is that continued trade liberalization helped China sustain its rapid growth. Till as late as the early 2000s, it was the decision by China to accept considerably opening up as a part of the conditions of its entry into the World Trade Organization that helped it sustain unprecedented growth in trade and double-digit growth.

The experience of India has been no different. It began opening up its economy in earnest in 1991. This early liberalization yielded positive results but by the late 1990s, growth began to falter yet again. It was another bout of reforms including trade liberalization during 1998–2003 that placed the country on a growth trajectory of 8% plus for nearly a decade beginning in 2003. But even this growth could not be sustained because trade liberalization came to a halt and some of the socialist era policies of the country found their way back into the policy regime during 2009–2014. The government that came to office in 2014 had to revive the reform agenda to bring high growth back to the country.

The Infant Industry Argument for Protection

The discussion of free trade and development will remain incomplete without at least a brief consideration of the much-abused infant industry argument. An influential early statement of this argument is found in a 1791 report authored by the first Treasury Secretary of the United States, Alexander Hamilton (1913). In this primitive form, the argument says that an industry, though viable in the long run, would fail to emerge if it is exposed to competition from established foreign counterparts in its early phase. The reason is that in contrast to the latter, it has not had the advantage of "learning" that takes place in the early phase and helps bring the costs down. Temporary protection in the early years of its existence would allow learning to take place allowing the industry to withstand competition against its foreign counterparts in the future.

Economists quickly realized, however, that the argument was logically invalid as long as learning was internal to the firm. If the activity is viable in the long run, the firm entering the market can cover its losses in the early years from profits in future years. This recognition led economists to reformulate the argument in terms of learning economies that are external to the firm.

In this revised form, the argument says that if the learning economies are external to the firm so that the future costs fall not just for the first entrant but future entrants as well, the firm that enters first and incurs losses during the learning phase will not be able to recover them in the future. For in the future, competition among the new entrants would drive the price down to the post-learning marginal cost of production. Therefore, anticipating net losses, no firm would want to be the first firm to enter the market. Temporary protection, which covers the losses of the firm during the learning phase, would overcome this problem.

It turns out, however, that even this reformulated argument works only if we assume that the learning takes place from the mere act of production by the incumbent firm and mechanically spills over to future entrants. The moment we specify the micro foundations of how learning takes place and gets transmitted to future entrants, the argument collapses.

To explain this critical but little appreciated point, consider a highly simplified, barebones example of widget industry that lasts for two periods. Widget manufacturing is subject to learning economies in period 1 that freely spill over to new entrants in period 2. Domestic demand is fixed at 1 million units in each period. Delivered import price is $90 and any exports are ruled out due to high transport cost or other barriers abroad. Per-unit cost at home is $100 in period 1 and $78 in period 2. The social rate of discount is 10%. With no capital-market distortions, the interest rate is also 10%.

In this setting, if widget is manufactured at home, there is loss of $10 million in period 1 and profit of $12 million in period 2. At 10% social discount rate, the profit in period 2 exceeds the loss in period 1 in net present value terms. Widget manufacture is a socially desirable activity. But it is easy to see that left to itself, the industry would fail to emerge.

The spill over of learning means that the cost in period 2 declines to $78 not just for the incumbent firm but new entrants as well. Because the latter have no period 1 losses to recover, competition among them would drive the domestic price down to $78. The incumbent would thus be unable to recuperate the losses incurred in period 1. Anticipating this outcome, no firm would enter the production activity in period 1 in the first place.

Protection in the form of $10 per unit tariff in period 1 can solve this problem. The tariff would raise the import price to $100, allowing the entrant in period 1 to recover its losses in that period. In period 2, the price would drop to $78 but that is no threat to the incumbent firm since it incurred no losses in period 1. Consumers would reap the benefit of the decline in price in the form of extra consumers' surplus of $12 million.

The conceptual issue this line of reasoning raises concerns the process via which learning takes place and transmits to the new entrants in period 2. It is rather heroic to postulate that the mere act of production by the incumbent firm leads to a fall in the production cost of period 2 entrants. It is essential that the argument stands up to the incorporation of one or more sources of learning and spill over such as innovation and worker training.

It turns out, however, that the moment we make the source of learning explicit, the case for protection on infant industry grounds collapses. To see this, modify the above example to allow for innovation as the source of learning. Suppose that the cost of widget production in period 1 is $95 instead of $100 and an innovation costing $5 million brings it down to $78 in period 2. The innovation cannot be held confidential so that it becomes available to new entrants in period 2 at no cost. The import price remains $90 per unit.

Once again, the widget manufacturing is a socially desirable activity but would fail to emerge own its own. To be sure a $5 per unit tariff will allow production but it would not result in cost-reduction innovation since the tariff would merely allow the entrant to break even. Will a tariff of $10 per unit to the trick? The answer is still in the negative since the firm makes zero profit if it invests in innovation and $5 million if it does not. No learning takes place. Free ridership on innovation de-incentivizes the firm from investing anything in it. Only a direct subsidy on innovation or patent protection can solve the problem. Replacing innovation by worker training that can spill over to new entrants in period 2 does not change this conclusion.[4]

Despite its logical flaws, the infant industry argument for protection has remained popular with policymakers who appeal to it even when subsidizing or extending increased protection to an industry that has existed for years. Some policymakers find the argument so plausible that economists advising them against it have little chance of gaining traction. The best that economists can do under such circumstances is to encourage them to support sectors that have the potential to become exporters. This approach has the advantage of picking sectors that are closer to the margin of comparative advantage. The opposite approach focusing on import substitution carries with it the danger of picking the highest cost industries to support.

Concluding Remarks

At the country level, all countries that have achieved high growth rates have done so in the presence of low or declining barriers to trade.[5] Using cross-country analysis, economists have also amassed considerable evidence not just of positive correlation but also causation flowing from trade to per-capita income or GDP growth. The infant-industry argument, often offered to justify protection in developing countries, fails to stand up to careful logical scrutiny.

Advocates of import substitution and industrial targeting have failed to provide similar evidence in favor of their position. They are yet to provide persuasive examples of countries that have grown rapidly behind high or rising trade barriers. Nor have they provided examples of countries experiencing rapid growth in the presence of low or declining trade-to-GDP ratio. As regards, cross-country evidence, they have made no serious effort to produce even a positive association, let alone explore

[4] Baldwin (1969) had originally made this point but subsequent authors have neglected it. As a result even many eminent trade economists continue to believe and teach to their students that a valid logical case for protection can be made on infant industry grounds.

[5] For detailed documentation, see Panagariya (2019).

causation, between high trade barriers or low import-to-GDP ration on the one hand and GDP growth on the other.

Pro-protection advocated hang their case principally on the existence of interventions in during phases of fast growth in countries such as South Korea, Taiwan, China and India. But they do not offer persuasive evidence to show that these interventions added to fast growth or subtracted from it. If anything, the available evidence points to the latter possibility. Hong Kong grew under complete free trade with no industrial targeting. Singapore and Taiwan intervened less than South Korea and grew faster than the latter. Even within South Korea, growth rate was higher during 1963–1973 when it did not engage in industrial targeting than during 1973–1982 when it did. Evidence thus does not lend support to the position of pro-protection advocates. In conclusion, it is difficult to resist quoting Frederic Bastiat who had written more than 160 years ago, "I believe that the opposition to free trade rests upon errors, or, if you prefer, upon *half-truths*" (Bastiat 1845 [1996]: p. 3).

References

Amsden A (1989) Asia's next giant: South Korea and late industrialization. Oxford University Press, New York.

Balassa B (1982) Development strategies in semi-industrialized economies. Johns Hopkins University Press, Baltimore.

Baldwin RE (1969) The case against infant-industry tariff protection. J Polit Econ 77:295–305.

Bastiat F (1845 [1996]) Economic sophisms. Foundation for Economic Education, Irvington-on-Hudson.

Bhagwati J (1978) Foreign trade regimes and economic development: Anatomy and consequences of exchange rate regimes. National Bureau of Economic Research, New York.

Chang H (2007) Bad samaritans: Rich nations, poor policies and the threat to the developing world. Random House Business Books, London.

Frankel JA, Romer D (1999) Does trade cause growth? Amer Econ Rev 89:379–399.

Frankel J, Rose A (2002) An estimate of the effect of common currencies on trade and income. Q J Econ 117:437–466.

Hamilton A (1913) Report on manufactures [1791]. Presented by Mr. Smoot. August 30. 63rd Congress, 1st Session, Document No. 172.

Irwin D (2019) Does trade reform promote economic growth? A review of recent evidence. National Bureau of Economic Research, Working Paper 25927.

Krueger A (1978) Foreign trade regime and economic development: Liberalization attempts and consequences. National Bureau of Economic Research, New York.

Krueger A (1997) Trade policy and economic development: How we learn. Amer Econ Rev 81:1–22.

Little IMD (1994) Trade and industrialization revisited. Pakistan Dev Rev 33:359–381.

Little IMD, Scitovsky T, Scott M (1970) Industry and trade in some developing countries. Oxford University Press, Londong.

Panagariya A (2019) Free trade and prosperity: How openness helps developing countries grow richer and combat poverty. Oxford University Press, New York.

Rodrik D (1995) Getting interventions right: How South Korea and Taiwan grew rich. Econ Policy 20:55–107.

Rodrik D (1999) The new global economy and developing countries: Making openness work. Overseas Development Council, Washington, DC.

Wade R (1990) Governing the market: Economic theory and the role of the government in East Asian industrialization. Princeton University Press, Princeton.

Wade R (2004) Governing the market: Economic theory and the role of the government in East Asian industrialization, second paperback edition with a new introduction. Princeton University Press, Princeton.

Westphal LE (1990) Industrial policy in an export-propelled economy: Lessons from South Korea's experience. J Econ Perspect 4(3):41–59.

7
The Case for Regulated Trade

Ronald B. Davies

Introduction

As a group, economists tend to be a hands-off lot that leans toward leaving people to make decisions for themselves. This reliance on free markets probably results from the way Economics is taught. When most people are introduced to Economics, one of the first concepts they learn is the Invisible Hand, an idea that says that under certain conditions an unregulated market will result in an outcome that is actually the best one for society. This is an appealing concept because of its ease of implementation—do nothing and what comes out of individual people doing their own things results in efficiency. This tendency to favor the unregulated market permeates a lot of economic thinking, including how economists approach the issue of international trade. To give an idea of the popularity of the Invisible Hand in international trade, we just need look to

R. B. Davies (✉)
University College of Dublin, Dublin, Ireland
e-mail: ronald.davies@ucd.ie

A. L. Kassens and J. C. Hall (eds.), *Challenges in Classical Liberalism*, Palgrave Studies in Classical Liberalism,
https://doi.org/10.1007/978-3-031-32890-9_7

a survey by the American Institute for Economic Research which found that more than four in five economists said that they supported the idea of free trade (Whaples 2009). Why is free trade as an idea so popular? It goes back to the Invisible Hand. If two people/cities/states/countries want to swap with each other—which is really what the act of international trade amounts to—and this swap makes both sides better off, why should we interfere with this? We don't need to because the Invisible Hand tells us that not only are they making each other happier, but this trade results in efficiency.

The problem here is that the Invisible Hand works, but only under a very specific set of assumptions. While an Economics degree may spend the first couple of years explaining why the Invisible Hand *can* work, the second half explores the limits those assumptions impose (as well as delving into advanced mathematical and statistical tools). For an unregulated market to achieve efficiency, two assumptions are especially important. The first assumption is that *everyone impacted by a choice has the right to put a stop to it*. A lot of choices create what economists call externalities, a bit of jargon which captures any effect from an action on third parties who are not directly involved in making the decision whether or not to do something. The classic example of an externality is pollution; while a company and its customer may decide between themselves to engage in business together, the pollution caused by this can affect people who are not part of this agreement. Now extend the idea to international trade. If a company in one country does business with an overseas customer, the Invisible Hand tells us that for this to automatically be efficient for society (which now means the whole planet), it should be the case that this transaction does not affect anyone else.

The second key assumption of the Invisible Hand is that, even if no third parties are impacted by an exchange, that everyone has *full and complete information*. This assumption requires that everyone involved knows everything there is to know about the transaction and its effects. For example, when importing a shirt from China, this would require that an American consumer knows where the cotton was grown, whether it was organic, how much the workers who sewed the shirt were paid, and a whole host of other things, including how buying a shirt from China affects American wages. If anything, these challenges are growing over time as global supply chains result in products containing inputs from across the globe.

Those are two big assumptions which, in reality, fail pretty much all the time. Nearly every action—including trade—affects third parties and clearly nobody knows everything. The real question, however, is whether the assumption violations are severe enough to require governments to step in and regulate international trade? The answer to that question—as with every question in Economics—is it depends. It is not hard to find examples where this is true. For example, consider human trafficking, an industry worth over $150 billion annually that pretty much every die-hard free trade economist would say needs government intervention (International Labour Organization 2017). Since human trafficking by definition involves people who did not voluntarily choose to participate in the transaction, this violates the first assumption of no externalities. Similarly, most people believe that trade in weapons of mass destruction should be heavily regulated, if not banned entirely. Again, because the point of such weapons is to kill people who presumably would rather not die, governments place strong limits on trade in military goods.[1]

Situations where incomplete information is grounds for regulation are equally easy to find. For example, agricultural imports are routinely inspected for pests, with fees charged at the border to cover the cost of inspection.[2] Since these fees are charged on imports only, they act as a barrier which reduces trade below its free trade level. Nevertheless, because of the dangers associated with unwittingly importing pests and diseases that can ravage domestic crops, there is a need for the government to intervene in free trade to try to resolve the imperfect information. Similarly, standards on the lead content of toys, the flammability of textiles, and a whole host of other concerns about potential unknowns about what is crossing the border are well-accepted methods of intervening in free trade.

It is important to remember that the Invisible Hand's need for no externalities and complete information applies to any economic choice,

---

[1] It is worth noting, however, that trade in military weapons remains legal. In 2020, the US led the world in weapons trade, exporting over $175 billion worth.

[2] For the US, you can find a list of fees at U.S. Customs and Border Protection (2022).

not just the decision to trade across borders. What makes international trade an interesting case for considering the limitations of the free market is the scale at which trade operates. When production occurs on the other side of the world, it can be difficult to ensure that a product meets your expectations. Many of us know the frustration of ordering something from the internet only to have it not fit right or be the wrong color. While those consequences of imperfect information are an annoyance, now imagine the potentially horrific consequences of a company that imports infant car seats which, unknown to them, suffer from serious design flaws. Because international trade involves distance in geography, time, legal systems, and culture, the information problems inherent to trade can dwarf those of local transactions and make it a hothouse for imperfect information.

Likewise, the externalities generated by international trade can be exacerbated because of the scale and distance at which trade operates. Here too, information plays a role since distance can impede information and make it difficult to see the links between action and outcome. For example, a US company may be importing chemicals produced by a firm that dumps waste in rivers, an action that the US firm does not see. Since the locals who suffer the effects of that pollution are far away, the importer may be completely unaware of who all is impacted by the product it buys. Labor markets are another area rife with trade externalities. Importing cheap toys from India would displace American toy workers in the US, lowering their wages. This is one externality from toy trade but there are others. In particular, when those former toy workers in the US go to find other jobs, this can push down wages in other industries. Thus, imports of one product can affect *all* wages, an externality that is hard to observe because it filters through the entire global economy. These "general equilibrium" effects show how the effects of trade percolate through economies and are at the heart of a lot of the research on trade as researchers try to follow the impacts of imports across industries, workers, and countries.

Thus, the distance involved in trade and the interconnected nature of global supply chains and overlapping markets mean that free trade is quite likely to fail the no externalities and full information in significant ways. This means that the Invisible Hand is unlikely to work as hoped and provides room for government intervention. On occasion, this regulation can be an outright ban on trade, as was the case for human trafficking.[3] Most of the time, however, regulation lands somewhere between unfettered free trade and a complete ban. With this in mind, and before moving on to discuss reasons to limit trade in more detail, it is first worth mentioning some of the policies governments use to do so.

Trade policies can take many forms, with tariffs (a tax when something crosses the border) and quotas (a limit on how many units can be imported) being two primary trade interventions. Over the past decades, both of these have fallen worldwide due to the efforts of the World Trade Organization. This has led to increased use of "non-tariff barriers," a catch-all category that includes safety regulations, license requirements to offer services in another country, and more. Currently, non-tariff barriers dominate international policy discussions, with a lot of debating about when they are needed and when they simply interfere with well-functioning markets. One reason for these debates is that non-tariff barriers are hard to define since they basically include any policy that affects trade, even when they're not explicitly about imported products themselves. For example, Ireland charges an annual road tax on all motor vehicles in use. While that may not sound like it has anything to do with trade, the road tax is a de facto tariff since Ireland imports all its cars. Another example is that in Japan, to get your motorcycle license you have to lay your bike on its side and pick it up. What does that have to do with trade? Japanese motorcycles are generally much lighter than American ones, meaning that if you want your license and you're not super-strong, you are better off buying a Japanese bike. Since this shifts Japanese consumers away from foreign motorcycles and toward home-made models, it acts as a non-tariff barrier. Thus, whether or not a policy counts as a non-tariff barrier is a bit of a slippery subject with some, such as anti-dumping duties (basically tariffs with special requirements),

---

[3] Another example of an outright ban is an embargo, that is, when a government tries to shut down all trade with a single country (as opposed to shutting down all trade in a single good). This is typically done to achieve political goals rather than correct externalities or address imperfect information.

looking very much like trade policy and others, such agricultural subsidies, less so.[4] In the end, however, non-tariff barriers, tariffs, and quotas all achieve the same thing—a reduction in imports from their free trade level.

Trade policy, like non-tariff barriers, is rarely straightforward. Modern trade policy attempts to balance the market forces of the Invisible Hand against important human and national interests arising from externalities and incomplete information. To dig deeper, let's focus on three particular types of externalities—wages, pollution, and homogenization—and how they relate to trade. The goal here is to provide a rationale for why the Invisible Hand may break down and therefore why regulation may be valuable. After that, we will explore why trade policy may be the best method of regulating the market, even when trade itself is not the root of the problem.

Wages

When talking about the downside of imports, nothing gets as much attention as its effects on workers. The impact of imports on wages is, on its surface, straightforward. If the US imports shirts made in China, it does not need to make as many shirts itself. As a result, some people that used to work in the US apparel industry will lose their jobs. Since the American tailor didn't agree to the transaction between the clothes store and the Chinese manufacturer, this counts as an externality. This initial job loss, however, is just the start of the wage effects of imports.

If imports are sizable—the US imported over $25 billion in apparel from China in 2020—then imports can displace a large number of shirt makers, meaning a significant excess supply of workers. This excess supply of workers pushes wages down, even for those tailors who did not lose their jobs. Further, and critically, this downward pressure on wages

---

[4] When a country subsidizes its farm production, this gives its farmers a cost advantage relative to foreign producers. Since this will tend to boost the subsidized farmers' exports and lower imports, this seemingly domestic policy can have sizable trade effects. Indeed, conflict about agricultural subsidies between the developed and developing countries is a major impediment in World Trade Organization discussions.

is not restricted to the apparel industry since some of the unemployed workers will look for jobs outside their original industry. For example, some workers who used to cut cloth for shirts, may move into cutting steel for cars, driving down assembly line wages in the auto industry. This means that shirt imports will drive down wages in multiple industries and this is why the scale of import trade can have significant and far-reaching effects on wages.[5]

To complicate the issue even further, the import shock that lowers wages for some workers can actually *increase* wages for others. Most companies hire both blue- and white-collar workers. For example, think about that auto company that hires some of the displaced textile workers. Although the bulk of its employment may be made up of assembly line workers, custodial staff, and the like, at the same time it has high-wage managers and engineers. These two groups are compliments, that is, they support each other in production. If wages go down for assembly line workers because of an influx of former shirt makers, this leads the auto firm to expand the assembly line, creating a need for more managers and engineers. Thus, the decrease in demand for blue-collar workers in the apparel industry leads to an increase in demand for white-collar workers in the auto industry. This is known as the Stolper–Samuelson effect and illustrates why import competition can hurt some workers while helping others. A side effect of this is that an increase in blue-collar intensive imports can increase wage inequality, leading to social conflict between groups of workers.

Two final implications add to the far-reaching effects of those shirt imports. First, just as increased imports have effects on the wages of the importing country, they have effects on the exporting country. If the US wage effects are driven by blue-collar intensive imports from China, that same exchange should boost blue-collar Chinese wages. Indeed, the past twenty years have seen both a dramatic rise in Chinese exports and Chinese wages. Second, the modern global economy is characterized by the global supply chain in which stages of production are spread across

[5] Note that this is a discussion of wages, not jobs. Even though there was a large influx of Chinese imports into the US which resulted in somewhere around 1.5 million job losses in US manufacturing (Autor and Dorn 2013), there is no clear evidence of a *net* effect in US jobs since those displaced workers tended to switch to service jobs (Bloom et al. 2019).

different countries to make the most of their local advantages. Thus, shirt imports from China can affect the wages of African workers who make the cloth that goes into those Chinese shirts. It can also affect American wages when, for example, US fashionistas are the ones creating the patterns for the Chinese companies. Thus, because global supply chains create complementarities across borders, trade and trade policy will have effects that reverberate far and wide.

Putting all of this together, the total effect on wages from trade is complicated and extends across industries and countries with some workers losing even as others gain. This web of linkages illustrates why trade can generate significant externalities since workers may be affected by imports they did not sanction, including those in industries that on the surface may have little connection to themselves. Because trade can create wage externalities (with low-income workers in the US particularly vulnerable), there is an argument to be made for trade intervention. By reducing the level of import competition, it is possible to minimize the disruption to labor markets.[6] In particular, if a sudden influx of imports displaces a lot of workers at once it may be better to allow imports to gradually rise in order to spread out these effects over time. Thus, at least in the short run, the wage effects of trade can provide a reason to regulate imports.

Pollution

Although the wage externalities of trade receive the most press, the links between international trade and pollution are gaining increased (and much needed) attention. When teaching externalities, pollution is the classic example because so many activities generate pollution, the effects of which are often felt by third parties. This then forms the basis for emission standards, carbon taxes, and nature preserves—regulations which force costs up and reduce production in order to limit pollution. Likewise, if tariffs lower imports, they can lower pollution.

[6] Gaston and Trefler (1994) among many others provide evidence of the effectiveness of government intervention in addressing the wage effects of import competition.

While the intuition for this is simple, three additional factors need to be considered. First, trade can have an impact on where production happens. Since regulation adds to costs, nations with weak pollution standards will have an advantage in global markets which can shift production to so-called pollution havens and increase global emissions (see Bagayev and Lochard 2017). Second, knowing this, governments may compete with one another by cutting environmental regulations (or not enforcing them) to gain an advantage in export markets. Therefore, trade can lead to more production where local environmental regulation is the worst. Further, both of these problems will be exacerbated by the difficulties in observing how an imported product is made and whether foreign governments are living up to their environmental promises. This then provides a rationale for intervention. By putting trade barriers on "dirty" products or countries, a government can shift demand toward more sustainable options.

The third factor is that many types of pollution are global in nature, meaning that carbon emissions in one country contribute to *global* warming. Thus, even if a country limits emissions to protect its own citizens it will too often ignore the consequences for people living outside its own borders. As a result, pollution levels will be too high relative to what is best for the planet as a whole. This points to the need for international agreements to reduce pollution to its efficient level.[7]

A final issue worth mentioning when it comes to trade and the environment is that trade means that consumers and producers are in different countries. When discussing limiting environmental impacts, it is important to remember that pollution is generated both by production and consumption. The estimates of Weiss et al. (2000) find that roughly 75% of the pollution created by passenger cars comes from driving them; only 6% is from production. Thus, to limit environmental damage, it may be just as important to address use as much as production. That, however, raises two issues. First, taxes on gasoline meant to lower driving will affect the demand for cars, including imported ones. Second, if both consumption and production drive pollution, international cooperation may be needed to address both sources of emissions. Finally, when

[7] See Davies and Naughton (2014) for evidence of this in environmental treaty participation.

global supply chains cross borders, again international cooperation may be needed to achieve efficient pollution levels.

Homogenization

One externality that trade critics bring up but that is not often discussed by economists is the role of trade in homogenization, that is, in a reduction of variety across countries. This is not to say that economists do not think about trade and variety. In fact, Paul Krugman (who took the 2008 Nobel Prize in Economics for his insights) spearheaded the discussion of precisely this more than four decades ago. In contrast to early trade models that would talk about trading beer for cars, Krugman's "New Trade Theory" aimed to describe why a country would both export and import the same product. His answer was found by allowing consumers to value variety as well as price. In this setting, access to imports from overseas gives consumers access to foreign beers, different car models, and so on. Since consumers like variety, this within-industry trade in variety creates a benefit for them.

The underbelly of this new gain is that imported varieties drive out some domestic ones, particularly those which are costly to make. Therefore, while trade increases the number of varieties in a single location, it reduces the number available globally as small, indigenous producers are driven by import competition. For consumers who really like those varieties, this can be a significant loss. In the context of cultural identity, this can be particularly keen and lead to a welfare loss.[8] Thus, once again, an externality provides an argument for regulating trade. For example, concerns that foreign artists may crowd local musicians off the airwaves motivate non-tariff barriers in Canada, France, and other countries that require that a certain percentage of airtime be given to home-grown musical acts.

[8] See Cole and Davies (2014) for a detailed discussion.

Other Considerations

While the above three externalities are perhaps the most common ones discussed for intervention in trade, they are by no means the only ones.

When talking about pollution and trade, imperfect information on how green an imported product was compounded the potential for externalities. This imperfect information over production methods is not limited to environmental issues. A host of concerns arise over how foreign firms make their goods, including their use of child labor, the work conditions they offer their workers, and whether their products are organically made. Since many consumers value and are willing to pay a premium for products meeting these standards, there is a need for verification of production methods. This then provides a reason for intervention to promote "fair trade" a designation that covers the environmental and ethical issues surrounding imported products. Although much of this is done by certification bodies such as FLOCERT, government efforts such as the European Union's electronic Certificate of Inspection act in similar ways to overcome imperfect information.

A second reason to limit trade, at least for some industries, is national security. A government may believe it wise to limit imports of medicines, food, and arms in order to ensure a domestic supply should events cut it off from its trade partners. Similarly, as shown by the limit on exports of personal protective equipment during the Covid-19 pandemic, policymakers may find it important to retain key products for use by their own people. Note that not all security issues have to be apocalyptic. When the Ever Given shipping vessel blocked the Suez Canal for weeks in 2021, this disrupted global supply chains and exposed vulnerabilities in obtaining key inputs in a timely fashion. Thus, if an overreliance on foreign producers leaves a country vulnerable, it may be desirable to limit imports.

Finally, an issue not typically discussed is that trade regulation raises government revenues. Remember that a tariff is just a tax on imports and the money raised from those ends up in government budgets. In Africa, these trade taxes make up about one-third of government revenues; in contrast, in the US they are less than two percent. Because of this, a push toward free trade would significantly hamper the ability of many developing countries to provide the services and infrastructure that are already in short supply. Thus, even without externalities or imperfect information, taxing trade may be warranted to provide public funds.

These reasons, and a host of others (such as the infant industry argument in which it may be beneficial to protect an emerging industry from foreign competition until it gets on its feet), provide a reason to intervene in free trade to improve societal outcomes.

Trade Policy

All of the above are reasons for a government to intervene, but they do not say anything about the best way to do so. Why should limiting imports be the optimal policy response? In principle, this actually *isn't* the best way to address the issue. If the concern over imports is the impact on wages, it is more efficient to address the problem directly via policies like the US's Trade Adjustment Assistance program which provides unemployment insurance and retraining opportunities to workers displaced by trade. If pollution or sweatshop labor is the worry, then it is more efficient to deal with the information problem directly via verification of how and where a product is made. Going at the problems created by externalities and imperfect information indirectly by limiting imports is a second best, roundabout way of dealing with the real problems. If that's the case, then why should *trade* be regulated rather than just implement the direct fix?

The short answer is sometimes the first-best, direct policy is just not possible. In the case of pollution, while it might be better to go in and observe overseas production this assumes that both the foreign producers and their governments welcome inspectors. When factors such as industrial secrets and other sensitive information are at play, this is unlikely to be the case. Even when those are not concerns, even just the cost of inspection can make direct observation prohibitively expensive. Thus, the first-best, direct policy may not be feasible.

Similarly, although wage subsidies may be a more efficient way of dealing with the labor market effects of trade, implementing them can be a nightmare. While an increase in shirt imports can put some textile workers out of a job, others may become unemployed for reasons that have nothing to do with trade. Identifying who was laid off due to Chinese shirts and who was let go for underperformance would be costly at best, and impossible at worst. Further, since the import-driven decrease in demand for textile workers will spread across industries, it would be necessary to judge where and how much those indirect effects are felt. Even under the best of circumstances, this would take data and careful analysis, meaning that targeted worker supports would likely come far too late.

By comparison, although trade policy may be a crude tool to address the concerns exacerbated by imports, it can be a lot easier to implement. Since imports generally come in through a limited number of ports and border crossings, it is relatively easy to observe how much comes in and from where. Thus, while it might be better to inspect production in the foreign country, it is probably easier and cheaper to do so at the border. Similarly, if a sudden rise in imports is expected to cause significant income shifts, swiftly restricting those imports can have major advantages over a targeted retraining scheme introduced years later.

Finally, do not forget that government policy cannot be separated from politics, both international and domestic. On the international front, agreeing to multi-lateral environmental policies can take years meaning that a swift-yet-crude limit on trade may be needed to achieve climate targets. Even for domestic policy, negotiations between different groups can bring the legislative progress to a crawl. This is one of the motivations for the US's Trade Protection Authority (TPA). Under the TPA, the President can negotiate a trade agreement with limited congressional input. As its nickname of "fast track authority" suggests, this is intended to streamline both the drawing up of the agreement and its movement through Congress since it requires only a simple majority rather than a two-thirds majority to be passed into law. Thus, if trade policy can move faster than other agreements for political reasons, again the second-best approach in theory may be the preferred one in practice.

Conclusion

Although economists on the whole favor the free market, they also understand that for the Invisible Hand to work several critical—and usually unrealistic—assumptions are necessary. When it comes to international trade, the problems from externalities and imperfect information can be amplified by the distance between exporters and importers, the veil of conflicting government policies, and the general equilibrium effects that spill over across industries and worker groups. These problems can push the free market far enough away from efficiency that there is a need for governments to step in and regulate the market. While trade policies may not be the optimal way to do so, they often can be the fastest and most feasible. Thus, a better description of general support of free trade by economists is that they support free trade as an ideal rather than a reality.

References

Autor DH, Dorn D (2013) The growth of low-skill service jobs and the polarization of the US labor market. Amer Econ Rev 103:1553–1597.

Bagayev I, Lochard J (2017) EU air pollution regulation: A breath of fresh air for Eastern European polluting industries? J Environ Econ Manage 83:145–163.

Bloom N, Kurmann A, Handley K, Luck P (2019) The impact of Chinese trade on U.S. employment: The good, the bad, and the apocryphal. Paper presented at the 2019 meeting of the Society for Economic Dynamics, St Louis, 27–29 June 2019.

Cole MT, Davies RB (2014) Royale with cheese: The effect of globalization on the variety of goods. Rev Dev Econ 18:386–400.

Davies RB, Naughton HT (2014) International cooperation in environmental policy: A spatial approach. Int Tax Public Finan 21:923–954.

Gaston N, Trefler D (1994) Protection, trade, and wages: Evidence from U.S. Manufacturing. Ind Labor Rev 47:547–593.

International Labour Organization (2017) Global estimates of modern slavery: Forced labour and forced marriage. International Labour Organization, Geneva.

U.S. Customs and Border Protection (2022) User fee table. U.S. Customs and Border Protection, Washington, DC.

Weiss MA, Heywood JB, Drake EM, Schafer A, AuYeung FF (2000) On the road in 2020—A life-cycle analysis of new automobile technologies. Massachusetts Institute of Technology, Energy Laboratory Report # MIT EL 00-003.

Whaples R (2009) The policy views of American Economic Association members: The results of a new survey. Econ J Watch 6:337–348.

Part IV

Labor Markets

8

How Job Creation, Job Destruction, and Match Capital Improve Worker Outcomes

Peter F. Orazem and Soumyadip Roy

There are large and persistent differences in labor productivity across countries that lead directly to persistent differences in per capita incomes (Syverson 2011). While some of the productivity gap reflects differences in natural resources, the majority is due to differences in physical capital and human capital across countries (Managi and Pushpam 2018). Moreover, the growth in per capita wealth and income is due to rising levels of physical and human capital per capita, even as per capita measures of natural resources have declined.

Differences in physical and human capital reflect differences in investments across countries. However, countries with similar levels of physical

P. F. Orazem (✉)
Iowa State University, Ames, IA, USA
e-mail: pfo@iastate.edu

S. Roy
Jindal School of Banking and Finance, Jagdishpur, India
e-mail: soumyadiproy@jgu.edu.in

A. L. Kassens and J. C. Hall (eds.), *Challenges in Classical Liberalism*, Palgrave Studies in Classical Liberalism,
https://doi.org/10.1007/978-3-031-32890-9_8

and human capital investments have experienced widely different returns to those investments, differences that have also persisted over time. Differences in allocative efficiency across countries play a major role in generating these productivity differences (Syverson, 2011). As Hsieh and Klenow (2009) demonstrated misallocation of capital and labor can have a dramatic effect on productivity, lowering output per unit input by over 30% in Chinese and Indian manufacturing.

Bartelsman and Doms (2000) showed that the process of productivity growth is heavily affected by dynamism in the economy. One-quarter of productivity growth is due to the entry of more productive firms and the exit of less productive incumbents. Decker et al. (2017) have documented declining rates of new firm entry across all sectors of the U.S. Government policies such as product and labor market regulations that protect incumbents against competition limit the pace of firm exits and job destruction. Local ordinances that restrict housing supply raise the costs of allocating sufficient workers to high productivity cities (Hsieh and Moretti 2019). These policies protect obsolete jobs and technologies, allocate too few inputs to high productivity opportunities, and slow the diffusion of new knowledge and techniques (Andrews et al. 2015).

This paper analyzes the effects of policies that constrain the formation of productive matches between firms and workers. We show that policies that make labor market search more costly or less efficient lower the productivity of matches. From a worker's perspective, such policies lower the returns to human capital. They also create monopsony power for firms by creating frictions in the process by which workers switch from less to more productive employers. From the economy's perspective, the policies reduce employment, per capita incomes, and productivity relative to the potential and give the distribution of skills in the population. We motivate the argument, using a standard search model, and then use that framework to evaluate various policies that constrain the range of possible matches between firms and workers. We argue that these policies reduce the dynamism in the economy, the process that fosters the most productive matches.

Theory

An individual's output depends on the attributes of the worker and attributes of the job. If the job search and contracting were costless, it would be possible for workers and employers to forge a first-best matching that would maximize the output of the society. This would never happen, not only because search and contracting are costly, but because new jobs are always being created, old jobs are being destroyed, and workers are entering and exiting the labor market. How closely the economy reaches the first-best matching depends on the constraints placed on free association and contracting between employers and workers.

Government regulation of job creation and job destruction will affect the efficiency of contracting. To illustrate, we adapt a model introduced by Stern (1989) to examine how labor or product market regulations alter the job search process. With optimal job search, a seeker will weigh the value of future search against the offers currently available. The job market specific to individual *i*'s skills has a wage distribution defined by the cumulative distribution function, $F(w_i)$. Each wage represents the productivity of a potential match between that worker's human capital, H_i, and an index of job *k* quality, J_k, represented by $M(H_i, J_k)$; $M_H > 0$; $M_J > 0$. The ith worker's wage in job *k* is $w_i = \theta M(H_i, J_k)$, where the parameter θ, $(0 < \theta < 1)$ defines the worker's share of the match productivity which could be viewed as workers' bargaining power. The job seeker knows the wage distribution but does not know the quality of the match *ex ante*, and so the search is conducted randomly across jobs.

Not all searches result in positive wage offers. The arrival rate of offers, δ_H, is treated as a parameter by individual job seekers. The arrival rate of offers varies by worker skills, H, and by government policies. As we will explain later, it will be larger when the cost of job creation or job destruction is low. Barriers to job creation may include business taxes, regulations on firm entry, and mandated benefits or wages. Barriers to job destruction included mandated severance, advance layoff notice, or other job protection requirements that are capitalized into the cost of job creation.

Workers decide how intensively to search in the labor market, as indicated by the number of applications. The compensation outcome from one application is distributed according to

$$G(w_i) = (1 - \delta_H) + \delta_H F(w_i) \tag{8.1}$$

Job seekers will submit A_i applications and then select the best match offer, valued at $\overline{W}_i = \max(\theta M(H_i, J_k))$. The probability that A_i applications will generate an offer of $\overline{W}_i$ is $[G(\overline{W}_i)]^{A_i}$. The applications' costs are increasing in the number of applications $C(A_i), C^{'}(A_i) > 0; C''(A_i) > 0)$, an assumption that insures a finite number of applications. The assumption presumes that job seekers face rising costs of acquiring information on jobs and perhaps growing disutility from the application process as the number of applications rises.

Define ξ_i as the reservation compensation level which is the lowest compensation package the applicant would accept. The optimum strategy is to set the reservation compensation level ξ_i equal to the discounted value of searching in the following period.

$$\xi_i = \beta \left\{ \int_{\xi_i}^{\infty} (1 - [G(w_i)]^{A_i}) dw_i + \xi_i \right\} - C(A_i), \tag{8.2}$$

where β is the discount factor. Equation (8.2) implies that seekers will set a constant reservation compensation level across all submarkets. Differentiating (8.2) with respect to A_i and setting $\frac{d\xi}{dA_i} = 0$ the first order condition for the number of applications is

$$-\beta \int_{\xi}^{\infty} G(w_i)^{A_i} lnG(w_i) dw_i \geq C'(A_i). \tag{8.3}$$

The left-hand side of (8.3) is the discounted expected marginal return from an additional application and the right-hand side is the marginal cost of the last application. Those for whom condition (8.3) is satisfied at $A_i = 1$ will be in the labor market. The ones whose search resulted in a realization of $\overline{W}_i \geq \xi_i$ will be employed. The unemployed are those for whom the inequality in (8.3) holds, and so the continued search is warranted.[1]

The efficiency of a country's labor market institutions can be judged by the productivity of the realized matches, given the distribution of human capital in the population. Total output across all successful seekers will be $Q = \sum_i \frac{\overline{W}_i}{\theta}$ possible matches available in the population, where the wage bill is $\sum_i \overline{W}_i$ and employers get $Q - \sum_i \overline{W}_i$. The maximum possible output, Q^{max}, would result if workers were assigned to jobs such that no worker could be reassigned and raise aggregate output.[2] More efficient labor markets would have higher values of Q/Q^{max}.

While Q^{max} is not observable, we can measure labor market outcomes that would be correlated with a more efficient matching process. The first is to examine how many matches occur. Note that if condition (8.3) is violated for all positive values of A_j, meaning that the value of search is below the cost, then the optimum strategy is to set $A_j = 0$ and the individual would be out of the labor force. This would happen, for example, if $\delta_H = 0$, meaning that at the individual's level of human capital, no employer would hire. One mark of a poorly performing labor market would be a low ratio of employed to population or a low labor force participation rate.

The second measure takes advantage of the fact that $Corr(\overline{W}, \xi_i) > 0$, and so the reservation wage becomes an index of match quality. While the reservation wage is not observable, simultaneous evaluation of Eqs. (8.1–8.3) shows that $\frac{d\xi_i}{d\delta_H} > 0, \frac{d\xi_i}{dH} > 0$, and $\frac{d\xi_i}{dC'(A_i)} < 0$. That means that raising human capital, raising the arrival rate of jobs, and lowering the marginal cost of search will raise reservation wages, the average productivity of matches, and the efficiency of the labor market. We can also evaluate how labor market policies affect efficiency by assessing how they affect human capital, the arrival rate of jobs, and the cost of search.

---

1 This is a point in time analysis. The model can be expanded to allow employed search. If the cost of search includes the current employed wage, and surges in labor demand lead to a faster arrival rate of jobs or a rightward shift in the wage distribution, workers will have an incentive to search again and potentially switch to a new match in future periods.

2 This is similar to Becker's (1981) positive assortative mating model of marriage.

Economic Freedom and Returns to Human Capital

The return to human capital depends on the quality of the match, $\frac{\partial \overline{W}}{\partial H} = \left(\theta \frac{\partial M}{\partial H} | \delta_H > 0\right)$, provided the human capital is high enough to attract job offers. In a free labor market, an individual has an incentive to match their human capital with the job offering the highest reward. T.W. Schultz (1975) advanced an important hypothesis for why returns to schooling might vary across markets. Human capital has its greatest complementarity with jobs that require decisions in the face of changing prices, tastes, productivity, technology, or other sources of disequilibrium. Economic systems that regulate prices, innovation, or consumer choices or that limit freedom to change jobs in response to opportunities will limit economic returns from those skills.

Free labor markets maximize the arrival rate of job offers which should maximize the rate of return to human capital. One test of that hypothesis is to compare rates of return to human capital as economies transitioned from centrally planned to market systems. Fleisher et al. (2005) summarized estimated rates of return in central and eastern European countries from 1975 to 2002, a period that spanned the transition that occurred in 1988–1989. The rate of return under the planned system averaged 3.2% per year of schooling. Rates of return to schooling rose quickly as market institutions were adopted, averaging over 8% per year of schooling by 2000. The rising returns reflect the increased opportunity to allocate skills to employer needs and the elimination of centrally dictated wage policies.

We can also illustrate the importance of free economic institutions as countries develop. King et al. (2012) examined how relative indexes of economic freedom affected returns to schooling and work experience across 86 different developing countries. The Heritage Foundation's Economic Freedom Index (Miller et al. 2022) evaluates the extent to which a country allows individuals to allocate labor, capital, and goods freely and protects individual returns to property. Returns to schooling average 9.7% per year of schooling for the countries ranking among the top quartile in economic freedom, while those ranked in the bottom quartile average 3 percentage points less. Returns to a year of work experience averaged 5% for countries in the top quartile and 4.2% for countries in the bottom quartile. The implication is that impediments to labor market search lower the efficiency of matches and limit incomes for individuals and for the country as a whole.

A parallel analysis examines how democratic institutions shape the fortunes of economies. Acemoglu et al. (2019) find a strong correlation between democratic institutions and the adoption of economic reforms that strengthen market forces, increased health and education, and a rising share of government in the economy. The strengthening democratic institutions also raise per capita incomes. The rising share of public goods is not inconsistent with market systems, as argued by Lazear (2020). Countries with high shares of state ownership grow slowly and generate lower incomes for the richest and poorest citizens. In contrast, countries with strong private ownership grow faster and raise incomes for the poorest and richest citizens. It is the free market economies that have the largest income transfer programs, presumably because they have individuals from whom income can be transferred.

Employment Protection

We can gain some insights into the effects of constraints on the matching process by examining differences in labor market outcomes across countries with different levels of employment protection. The OECD (2020) provides estimates for 2019 based on prior notice requirements, mandated severance, regulation of unfair dismissals, limitations on term employment, and enforcement. The index ranges from 0 to 6 with higher values indicating greater employment protection. For protections against individual dismissals, the value for the U.S. was 0.09 and the European average was 2.3.[3] The U.S. offers the least protection against group dismissals as well.

The intent of these policies is to preserve jobs. However, restrictions on individual or group layoffs impose costs on firms. As initially shown by

[3] The range of values in Europe is from 1.2 in Ireland to 4.3 in Portugal.

Lazear (1990), these policies can be viewed as raising the cost of hiring because firms must incorporate the expected cost of retaining workers who may not be needed in the future when adding personnel. In the context of the model, countries with greater employment protection will have a lower arrival rate of job offers, lowering the expected value of the match and reducing the labor force participation rate.

The differences in labor force participation rates for individuals aged 25–64 between Europe (80.3%) and the U.S. (78.2%) are not large and do not suggest problems with the matching process. However, the gap for those aged 15–24 is much larger, with Europe (42.6%) averaging well below the U.S. (55.9%). While some of the difference is due to a high fraction of European youth in post-secondary education, some argue that Europe is producing too many college graduates relative to demand (Delaney et al. 2020) and that overeducation is less problematic in the countries with more flexible labor market policies (McGuinness et al. 2018). Weak employment prospects induce more youth to stay in school.

The differences in labor force participation mask further differences in the successful conclusion of job search. Duration of search differs dramatically between countries depending on their employment protection. In Fig. 8.1, we plot the 25-year average share of long-term unemployed (12 months or more) among all unemployed. Raising the cost of layoffs creates impediments to a successful search.

Consistent with the apparent low rate of labor force participation among European youth, Fig. 8.2 shows that the cost of unemployment is borne disproportionately by the young in countries with high levels of employment protection. Eventually, the youth find their way into employment, as employment rates for those aged 25–64 are nearly identical in the U.S. and Europe. However, in the U.S., young workers are more likely to engage in a period of job shopping in which they can sample jobs in search of a better match. In Europe, a smaller share of youth is employed, and those with jobs are less likely to switch jobs (Pries and Rogerson 2005). The less efficient search in Europe will result in lower wages relative to their potential, consistent with the findings reported by Cervini-Plá et al. (2014) who studied wage growth after Spain relaxed its employment protection provisions.

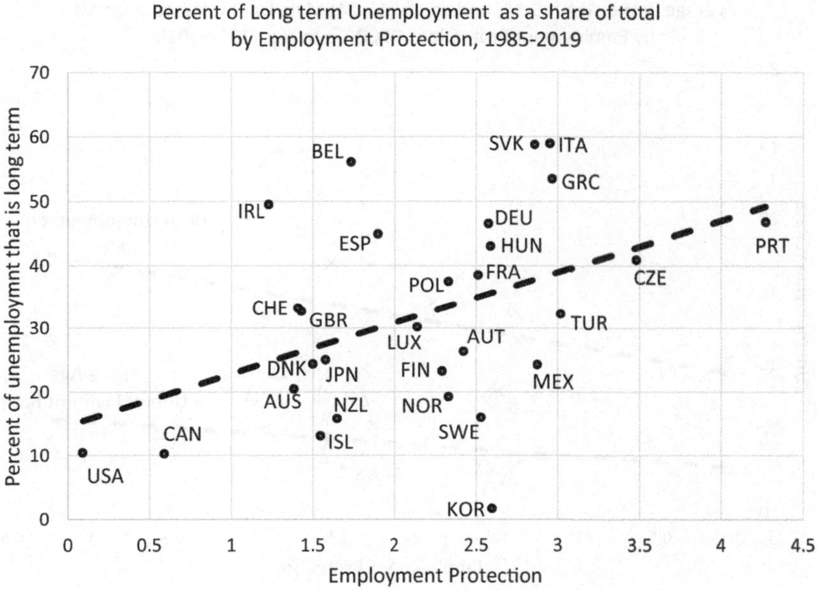

Fig. 8.1 Long-term unemployment and employment protection laws, OECD countries, 1985–2019

Restrictions on layoffs are particularly costly during cyclical downturns in the economy where workers leaving the least productive firms raises overall productivity (Haltiwanger et al. 2021). However, they also slow the pace of new offers during expansions that limit the transfer of workers from low to high productivity establishments (Haltiwanger et al. 2021). As a result, employment protection slows the pace of the recovery. In Fig. 8.3, we show the pattern of long-term unemployment by year. The share is always lower in the U.S. than in Europe, but the U.S. long-term share rose during the recessions of 1990–1991, 2001, and 2007–2009 downturns while changing only modestly in Europe. The U.S. rate falls dramatically in the U.S. recoveries as workers can switch from declining to growing sectors, but limitations on job creation in Europe do not match that pace of reallocation.

The U.S. experiences high rates of worker turnover, even during expansions. The average annual rate of private workers changing jobs was 48% between 2016 and 2019. As shown by Haltiwanger et al. (2014),

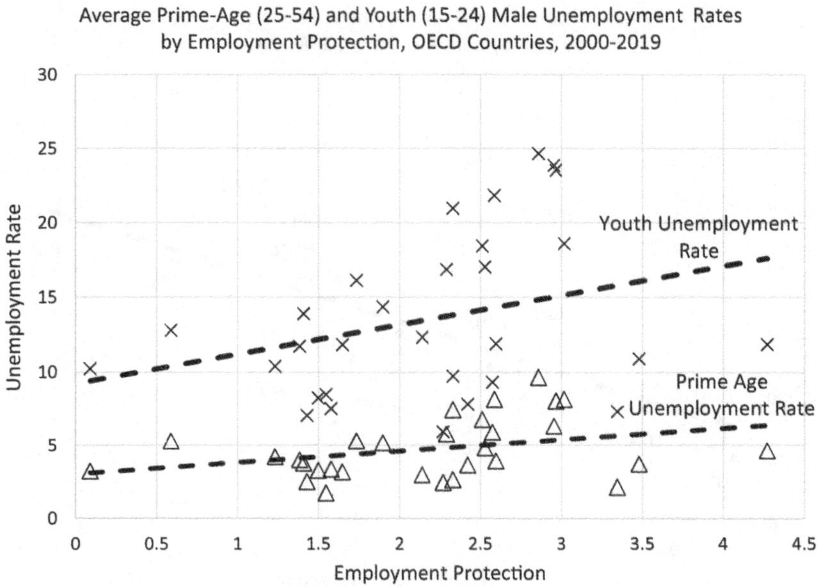

Fig. 8.2 Employment protection and youth and prime age unemployment, 2000–2019

the employed in Europe are significantly less likely to switch jobs. While 22% of workers in the U.S. have less than one year of job tenure, only 14% of European workers are in their first year with their firm.

This constant churning in the U.S. market should raise productivity as unproductive matches are replaced by productive ones. Empirical tests of this allocative efficiency proposition are generally supportive (Davis and Haltiwanger 2014). Declines in labor market churning in the U.S. have contributed to the slowing of allocative efficiency gains since the late 1990s (Decker et al. 2017). Caballero et al. (2013) provide evidence that job security regulations hinder the process of creative destruction (Schumpeter, 1942) more generally across a sample of 60 countries.

For the most part, the lack of employment protection in the U.S. does not cause serious issues in the labor market because displaced workers can quickly find new matches. While a large fraction of the labor force

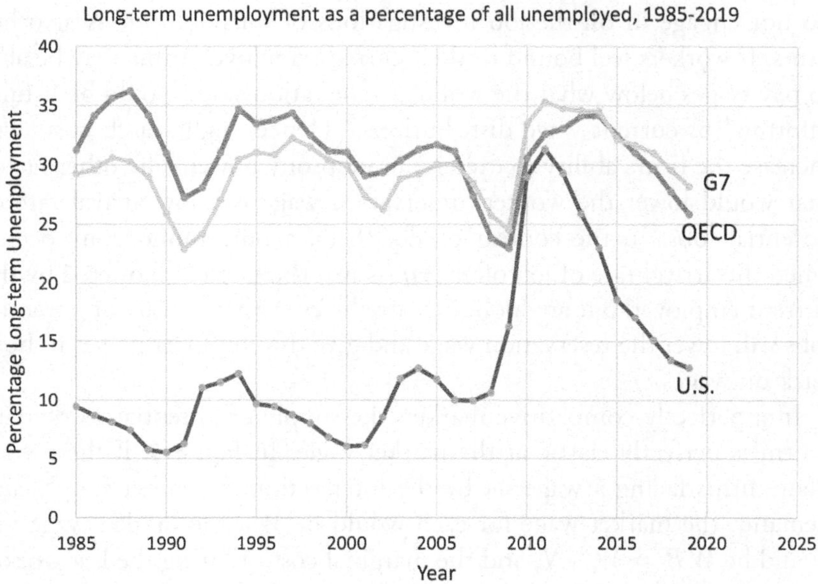

Fig. 8.3 The share of long-term unemployed by year, Europe, the G7, and the U.S., 1985–2019

experiences spells of unemployment in a given year,[4] the length of unemployment spell is short and the fraction of unemployed at a point in time is small. In Europe, unemployment is borne disproportionately by a smaller share of the labor force who remain unemployed for an extended period, resulting in a larger fraction who are unemployed at a point in time.

Monopsony

Frictions in the job search process mean that the labor market will not perfectly solve the job assignment problem. As most prominently advanced by Manning (2013), search frictions can lead to a degree of monopsony power that can be exercised by firms, particularly if workers

[4] The average annual rate of private workers changing jobs was 48% between 2016 and 2019.

do not engage in on-the-job investigations of outside options at other firms. If workers feel bound to their current employer, firms may be able to pay wages below what the worker's reservation wage would be if fully informed of current wage distributions.[5] Hence, high search costs will increase the firm's ability to exercise monopsony power. The other factor that would lower the worker's reservation wage is a low arrival rate of potential jobs. In the context of Eq. (8.1), a pure monopsony occurs when the arrival rate of job offers,δ_H, is just the single job offered by the current employer, but any policy that reduces the arrival rate of potential jobs will lower the reservation wage and give the employer power to hold back on wages.

In a perfectly competitive market, the supply of potential workers to a firm is perfectly elastic at the market wage. In Fig. 8.4, if there were many firms facing a wage set by the intersection of market supply and demand, the market wage for each would be W_o, the market wage bill would be $WB = W_o \cdot N$, and the marginal cost of hiring the last worker would be $\frac{\partial WB}{\partial N} = W_o$. If this were a monopsony, the single firm faces the upward sloping market labor supply curve OACC' in Fig. 8.4. Each point on the supply curve represents the reservation wage, ξ_i, of the last worker induced to accept employment. As a result, as the monopsonist's hiring increases, wages are bid up $\left(\frac{\partial W}{\partial N} > 0\right)$, and the wage bill is $WB = W(N) \cdot N$. If the firm cannot pay different wages to different workers, it must raise the wage for all workers as it increases employment, and so the marginal cost of the last hire is $\frac{\partial WB}{\partial N} = \frac{\partial W}{\partial N} N + W(N) > W(N)$. A profit maximizing firm with monopsony power will set employment where marginal cost of the last hire equals that worker's marginal revenue product: $\frac{\partial WB}{\partial N} = \frac{\partial W}{\partial N} N + W(N) = P\frac{\partial Q}{\partial N}$. That corresponds to employment level, N_{min}, and workers are paid W_{min}, the reservation wage for the last worker hired. Workers are exploited because they are paid below the value of their work. In addition, too few workers are employed compared to the social optimum because we would want to keep hiring

[5] Monopsony power also exists in large firms with internal labor markets. In firms where worker productivity depends on firm-specific knowledge and experience, worker productivity in the firm will rise relative to their productivity in other firms. As long as the firm pays above what the worker can earn in other firms, the firm can pay below the worker's marginal product.

as long as the value of the workers' output is above the workers' reservation wage. The first-best social solution would be to hire N_{max} workers at wage W_o, the wage that would obtain if the firm could not prevent its workers from seeking employment in other establishments offering pay equal to their productive value.

Researchers often equate the existence of an upward sloping firm supply curve as evidence of monopsony power (Sokolova and Sorenson, 2021), but there is no guarantee that the firm can pay W_{min}. First, the firm may not have the information necessary to identify the worker with the reservation wage equal to W_{min}. In general, firm profit rates are well below that implied by existing estimates of firm labor supply, suggesting that the costs of exercising monopsony power outweigh the benefits. More generally, Fig. 8.4 suggests that any combination of wages and employment in the contract zone *ABC* could be negotiated, and so wages could range between $[W_{min}, W_{max}]$ as employment ranges between $[N_{min}, N_{max}]$.

It is not clear how important monopsony power is in setting labor market outcomes. Azar et al. (2022) found that local labor markets

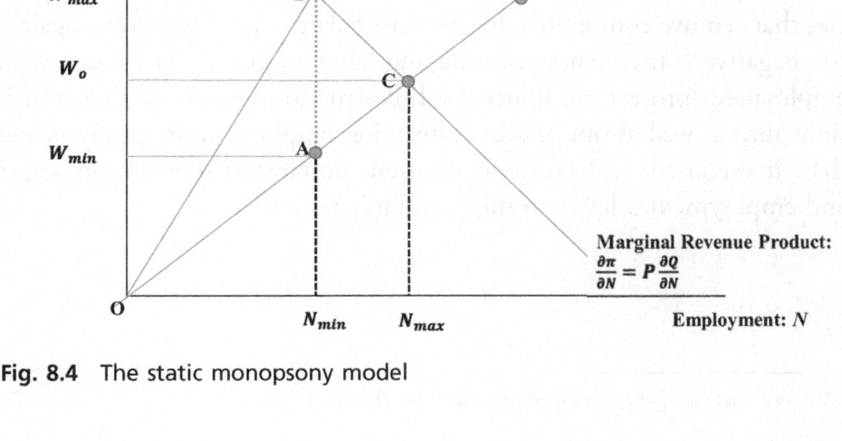

Fig. 8.4 The static monopsony model

can be highly concentrated by sector, and that real wages in the more concentrated labor markets are lower. Rinz (2022) reported that the importance of local market concentration has decreased over time, and so the effect of monopsony on wages has not been increasing. In addition, the markets identified as having the greatest monopsony power are those in rural areas and small cities that also have low levels of productivity enhancing agglomeration. It is possible that the lower wages attributed to monopsony power may be explainable, at least in part, by differences in labor productivity across less and more populated markets.

We should note that, in general, workers seem very able to leave employers voluntarily for other options, a tendency that should limit monopsony power. In 2019, the annual quit rate for nonfarm employees was 27.9%, 31.1% in the private sector, and 9.8% in the government sector. The lowest quit rate was 13.2% in February 2009 near the trough of the Great Recession when vacancy rates were low.[6] Quit rates respond positively to the rising arrival rate of job vacancies during expansions, with the highest rate of 34.8% occurring in July 2019 toward the end of the long recovery. While a minority of local markets may be characterized by low turnover rates that would support monopsony power, the labor market has high rates of voluntary worker mobility overall.

Our intent is not to debate the quality of evidence on the importance of monopsony in the labor market. Instead, we want to indicate how government policies can create the conditions in which monopsony can occur. Because monopsony can lead to exploitative labor contracts and underemployment of workers relative to the socially efficient level, policies that remove competitive forces must balance those objectives against the negative consequences of reducing labor mobility. As we saw with employment protection, limiting job destruction reduces worker transitions into as well as out of jobs. This raises employer monopsony power that, if exercised, will create a persistent downward pressure on wages and employment relative to the economy's potential.

[6] Authors' analysis of the Job Openings and Labor Turnover Survey.

Licensing

Occupational licensing provides an important example of how limits to worker mobility due to government policies create inefficient resource allocations and monopsony rents. One-quarter of the U.S. workforce is covered by licensing regulations that govern the supply of workers to the occupation (Kleiner, 2017). To supply labor to the market, workers have to meet minimum standards aimed at ensuring consumers receive high-quality services. For services where lack of credentials could result in life threatening failures such as engineering, architecture, or medicine, the consumer benefit from a certification process is easily defended although educational credentials might be sufficient. For other occupations such as beauticians, auctioneers, bartenders, or unarmed security guards, the consumer benefits are less obvious. In practice, studies have not been able to show an impact of licensing on service quality (Kleiner, 2017).

The other possible reason for licensing is to restrict supply of labor relative to the unrestricted supply. In Fig. 8.4, the unrestricted supply is characterized by line OAC. If the licensing is set to restrict entry to the occupation, the licensed supply may be more like OAB, reducing the elasticity of supply and creating a form of monopsony. The difference between the licensed occupation versus the traditional monopsony is that the licensed laborer may also be the employer. If the licensed worker is employed by a firm, the firm will want to pay W_{min} and capture the rents from the licensing equal to $W_{max} - W_{min}$. If the licensed worker is self-employed, they capture all the rents from the restricted supply and pay themselves W_{max}. As a result, the worker's return from licensing depends on whether they are self-employed, or if not, whether they have power to bargain for wages above W_{min}. In his review of studies measuring the effect of licensing on wages, Kleiner (2017) found large positive wage effects for physicians, dentists, accountants, and lawyers who are frequently self-employed or equity partners in their firms. Returns were negligible for teachers, nurses, and cosmetologists, occupations that are less frequently self-employed. Corroborating evidence is found in Kleiner and Vorotnikov (2017) who found that average pay gains from licensing were nearly 25%, but the gains from self-employment was 19%, leaving an average gain of only 10% for those who are not self-employed.

Occupational licensing distorts labor markets in several important ways. It creates a barrier to entry that lowers occupational employment relative to the efficient level. Kleiner and Volotnikov (2017) estimate that licensing reduces employment by 1.6 million jobs. Because many occupations are licensed at the state level, they create artificial wage differences within occupations across states. Kleiner and Volotnikov (2017) found that the barriers raise pay significantly in 16 states with insignificant effects in the remaining 34 states, meaning that there is too little cross-state migration toward the states with higher returns. Finally, licensed workers are 24% less likely to switch occupations (Kleiner and Xu, 2020) because they do not want to sacrifice the rents earned from the entry barriers created by state regulations. The dead-weight loss from these limits to labor mobility are not small, totaling $170 billion or about $1400 per household (Kleiner and Volotnikov 2017).

Minimum Wages

Government labor market policy can also affect the efficiency of the matching process by truncating the distribution of wages. An increase in the minimum wage will alter the wage distribution depending on the worker's skill level, *H*. For the subminimum population whose marginal revenue products are below the new minimum wage, the arrival rate of job offers , δ_H will fall,[7] but the expected wage, conditional on an offer, will rise. The impact on applications is ambiguous as the falling arrival rate of offers discourages applications even as the higher conditional wage increases search intensity. However, a larger share will find condition (8.3) violated and will drop out of the labor market. For the near-minimum population whose marginal revenue products are just above the minimum, the offer rate will rise, as will their reservation wages. For the super-minimum population whose skills place them well above the new minimum wage, there will be little effect.

[7] The offer rate will not necessarily fall to zero because firms may expect a worker's skill level to rise above the minimum wage with sufficient work experience or job training.

The mixture of effects on offer rates based on skill explain why the impact of minimum wages on employment are so uncertain.[8] Studies that pool the subminimum and near-minimum groups are more likely to find negligible or even positive effects from minimum wageminimum wage increases, while studies that separate these groups are more likely to find negative employmentemployment effects on the subminimum population.[9] The imprecision is also due to the modest size of most changes in the minimum wage so that relatively few workers are directly affected. Finally, if the search frictions create monopsony power for firms that employ subminimum workers, as proposed by Manning (2013), the minimum wage set above W_{min} would create a perfectly elastic range of the firm supply curve. For example, if the minimum wage were set at W_o in Fig. 8.4, the firm supply curve becomes W_oCC', the marginal cost of labor becomes W_o, and employment rises to N_{max}.

The effects of the minimum wage on other firm decisions are not as uncertain. For example, firm profits fall unambiguously if its workers receive mandated wage increases, whether the firm is a monopolist, monopsonist, or a perfectly competitive firm. Draca et al. (2011) found a large significant negative effects of increases in minimum wage on firm profitability in low-wage residential care homes as well for firms in general. Bell and Machin (2018) showed a large increase in minimum wages on firm market capitalizations. Decreased profitability would lower the rate of firm entry, as found by Rohlin (2011), Draca et al. (2011), Luca and Luca (2019), and Chen et al. (2021). The last two papers also find that minimum wages hasten firm exits. The evidence points strongly to a general decrease in the arrival rate of job offers when minimum wages rise.

The reduced rate of offer arrivals should slow the pace of hiring and voluntary exits. Brochu and Green (2013), Dube et al. (2016), and Gittings and Schmutte (2016) found that minimum wages reduce both

---

[8] See Manning (2013) who concludes that the weight of the evidence is for negligible employment effects and Neumark and Shirley (2022) who conclude that the weight of the evidence is for modestly sized negative employment effects.

[9] For example, Aaronson and Phelan (2019) and Lordan and Neumark (2018) find that minimum wages reduce the number of automatable or cognitively repetitive jobs for low-skilled workers.

the rate of separations and new hires. The resulting slower churning rate in the labor market would lower the rate of productivity growth as unproductive matches will persist and potentially productive matches will not occur. However, as proposed by Acemoglu and Pischke (1999, 2003), the reduced labor turnover rate from the minimum wage generates a source of monopsony power that may allow firms to capture investments in worker training by paying them below their marginal revenue products.

Evidence on how the minimum wage affects training is quite thin. Neumark and Shupe (2019) found that minimum wages increase the share of teens enrolled in school, but Neumark and Nizalova (2007) found that high school graduates were less likely to attend college in high minimum wage states. There is consistent evidence that working while in high school raises earnings as an adult (Ruhm 1997; Light 2001; Baum and Ruhm 2016) which suggests that high school jobs involve useful training. Minimum wages may limit such on-the-job training if they limit job opportunities for high school students.

Poverty and Inequality

Many of the government interventions in the labor market, including employment protection, minimum wages, redistributive tax and transfer policies, mandatory leaves, or other mandated benefits are aimed at improving the incomes of those at the lower tail of the income distribution. An important question is whether the poor do better in economic systems that regulate the labor market in ways that limit mobility or whether the poor do better in a free market system.

Lazear (2020) examined the incomes of the lowest 10th percentile of the populations for 162 countries ranked from the most to the least adherent to free market principles. The poor do significantly better in economies with free markets, competition, and low state ownership. In addition, while all income groups benefit from a freer economy, the poorest benefit more than the wealthiest, and so inequality falls.

In Fig. 8.5, we illustrate the thrust of his argument. We rank countries from the least to the most unequal as indicated by their Gini coefficients.

We then examine how inequality corresponds to their average income, measured by GDP per capita, and Economic Freedom, measured by the index reported by the Heritage Foundation. Every unit increase in the Gini coefficient is associated with a drop of almost $1000 in income. Of course, the causality may go the other way—that richer countries can afford less inequality. As Lazear shows, it is only the richest countries that engage in income redistribution through their tax and transfer policies. However, over the longer period, it is not the aggressive tax and transfer policies that are associated with improved incomes of the poor, but the faster growth of the overall economy. This last point is illustrated by the negative correlation between economic freedom and inequality. Limitations on contracting, whether in the markets for labor, land, foreign or domestic goods and services, debt, or equity limit incomes for all groups, but atypically harm the poor.

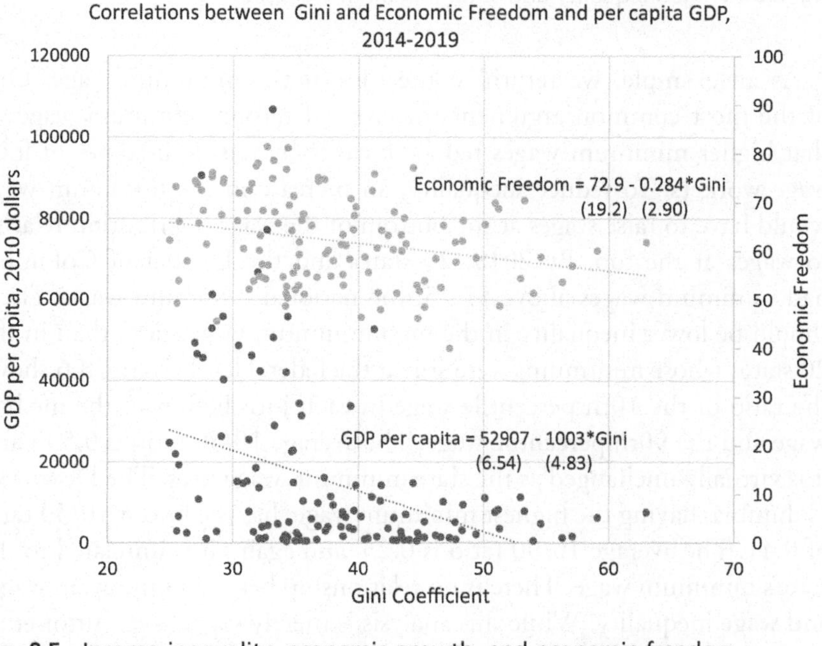

Fig. 8.5 Income inequality, economic growth, and economic freedom

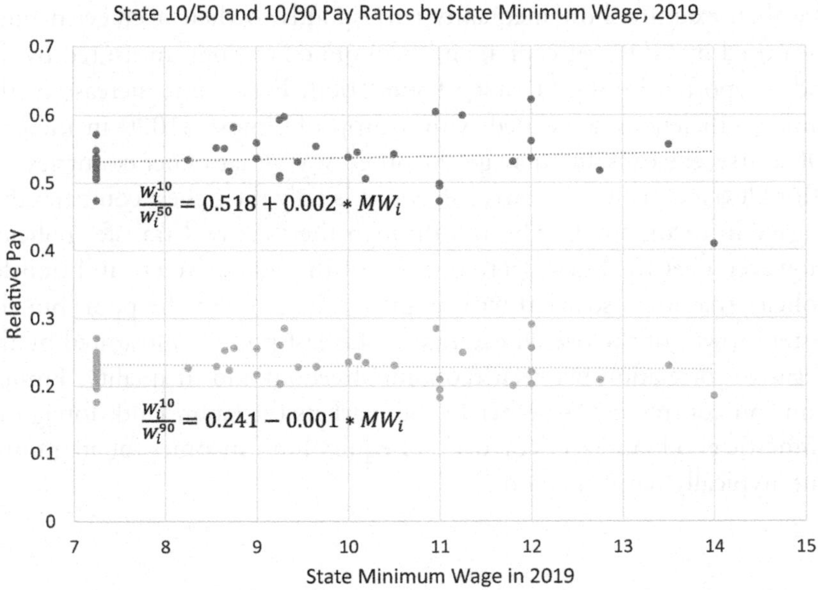

Fig. 8.6 Wage inequality and state minimum wages, 2019

As an example, we return to the case of the minimum wage. One of the most common arguments in favor of raising minimum wages is that higher minimum wages reduce poverty by raising incomes of low-wage workers. To reduce inequality, an increase in the minimum wage would have to raise wages at the bottom of the wage distribution relative to wages at the top. By 2019, 29 states and the District of Columbia had minimum wages above $7.25, the national minimum wage. There should be lower inequality in the high minimum wage states than in the 20 states whose minimums were still at the federal level. Figure 8.6 shows the ratio of the 10th percentile wage in each jurisdiction to the median wage and the 90th percentile wage. The average 10/50 ratio is 0.535 and it is virtually unchanged as the state minimum wage rises. The District of Columbia, having the highest minimum wage, has the lowest 10/50 ratio of 0.41. The average 10/90 ratio is 0.23, and again, it is unrelated to the state's minimum wage. There is no relationship between minimum wages and wage inequality. While this analysis is merely suggestive, Autor et al.

(2016) found that minimum wages had only a modest effect on income inequality since the 1980s.[10]

Conclusion

The U.S. labor market is based on the at-will philosophy under which firms can dismiss workers without cause and workers can quit a job without consequence. Strict adherence to the philosophy would minimize constraints on searching for new matches. Relatively frictionless contractual adjustments to changing technologies, product demands, input supplies, and other economic shocks speed the efficient reallocation of inputs and maximize the productive value of matches. This generates more surplus that can be shared among firms and workers.

Government policies can move the labor market closer to or farther from the frictionless contracting outcome. Policies that limit the length or ease the other terms of noncompete clauses increase worker mobility between jobs. Policies that improve the flow of information on job opportunities lower the cost of search and speed up the matching process. Departures from the at-will doctrine create frictions in the search process that slow the arrival rates of new job offers, raise the cost of search, or truncate the distribution of potential contracts. For example, high marginal tax rates on wages open a wedge between the firm's cost of hiring a worker and the worker's compensation will reduce the number of vacancies. Mandated benefits such as paid leaves, or minimum health insurance or pension benefits affect labor market outcomes in the same way as mandated severance or advance notice. High barriers to firm entry such as protracted permitting processes or unnecessary regulatory requirements raise the cost of job creation.

Evidence shows that countries whose policies hew closer to employment at-will on the worker and firm side have better labor market outcomes on average than do those with more interventionist strategies.

---

[10] Our analysis only considers wages for those who remain employed. If the minimum wage lowers employment for the subminimum population, then the lack of a change in the wage distribution conditional on employment would suggest an increase in inequality when nonemployment was taken into account.

Beyond the practical value of generating more stable employment and higher wages, policies that reduce the costs of job search minimize the firm's monopsony power. Greater competition between firms wanting to attract and retain workers raises worker bargaining power in contracting for a share of the larger output due to greater match quality and allocative efficiency.

References

Aaronson D, Phelan BJ (2019) Wage shocks and the technological substitution of low-wage jobs. Econ J 129:1–34.

Acemoglu D, Naidu S, Restrepo P, Robinson JA (2019) Democracy does cause growth. J Polit Econ 127:47–100.

Acemoglu D, Pischke J (1999) Beyond Becker: Training in imperfect labour markets. Econ J 109:112–142.

Acemoglu D, Pischke J (2003) Minimum wages and on-the-job training. Res Labor Econ 22:159–202.

Andrews D, Criscuolo C, Gal PN (2015) Frontier firms, technology diffusion and public policy: Micro evidence from OECD countries. OECD, OECD Productivity Working Paper No. 2.

Autor D, Manning A, Smith CL (2016) The contribution of the minimum wage to US wage inequality over three decades: A reassessment. Amer Econ J Appl Econ 8:58–99.

Azar J, Marinescu I, Steinbaum M (2022) Labor market concentration. J Human Res 57:S167–S199.

Bartelsman EJ, Doms M (2000) Understanding productivity: Lessons from longitudinal microdata. J Econ Lit 38:569–594.

Baum CL, Ruhm CJ (2016) The changing benefits of early work experience. South Econ J 83:343–363.

Becker GS (1981) A treatise on the family. Harvard University Press, Cambridge.

Bell B, Machin S (2018) Minimum wages and firm value. J Labor Econ 36:159–195.

Brochu P, Green DA (2013) The impact of minimum wages on labour market transitions. Econ J 123:1203–1235.

Caballero RJ, Cowan KN, Engel EM, Micco A (2013) Effective labor regulation and microeconomic flexibility. J Dev Econ 101:92–104.

Cervini-Plá M, Ramos X, Silva JI (2014) Wage effects of non-wage labour costs. Eur Econ Rev 72:113–137.

Chen Y, Ma L, Orazem PF (2021) Minimum wages and rural and urban firm entry and exit. Ag Pol Rev, Winter, Center for Agricultural and Rural Development, Iowa State University.

Davis SJ, Haltiwanger J (2014) Labor market fluidity and economic performance. National Bureau of Economic Research, Working Paper No. w20479.

Decker RA, Haltiwanger J, Jarmin RS, Miranda J (2017) Declining dynamism, allocative efficiency, and the productivity slowdown. Amer Econ Rev 107:322–326.

Delaney J, McGuinness S, Pouliakas K, Redmond P (2020) Educational expansion and overeducation of young graduates: A comparative analysis of 30 European countries. Oxford Rev Educ 46:10–29.

Draca M, Machin S, Reenen J (2011) Minimum ages and firm profitability. Amer Econ J Appl Econ 3:129–151.

Dube A, Lester TW, Reich M (2016) Minimum wage shocks, employment flows, and labor market frictions. J Labor Econ 34:663–704.

Fleisher BM, Sabirianova K, Wang X (2005) Returns to skill and the speed of reforms: Evidence from Central and Eastern Europe, China, and Russia. J Comp Econ 33:351–370.

Gittings RK, Schmutte IM (2016) Getting handcuffs on an octopus: Minimum wages, employment, and turnover. Ind Labor Rel Rev 69:1133–1170.

Haltiwanger JC, Hyatt HR, McEntarfer E, Staiger M (2021) Cyclical worker flows: Cleansing vs. sullying. National Bureau of Economic Research, Working Paper No. w28802.

Haltiwanger JC, Scarpetta S, Schweiger H (2014) Cross country differences in job reallocation: The role of industry, firm size and regulations. Lab Econ 26:11–25.

Hsieh C, Klenow PJ (2009) Misallocation and manufacturing TFP in China and India. Q J Econ 124:1403–1448.

Hsieh C, Moretti E (2019) Housing constraints and spatial misallocation. Amer Econ J Macro 11:1–39.

King EM, Montenegro CE, Orazem PF (2012) Economic freedom, human rights, and the returns to human capital: An evaluation of the Schultz hypothesis. Econ Dev Cult Change 61:39–72.

Kleiner MM (2017) The influence of occupational licensing and regulation. IZA World Lab 392:1–10.
Kleiner MM, Vorotnikov E (2017) Analyzing occupational licensing among the states. J Reg Econ 52:132–158.
Kleiner MM, Xu M (2020) Occupational licensing and labor market fluidity. National Bureau of Economic Research, Working Paper No. w27568.
Lazear EP (1990). Job security provisions and employment. Q J Econ 105:699–726.
Lazear EP (2020) Socialism, capitalism, and income. Hoover Institution, Palo Alto.
Light A (2001) In-school work experience and the returns to schooling. J Labor Econ 19:65–93
Lordan G, Neumark D (2018) People versus machines: The impact of minimum wages on automatable jobs. Lab Econ 52: 40–53.
Luca DL, Luca M (2019) Survival of the fittest: The impact of the minimum wage on firm exit. National Bureau of Economic Research, Working Paper No. w25806.
Managi S, Pushpam K (eds) (2018) Inclusive wealth report 2018: Measuring progress towards sustainability. Taylor and Francis, New York.
Manning A (2013) Monopsony in motion. Princeton University Press, Princeton.
McGuinness S, Bergin A, Whelan A (2018) Overeducation in Europe: Trends, convergence, and drivers. Oxford Econ Pap 70:994–1015.
Miller T, Kim AB, Roberts JM (2022) 2022 index of economic freedom. Heritage Foundation, Washington, DC.
Neumark D, Nizalova O (2007) Minimum wage effects in the longer run. J Hum Res 42:435–452.
Neumark D, Shupe C (2019) Declining teen employment: Minimum wages, returns to schooling, and immigration. Lab Econ 59:49–68.
Neumark D, Shirley P (2022) Myth or measurement: What does the new minimum wage research say about minimum wages and job loss in the United States? Ind Relat 61: 384–417.
OECD (2020) Recent trends in employment protection legislation. In: OECD (ed) OECD employment outlook 2020: Worker security and the COVID-19 crisis. OECD Publishing, Paris.
Pries M, Rogerson R (2005) Hiring policies, labor market institutions, and labor market flows. J Polit Econ 113:811–839.
Rinz K (2022) Labor market concentration, earnings, and inequality. J Hum Res 57:S251–S283.

Rohlin SM (2011) State minimum wages and business location: Evidence from a refined border approach. J Urban Econ 69:103–117.

Ruhm CJ (1997) Is high school employment consumption or investment? J Labor Econ 15:735–776.

Schultz TW (1975) The value of the ability to deal with disequilibria. J Econ Lit 13:827–846.

Schumpeter JA (1942) Capitalism, socialism, and democracy. Harper & Brothers, New York.

Sokolova A, Sorensen T (2021) Monopsony in labor markets: A meta-analysis. Ind Labor Rel Rev 74:27–55.

Stern S (1989) Estimating a simultaneous search model. J Labor Econ 7:348–369.

Syverson C (2011) What determines productivity? J Econ Lit 49:326–365.

9

Labor Market Regulations and Outcomes for American Workers

Amanda Novello

Introduction

The COVID-19 pandemic and related economic crisis exposed the need for labor market regulations. Safe workplaces, time off for workers to care for themselves and others, and livable wages that allow workers to save, are not natural features of today's labor market, but can be required by policy. Over the past year, lax and unenforced regulations from the Occupational Safety and Health Administration (OSHA) were responsible for thousands of COVID-19 cases in workplaces, lack of comprehensive paid sick leave made it impossible for millions of workers, especially parents, to care for family members while keeping their jobs, unemployment insurance regulations provided a safety net for millions but still left many out, and widespread low wages meant millions with

A. Novello (✉)
Economic Policy Researcher, Jersey City, NJ, USA
e-mail: novelloab@gmail.com

A. L. Kassens and J. C. Hall (eds.), *Challenges in Classical Liberalism*, Palgrave Studies in Classical Liberalism,
https://doi.org/10.1007/978-3-031-32890-9_9

few savings had to continue working despite unsafe conditions. Inequalities of access to labor market regulations exacerbated existing disparities across socioeconomic and racial groups.

However, what so many workers needed during the pandemic is what workers need all the time—a decent and fair pay standard, the right to collectively bargain, and to be covered by labor law. The rest of this chapter will delve into some of the key policy debates regarding labor market regulations in the twenty-first century, offering evidence and insight into the economics, politics, and policy. In general, I am making the case for strengthened and universal protections that would correct for decades of deregulation, ensure dignity and decency at work, and move toward eradicating working poverty—outcomes that the free market will not produce on its own.

I will start with key terms and concepts, followed by a sketch of labor market outcomes that coincide with decades of deregulation, before getting into a discussion of a few critical labor market policy debates.

Key Terms and Concepts

What Is the Economy?

In capitalism, and the neoclassical economic school of thought that supports a capitalist economy and ideology, the economy is synonymous to markets, or the buying and selling of goods (Harvey 2005).[1] In recent times, the economy is commonly equated with the stock market—a measurement of wealth of the owners of capital—especially when assessing the strength of the economy.[2]

Before diving into the workings of the labor market, it's important to understand that the labor market is not separate from the economy, as stock market watchers would like you to believe. Rather, the labor

[1] See David Harvey, *A Brief History of Neoliberalism*. Oxford: Oxford University Press, 2005. Print.

[2] Many academic studies attempt to define a direct relationship between a nation's stock market and macroeconomic conditions, e.g., Adebayo et al. (2020), Boon (2005), Pilinkus (2010), and more.

market, consisting of workers selling their time and labor and employers buying that labor, is foundational to the economy. The economy is made up of people who are accessing the things they need (or not), and the strength of the economy should be assessed by the extent to which people are able to do so. Rules and regulation of production should ensure humane, dignified, equitable economic life for those who comprise the economy.

Is GDP the economy? Gross Domestic Product, or GDP, is defined as the aggregate value of all goods and services produced in an economy in a given amount of time (commonly one year). While commonly confused with a measure of economic well-being or success, it was never intended to be—Kuznets, the "founder" of the indicator, was adamant that it should not be used as such. Why? The most obvious reason is that GDP cannot tell you how the people that comprise the economy are doing, or how that aggregate value is distributed. It can tell you the size of the pie, but not if everyone gets a slice. As all types of inequality have increased in the United States and many other developed countries, GDP has been increasingly assessed as a poor indicator of well-being (Bleys 2012; Costanza et al. 2005; Giannetti et al. 2015). For this reason, I will not be focusing on the impact of regulations on GDP, as some might do in order to examine the viability of a policy.

This is also an example that demonstrates that the ways in which we assess the economy, and the indicators we use to do so, have a lot to do with values. Do we care about inequality and distribution or not? As conditions change over time, issues come to light, and previously held norms and beliefs change. That's because economics is not a hard, physical science like physics or biology. Rather, it's a social science that requires understanding behavior and psychology, sociology and politics, and ultimately an analysis of power (who has it, who doesn't). It will be important to keep in mind what our values are when discussing regulations, and who matters when we are talking about "the economy."

What Are Labor Market Regulations?

According to the Organisation for Economic Cooperation and Development (OECD), labor market regulations are simply regulations meant to protect workers and their rights. They include rules related to wage levels and benefits provided to workers by the state or required by employers. At a macro level, they can also be viewed as tools to maintain productivity (Storm 2007) and influence employment levels (Bertola 2009).

Flexible labor markets refer to those with few regulations and/or little enforcement of those regulations. Common features include high turnover as companies and workers are able to shift and adapt to changing conditions more easily. In mainstream economics, flexible markets, often leaning toward laissez-faire systems of governance, are seen as "efficient," or without frictions, as there is little imposing on anyone's ability to adapt to changing circumstances, to seek higher utility through changing jobs or locations (on the worker side) or prohibit employers from making hiring or firing decisions.[3] Many have said that the united States has a highly flexible labor market, although that is a complicated debate.[4] I do feel confident, however, saying that the U.S. labor market has become more flexible over time, in the sense that labor market regulations have weakened, and that the costs to workers far outweigh any gains in terms of "efficiency." Evidence for this conclusion is provided throughout the rest of this paper.

Regulations can determine who has labor market power (or a lack of it), or who has the ability to influence outcomes in the labor market. E.g., when there are higher rates of unionization, workers collectively have the power to set wages and conditions. When there are lower rates of unionization and/or higher rates of unemployment, employers tend to have more power to set wages and working conditions. Labor market regulations that set decent minimum wages or encourage unionization

---

3 For a review of the literature, see Betcherman (2012).

4 For an introduction to this debate, see Freeman (2013).

can enhance worker bargaining power (e.g., ability to negotiate for higher pay and better conditions) and increase workers' collective labor market power.

U.S. Outcomes of Concern

The U.S. labor market, while classified at the international level as "flexible," or without stringent regulation relative to other countries, has massive shortcomings and continuously fails millions of American workers. Wages have stagnated. Real hourly wages have stagnated for middle-income earners, and have fallen for low-income earners, since 1979, and only those with high incomes (the ninety-fifth percentile and higher) have seen gains. Average wage growth in the United States has been lower than in all other rich countries since the early 1990s (Novello and Madrick 2018).

Despite what most econ 101 textbooks would explain, wages do not equal productivity on a macro- or micro level.[5] Why? Because, as we will see in this chapter, there are policies that make employers pay fair wages, but as those regulations have eroded, employers have gained the power to set wages and conditions (monopsony power), and have been paying wages equal to less than the value of what workers produce (Marinescu 2021). The classic piece of evidence to prove this point is that productivity, or the average output per hour worked, has increased much more than real wages (Economic Policy Institute 2021a).

While wages have held constant, bosses and corporations have increased their income and wealth dramatically (Tsui et al. 2018). CEO compensation has grown 940% since 1978, while typical worker compensation has risen only 12%—and that was before the coronavirus pandemic hit (Mishel and Schieder 2016). As millions struggled during the pandemic, billionaires increased their wealth by 55% (Americans for Tax Fairness and Institute for Policy Studies 2021). If they were countries, mega-corporations like Amazon and Apple have become richer

---

[5] See Mankiw (2016). Mankiw himself shows how wage and productivity data do not align (Mankiw 2006).

than most other countries in the world (Dughi 2021). The number of multinational corporations has more than doubled in the past 20 years, profiting greatly from finding the lowest labor costs in countries with the fewest regulations.[6]

The crises of low wages, growing income inequality, and too-slow progress on racial and gender inequality, are moral crises that were created by policy decisions that allow this exploitation to continue, and can only be solved through policy change. But it's clear that the federal government has not done enough, and that these outcomes are unique to the United States in large part because of a lack of labor market support that workers in other countries enjoy (Brown and Freund 2018), in addition to regressive taxation, and smaller social expenditures than most other countries, as a percentage of national GDP.[7]

These worsening outcomes correlate with the deregulatory turn and the rise of neoliberal ideology in the 1970s and 1980s, which persists today (Harvey 2005). This neoliberal era can be characterized by a shift away from the prior era of shared prosperity following the New Deal, the strong welfare state and pro-labor policies that followed, and the implementation of the National Labor Relations Act that included comprehensive protections for workers. And unlike the mid-twentieth-century era of relatively shared prosperity, the neoliberal era has seen policies steadfast in stripping protections for workers while reducing the responsibility and accountability of corporations.[8] Specific to the labor market, we have seen a reduction in the real (inflation-adjusted)

---

[6] The trend of increasing wages, benefits, bonuses, options, etc., for corporate bosses and executives, while shedding labor costs, has a lot to do with the rise in private equity and financialization of corporations in which private shareholder interests are primary to business decisions, rather than stakeholder interests. This is not a focus of this chapter, due to word count limitations, however it is an important piece of context in explaining the rise of low-wage work that is worthy of investigation. For more data, see Organisation for Economic Cooperation and Development (2018).

[7] In the united States these programs include Medicare and Medicaid, food stamps, disability insurance, and Social Security, as well as tax credits like the Earned Income Tax Credit and the Child Tax Credit. Spending on programs for the poor, in particular, has declined in the past few decades. See Organisation for Economic Cooperation and Development (2020).

[8] For a wealth of context and sources, see Peters (2008).

minimum wage, a decline in union membership and union-supportive policies, a rise in misclassification of workers, and more, all of which is explored below.

Key Policy Debates in U.S. Labor Market Regulations

Minimum Wage

The minimum wage was originally designed to provide a higher standard of living and to boost the economy during the Great Depression (Doody 2021). Now, the value of the minimum wage has eroded so much that it is a poverty wage for a full-time worker. In fact, at an annual pay of $15,000 for a full-time worker, the minimum wage is a poverty level wage for any worker with a dependent,[9] leaving millions of minimum wage workers and their families reliant on government support to survive.

The United States is an outlier in this area of policy. Nearly 25%, or one out of four workers in America get paid "low wages," which is defined by the OECD as two-thirds of the national median wage. This is the highest share of workers earning low wages than any other country in the OECD—in Germany, 18% of workers get paid low wages, in Japan it's 12%, in Denmark, 9%, and in Italy, 8% (Organisation for Economic Cooperation and Development 2019). 1 in 4 Americans cannot afford a $400 expense, according to a 2019 Federal Reserve Bank study, and that was before the COVID-19 pandemic and recession hit (Board of Governors of the Federal Reserve System 2019).

It's no wonder that so many workers make low wages when the floor on what wages companies can legally pay is so low. Compared to other developed countries, the current federal minimum wage is the lowest, relative to median pay. Across OECD countries, the minimum wage is equal to 50% of median pay, on average. Only a handful of OECD

[9] More than half of minimum wage workers are above age 25 despite the idea that most minimum wage jobs are "youth" jobs, according to Bureau of Labor Statistics (2021).

countries have minimum wages equal to less than half of that nation's median pay, and those include Ireland (42%), Czech Republic (43%), Estonia (43%), Japan (44%), and Mexico (46%). In the United States, the minimum wage of $7.25 per hour is equivalent to merely 32% of the nation's median pay.[10]

The rate of $7.25 per hour, which has not been raised at the federal level since 2009, is worth 17% less than it was 10 years ago and 31% less than in 1968 when adjusted for inflation (Cooper et al. 2019). That means the policy used to be stronger and more in line with the cost of living than it is today. 30 states and D.C. have raised minimum wages above the federal minimum, but millions in other states are continuously left behind by lack of reform (Economic Policy Institute 2022). Raising the minimum wage (to at least $15/hr) would reduce poverty (Dube 2019) and reduce the cost of government programs (Jacobs et al. 2021), making it possible for families to make more than $30 k in a year (compared with the current poverty threshold of roughly $25,000) (Rodgers and Novello 2019).

Meanwhile, there are also millions of workers who are not even covered by minimum wage regulations, such as agricultural workers, domestic workers (e.g., home care), and many others who are covered by a subminimum wage, such as tipped workers (e.g., waiters) and disabled workers. The Raise the Wage Act would phase out subminimum wages and work to ensure all workers are covered by the new, higher wage floor. Altogether, 1 in 5 workers, or 32 million individuals, would benefit from raising the minimum wage to 15 by 2025 (Cooper et al. 2021). Doing so would increase wages for low-wage workers and those who are not currently covered by the minimum wage, who are disproportionately women and workers of color, and would help to narrow gender and racial wage gaps. Almost 60% of workers who would benefit from the raised wage are women, including a disproportionate number of black and latina women, compared with their share of the workforce (Boesch et al. 2021).

[10] Author's calculation based on 2019 Organisation for Economic Cooperation and Development (2021) data.

Why has the minimum wage not been raised in more than 10 years? Econ 101 theory would posit that increasing the price of anything will decrease demand for that good, and therefore increasing the minimum wage will decrease the demand for low-wage labor.[11] However, research shows that this theory does not hold true, mainly because increasing wages for workers increases their demand for goods and services, and also raises worker productivity. Empirical findings demonstrate that there are small, if any, employment changes when minimum wages have been raised. As I've written previously (Rodgers and Novello 2019):

> A meta-analysis that combined the results of hundreds of studies showed that job loss estimates [of raised minimum wages] cluster around zero. In other words, decades of research findings, when combined, show little to no negative employment effects in localities that have raised the minimum wage. Similarly, a team of economists from UC Berkeley led by Sylvia Allegretto examined the most recent outcomes in six major cities that have significantly raised the minimum wage. By comparing these cities (among them Seattle, Chicago, and Washington, D.C.) with similarly sized areas that haven't raised the minimum wage, they found no statistically significant employment effects after the policies were enacted.

But this area of minimum wage research also begs other questions: even if a marginal number of jobs were lost, does it not negate the dramatic increase in quality of life for the millions of workers and their families earning better pay, and the reduction of working poverty? And if a business cannot afford to pay a decent wage, do they have a sustainable business model? These questions are hard to answer, but differing opinions on the answers to these questions are at the heart of the debate on the minimum wage.

There is also a prevalent narrative that higher labor costs due to an increased minimum wage will incentivize companies to invest in labor-saving technologies[12] that in the long run cost them less. While there is some evidence that certain repetitive tasks are being automated (e.g., cashier check-out), increased minimum wages actually create other

---

[11] For discussion, see Leonard (2000).

[12] For example, see Schlogl and Sumner (2018).

lower-wage jobs because of increased demand for services like food and leisure. Further, companies should understand that paying more makes workers more productive (Bassanini and Venn 2008) and reduces turnover which costs companies. Low retention, or high turnover, is expensive for businesses, especially for those in low-wage industries like retail and hospitality, which both have notoriously high turnover rates. Businesses typically spend a fifth of an employee's salary to replace one that left the company, due to search costs and lower productivity during training (Boushey and Glynn 2021). That's why many corporations have taken it on themselves to even go beyond the federally mandated minimum wage. Walmart and others have cited improved recruitment and retention as part of their rationale behind raising pay (Rodgers and Novello 2019).

Finally, some have advocated for "regional" minimum wages rather than the federal $15 minimum, but that ignores the reality of life in those regions. In every region of the United States, a single adult without children needs at least $30 k (what a $15/hr wage earner makes annually) to afford to live (Economic Policy Institute 2021b). By 2025, workers, especially those with children, will need even more than that, due to rising costs of living, according to projections based on the Economic Policy Institute's (2021c) Family Budget Calculator. Further, having different minimum wages in different states and localities would intensify the already rampant corporate race to the bottom, in which companies relocate to places where they can most exploit workers most, exploiting already vulnerable workers, while putting downward pressure on wages everywhere.

Collective Bargaining

Collective bargaining is when workers, typically at the same company or institution, come together to negotiate with management over benefits and working conditions. While there are various forms this can take, the most common way to access collective bargaining rights is through joining a labor union. In the United States, a labor union is formed by filing a petition with the National Labor Relations Board (NLRB), and holding a vote to form a union, that passes if at least 30% of workers vote to form the union. Alternatively, an employer can voluntarily recognize the union. As the National Labor Relations Board (2021) states, "Once a union has been certified or recognized, the employer is required to bargain over your terms and conditions of employment with your union representative."

At an individual level, as someone who's been part of a union, I know firsthand how unions benefit workers. Our collective bargaining contract, which was negotiated between my unionized coworkers and our organization's management and is a legally binding document, made fair pay and annual raises a given. Our contract included baseline wages for new workers that ensured equal pay for workers of different races, genders, and education and experience levels, which guarded against wage discrimination that was already present within the organization. We put in place a disciplinary plan for workers who were said to be underperforming to make sure no one was unfairly laid off or disciplined, which stands in stark contrast with most workers in America who are "at will" employees and can be laid off at the employer's discretion at any time. We were able to file a grievance—a legal binding procedure for holding a company accountable when it violates a collective bargaining contract—and win thousands of dollars in increased base salaries for more than half of our members. Other organizations do much more egregious things, and workers, for the most part, have little agency or legal recourse.

How do unions help workers and the economy? At the height of union power in the twentieth century, unions collectively fought for and won benefits for workers that most enjoy today: the weekend, 40-hour work week, holidays, a ban on child labor, and more. And unions now, while weaker than in the past, still fight for decent pay and conditions for their members. Unionized workers get paid more than non-unionized workers—on average, a worker covered by a union contract earns 13% more than a peer with similar education, occupation, and experience in a non-unionized workplace in the same sector (Farber et al. 2021; Budd and Na 2000).

But the right to collective bargaining is not only important for individuals' wages and benefits, but it's also key to solving the crisis of economic inequality. When workers have the ability to bargain collectively with their employers, the distribution of corporate profits is more equally shared between employees, management, and shareholders. When workers don't have this right, inequality grows, and wages stagnate (Farber et al. 2021). According to regression analyses that control for other factors, the erosion of collective bargaining lowered the median hourly wage by $1.56, an 8% decline, from 1979 to 2017 (Mishel 2021). In other words, if unionization were at the level it was in the late 70s, the gap between the rich and poor would be much smaller (Peters 2008).

Beyond wages, because of collective bargaining agreements, union workers are more likely to have employer-sponsored health insurance, and to have paid vacation and sick leave. Union workers are more likely to have retirement plans, with higher employer contributions. And they are more likely to be safe at work because employers can be held accountable for unsafe conditions (Donado and Wälde 2012).

During the COVID-19 pandemic, these benefits were especially critical, sometimes in unforeseeable ways. For example, because of better access to PPE, unionized nursing homes had lower mortality rates than non-unionized nursing homes (Dean et al. 2020); the United Auto Workers union pushed major firms—General Motors, Ford, and Fiat Chrysler—to partially shut operations to slow the spread of the virus (Wayland 2020) while negotiating safe work practices and PPE (meanwhile, other union workers produced PPE for the rest of the country [Green 2021]); having access to sick leave kept unionized workers from going to work and spreading the virus; and fewer unionized workers lost their jobs during 2020 than non-unionized workers, and that was the case in every sector (McNicholas et al. 2019).

What's on the horizon for U.S. labor unions? Surveys show that most American workers want a union (Economic Policy Institute 2021d) in their workplace but very few are able to form or join a union, largely due to a combination of legal and illegal employer intimidation tactics. Workers face multiple hurdles when they try to organize, including but not limited to captive audience meetings, retaliation, layoffs and facing the threat of layoff, and other forms of aggressive employer-directed antiunion campaigns (Lafer and Loustaunau 2020).

Many workers have fought back, filing lawsuits or complaints with the NLRB. Based on these reported cases alone (many more cases are certainly unlawful but are not reported), data show that employers violate federal labor law in nearly half—42%—of all union election campaigns. One out of five union election campaigns involves a charge that a worker was illegally fired for union activity, and in one-third of union drives, employers illegally threaten to retaliate or fire workers trying to unionize (McNicholas et al. 2019).

Under the NLRA, employers are prohibited from interfering with workers' rights to organize (Sect. 8(a)(1)), employers are prohibited from discriminating against any worker because of union activity (Sect. 8(a)(3)), and more. However, corporations get around the law because there is little to no enforcement, and penalties are small (e.g., deciding back pay is owed to workers). But with help from anti-union lawyers and consultants, instead of allowing workers to have a voice at work, companies have collectively spent hundreds of millions of dollars on "union avoidance" consultants to implement these anti-union tactics and to get around weak laws.[13]

Flaws in this system have been well understood for a long time, but it of course takes political will to change laws. Transformative legislation in hopes of being passed, called the Protecting the Right to Organize (PRO) Act, would repeal anti-union right-to-work laws that exist in many states. It would also streamline the process of forming a union, bolster workers' chances of success at negotiating a first agreement, and hold employers accountable when they violate workers' rights. As of early 2021, the legislation has passed the House of Representatives.

Misclassification and Alternative Work Arrangements

There have always been "gig workers"—from your local handyperson or babysitter to your lawyer or accountant—it's not uncommon to hire

[13] Big-name employers using union avoidance consultants have included FedEx, Bed Bath & Beyond, LabCorp, Caterpillar, Pier 1 Imports, Nestle, Hilton, and more. Gordon Lafer and Lola Loustaunau (2020).

someone for pay to do a task. However, now that a significant portion of work being done is labeled as "gig" work, and the use of contract and temp work is rising in every industry from tech to manufacturing, it's important to understand what's at stake and how regulations can keep workers from losing benefits by being misclassified.

How many gig workers are there, and how many are misclassified? According to a peer-reviewed article by political scientist John Peters (2008: p. 96), "one of the most telling signs of labor market deregulation and the declining strength of workers and unions has been in the rise of part-time and temporary employment and the decline in good paying jobs and job security." The exact number of temporary and "gig" workers is widely disputed—comprising anywhere from 7 to 36% of the nation's workforce—and aside from state-level studies, it's unclear exactly how many of those workers are misclassified.[14]

Gig and misclassified contract workers are increasingly composed of women, people of color, and immigrants (Bernhardt and Thomason 2017). Therefore, correcting for widespread misclassification and enforcing the law will be an act of justice. The work will be to ensure that those who face multiple levels of discrimination in the labor market can start on a more level playing field, with the protections that come with employee status, as opposed to facing exploitation as a contract worker.

Why does it matter: what's the difference between a contract worker and an employee? Employees get protected by labor laws through various policies including but not limited to the Fair Labor Standards Act of 1938 that included the right to a minimum wage, overtime pay rules, and limitations on child labor; the Occupational Safety and Health Act (OSHA) of 1970 that provided legal recourse for unsafe work conditions; access to unemployment insurance; the option to take unpaid leave (for most employees); and much more. Workers who do not have employee

[14] An NPR/Marist poll found that that 1 in 5 jobs in America is held by a worker under contract (Noguchi 2018); an estimated 57 million Americans, or 36 percent of the workforce, are freelancing, according to a 2017 report by Upwork (2017); Weil and Goldman (2016) estimated there are 29 million workers in ten industries alone who are affected by the fissured workplace; and Katz and Krueger (2019) show that between 6.9 percent and 9.6 percent of all workers are independent contractors, or 10.5 to 15 million workers—an estimated 30 percent increase since the early 2000s, in large part due to misclassification of workers as independent contractors.

status are not covered by any of these laws and do not have access to their benefits.

Companies that use contractors to avoid paying for paid time off, taxes (e.g., payroll), health care, unemployment benefits, or having to comply with important labor standards like minimum wage and overtime pay, safety, and anti-discrimination protection, have gone to great lengths to avoid calling workers "employees" (Smith 2019). A 2000 study commissioned by the U.S. Department of Labor found that the number one reason employers misclassify employees as independent contractors are these savings, as well as not being subject to injury and disability-related disputes (Planmatics 2000). According to researchers, "contracted work is an often overlooked driver of eroding labor standards, rising income and wealth inequality, persistent structural racism and occupational segregation, and the shifting of power away from workers and toward corporations (Smith 2019)."

Regulating Employee Classification: How to Determine if a Worker is a Contractor or an "Employee"

To ensure workers are fairly treated and get the benefits they are owed, there should be a federally mandated "ABC" test and misclassification should be monitored and laws should be properly enforced (note that the PRO Act would implement a federal ABC test). The existing test used in some states and cases uses the following three questions to determine if a worker is in fact "independent": if they are (A) are free from control by the putative employer, (B) are doing work that is outside the usual course of business of the putative employer, and (C) are engaged in an independently established business (Smith 2019).

Four states, including California, New Jersey, Massachusetts, and Connecticut, already use the test in their wage and hour laws. About half the states, including Washington, use some version of it in their unemployment laws, and 10 other states apply it to labor laws within particular sectors such as construction (Smith 2019). But companies have fought hard against passing and implementing such laws. In California, an ABC test was implemented through California Assembly Bill 5 (AB5) in 2019. One year later, corporations that depend on misclassifying their workforce spent almost $200 million to pass Proposition 22 that gave exemptions from AB5 that would allow them to continue misclassifying their workers (Hartnett 2020). Lead corporate backers of Prop 22 included Uber and other ride-sharing companies that are determined to avoid responsibility and liability for their workers' subminimum wages and their high likelihood of harassment and even being killed on the job (Parrot and Reich 2018; Jacobs and Reich 2019; Conger 2019; Menéndez et al. 2017).

Conclusion

All of the trends mentioned thus far are interconnected and feed off of one another, and without regulatory reform as a backstop, they will only continue. When people can't make enough pay to only have one job, it is inevitable that they have to find other part-time or gig work in order to make ends meet, and contribute to the growth of precarious work with few benefits or protections. Solid minimum wages and unions would allow people to have more security in one job, but those areas of regulation have eroded over time. The American labor market, although deemed "flexible," is in fact deregulated to a level that is unparalleled compared to other developed countries, and causes harm that is unique in scale and scope to American workers. Too many are burdened by insufficient protections and many are left out of protections altogether. This hurts those individuals, their careers, and their families, but also the economy at large by diminishing their contributions to local economies. While deregulation hurts everyone, it harms those who are systematically disadvantaged and more likely put into precarious and deregulated working conditions with fewer ways out. Thus implementing labor market reforms such as raising the minimum wage and making it easier to join unions would be a step toward equity and justice in the United States.

References

Adebayo TS, Awosusi AA, Eminer F (2020) Stock market-growth relationship in an emerging economy: Empirical finding from ARDL-based bounds and causality approaches. J Econ Bus 3:903–916.

Americans for Tax Fairness and Institute for Policy Studies (2021) Billionaire pandemic wealth gains of 55%, or $1.6 Trillion, come amid three decades of rapid wealth growth. Americans for Tax Fairness and Institute for Policy Studies, Washington, DC.

Bassanini A, Venn D (2008) The impact of labour market policies on productivity in OECD countries. Int Prod Monit 17:3–15.

Bernhardt A, Thomason S (2017) What do we know about gig work in California? An analysis of independent contracting. UC Berkeley Labor Center, Berkeley.

Bertola G (2009) Labour market regulation: Motives, measures, effects. International Labour Organization, Conditions of Work and Employment Series No. 21.

Betcherman G (2012) Labor market institutions: A review of the literature. World Bank, Policy Research Working Paper 6276.

Bleys B (2012) Beyond GDP: Classifying alternative measures for progress. Soc Indic Res 109:355–376.

Board of Governors of the Federal Reserve System (2019) Report on the economic well-being of US households in 2018. Board of Governors of the Federal Reserve System, Washington, DC.

Boesch D, Bleiweis R, Haider A (2021) Raising the minimum wage would be transformative for women. Center for American Progress, Washington, DC.

Boon TK (2005) Do commercial banks, stock market and insurance market promote economic growth? An analysis of the Singapore economy. Nanyang Technological University, School of Humanities and Social Studies, Working Paper.

Boushey H, Glynn S (2021) There are significant business costs to replacing employees. Center for American Progress, Washington, DC.

Brown CP, Freund CL (2018) Active labor market policies: Lessons from other countries for the United States. Peterson Institute for International Economics, Working Paper No. 19–2.

Budd JW, Na IG (2000). The union membership wage premium for employees covered by collective bargaining agreements. J Labor Econ 18:783–807.

Bureau of Labor Statistics (2021) Characteristics of minimum wage workers, 2019. Bureau of Labor Statistics, Washington, DC.

Conger K (2019) Uber says 3,045 sexual assaults were reported in U.S. rides last year. New York Times, 5 December.

Cooper D, Gould E, Zipperer B (2019) Low-wage workers are suffering from a decline in the real value of the minimum wage. Economic Policy Institute, Washington, DC.

Cooper D, Mokhiber Z, Zipperer B (2021) Raising the federal minimum wage to $15 by 2025 would lift the pay of 32 million workers. Economic Policy Institute, Washington, DC.

Costanza R, Hart M, Talberth J, Posner S (2005) Beyond GDP: The need for new measures of progress. The Frederick S. Pardee Center for the Study of the Longer-Range Future at Boston University, Working Paper (Pardee Paper) No. 4.

Dean A, Venkataramani A, Kimmel S (2020) Mortality rates from COVID-19 are lower in unionized nursing homes: Study examines mortality rates in New York nursing homes. Health Affair 39:1993–2001.

Donado A, Wälde K (2012) How trade unions increase welfare. Econ J 122:990–1009.

Doody C (2021) The missing piece of the minimum wage debate. Washington Post, 25 February.

Dube A (2019) Minimum wages and the distribution of family incomes. Amer Econ J Appl Econ 11:268–304.

Dughi P (2021) Apple, Amazon wealthier than more than 90% of the world's countries. Medium, 29 March.

Economic Policy Institute (2021a) The productivity-pay gap. Economic Policy Institute, Washington, DC.

Economic Policy Institute (2021b) Why the U.S. needs a $15 minimum wage, how the Raise the Wage Act would benefit U.S. workers and their families. Economic Policy Institute, Washington, DC.

Economic Policy Institute (2021c) Family budget calculator. Economic Policy Institute, Washington, DC.

Economic Policy Institute (2021d) Working people want a voice at work. Economic Policy Institute, Washington, DC.

Economic Policy Institute (2022) Minimum wage tracker. Economic Policy Institute, Washington, DC.

Farber HS, Herbst D, Kuziemko I, Naidu S (2021) Unions and inequality over the twentieth century: New evidence from survey data. Q J Econ 136:1325–1385.

Freeman RB (2013) Failing the test? The flexible US job market in the Great Recession. Ann Am Acad Polit SS 650:78–97.

Giannetti BF, Agostinho F, Almeida CM, Huisingh D (2015) A review of limitations of GDP and alternative indices to monitor human wellbeing and to manage eco-system functionality. J Clean Prod 87:11–25.

Green K (2021) Filling supply shortages during the pandemic: 'Union workers are our heroes.' Union Track, 9 March.

Hartnett S (2020) Prop 22 explained: Why gig companies are spending huge money on an unprecedented measure. KQED, 26 October.

Harvey D (2005) A brief history of neoliberalism. Oxford University Press, Oxford.

Jacobs K, Perry IE, MacGillvary J (2021) The public cost of a low federal minimum wage. UC Berkeley Center for Labor Research and Education, Berkeley.

Jacobs K, Reich M (2019) The Uber/Lyft ballot initiative guarantees only $5.64 an hour. UC Berkeley Labor Center, Berkeley.

Katz LF, Krueger AB (2019) The rise and nature of alternative work arrangements in the United States, 1995–2015. Ind Lab Relativ Rev 72:382–416.

Lafer G, Loustaunau L (2020) Fear at work: An inside account of how employers threaten, intimidate, and harass workers to stop them rom exercising their right to collective bargaining. Economic Policy Institute, Washington, DC.

Leonard TC (2000) The very idea of applying economics: The modern minimum-wage controversy and its antecedents. Hist Polit Econ 32(Suppl 1):117–144.

Mankiw G (2006) How are wages and productivity related? Greg Mankiw's Blog, 29 August.

Mankiw G (2016) Principles of macroeconomics. Cengage, Mason.

Marinescu I (2021) Boosting wages when U.S. labor markets are not competitive. In: Boosting wages for U.S. workers in the new economy: Ten essays on worker power, worker well-being, and equitable wages. Center for Equitable Growth, Washington, DC.

McNicholas C, Poydock M, Wolfe J, Zipperer B, Lafer G, Loustaunau L (2019). Unlawful: US employers are charged with violating federal law in 41.5% of all union election campaigns. Economic Policy Institute, Washington, DC.

McNicholas C, Shierholz H, Poydock M (2021) Union workers had more job security during the pandemic, but unionization remains historically low. Economic Policy Institute, Washington, DC.

Menéndez CK, Socias-Morales C, Daus MM (2017) Work-related violent deaths in the US taxi and limousine industry 2003 to 2013: Disparities within a high-risk working population. J Occup Environ Med 59:768–774.
Mishel L (2021) The enormous impact of eroded collective bargaining on wages. Economic Policy Institute, Washington, DC.
Mishel L, Schieder J (2016) As union membership has fallen, the top 10 percent have been getting a larger share of income. Economic Policy Institute, Washington, DC.
National Labor Relations Board (2021) Your right to a union. National Labor Relations Board, Washington, DC.
Noguchi Y (2018) Freelanced: The rise of the contract workforce. NPR, 22 January.
Novello A, Madrick J (2018) 11 ways American workers are falling behind the rest of the world. Century Foundation, Washington, DC.
Organisation for Economic Cooperation and Development (2018) Multinational enterprises in the global economy. Organisation for Economic Cooperation and Development, Paris.
Organisation for Economic Cooperation and Development (2019) Data: Wage levels. Organisation for Economic Cooperation and Development, Paris.
Organisation for Economic Cooperation and Development (2020) Social expenditure update 2020. Organisation for Economic Cooperation and Development, Paris.
Organisation for Economic Cooperation and Development (2021) OECD: Stat: Real minimum wages. Organisation for Economic Cooperation and Development, Paris.
Parrot J, Reich M (2018) An earnings standard for New York City's app-based driveers. Center for New York City Affairs, New York.
Peters J (2008) Labour market deregulation and the decline of labour power in North America and Western Europe. Policy Soc 27:83–98.
Pilinkus D (2010). Macroeconomic indicators and their impact on stock market performance in the short and long run: The case of the Baltic States. Technol Econ Dev Eco 16:291–304.
Planmatics (2000) Independent contractors: Prevalence and implications for unemployment insurance programs. US Department of Labor, Washington, DC.
Rodgers W, Novello A (2019) Making the economic case for a $15 minimum wage. Century Foundation, Washington, DC.

Schlogl L, Sumner A (2018) The rise of the robot reserve army: Automation and the future of economic development, work, and wages in developing countries. Center for Global Development, Working Paper 487.

Smith R (2019) Washington state considers ABC test for employee status. National Employment Law Project, New York.

Storm S (2007) Why labour market regulation may pay off: Worker motivation, coordination and productivity growth. International Labour Organization, Economic and Labour Market Paper No. 4.

Tsui AS, Enderle G, Jiang K (2018) Income inequality in the United States: Reflections on the role of corporations. Acad Manage Rev 43:156–168.

Upwork (2017) Freelancing in America: 2017. Upwork, San Francisco.

Wayland M (2020) UAW, Detroit automakers negotiate rotating partial shutdowns of US plants. CNBC, 17 March.

Weil D, Goldman T (2016) Labor standards, the fissured workplace, and the on-demand economy. Persp Work 20:26–77.

Part V

Health Care

10

Should We Trust Consumers or Bureaucrats with Health Insurance Choices?

Aaron Yelowitz

Introduction

The market for health care is different from most other markets that economists think about. Health shocks are unpredictable and expensive, leading to demand for health insurance to smooth consumption. Demand for health insurance then leads to a host of other economic issues. One issue is that adverse selection has the potential to unravel insurance markets or limit the menu of plans that are offered, a market failure that may motivate government intervention such as mandating insurance purchases.[1] Another important issue is that by its very nature,

[1] Cutler and Reber (1998) provide a compelling example of an adverse selection death spiral after Harvard changed the pricing structure across the menu of health insurance plans it offered.

A. Yelowitz (✉)
Gatton College of Business and Economics, University of Kentucky, Lexington, KY, USA
e-mail: aaron.yelowitz@uky.edu

A. L. Kassens and J. C. Hall (eds.), *Challenges in Classical Liberalism*, Palgrave Studies in Classical Liberalism,
https://doi.org/10.1007/978-3-031-32890-9_10

health insurance insulates consumers from the expenditure risk, which in turn lowers the out-of-pocket price of health care utilization. Moral hazard—the notion that insurance enables consumers to use more health care than they otherwise would—is thought to make consumers less prudent shoppers leading to wasteful and inefficient medical decisions.[2]

In the United States and other countries, there is far greater government involvement in the health insurance sectors than in most other insurance markets. The government's tax-exclusion for employer contributions to health insurance leads to an implicit preference away from private, non-group plans; more than 80–90% of private insurance is provided through the employers. There has been constant growth in government involvement in health insurance markets over the last 50 years. The 1960s saw the initial implementation of Medicare and Medicaid. The 1980s and 1990s saw large expansions in eligibility for the means-tested Medicaid program and SCHIP for children under 18 with incomes far exceeding the Federal Poverty Level (FPL). The 2000s saw the Medicare program become more comprehensive with Medicare Part D insurance for prescription drugs. And the 2010s saw dramatic increases in insurance coverage from the Patient Protection and Affordable Care Act (ACA) through both adult Medicaid expansions and taxpayer-subsidized private coverage on exchanges in the Federally Facilitated Marketplace (Courtemanche et al. 2017). By 2020, Medicare and Medicaid spending totaled approximately $800 billion and $600 billion, respectively, or 37% of national health expenditure Center for Medicare and Medicaid Services (2022).

For those who advocate for a dynamic, open market in health care, both the extensive government involvement in promoting insurance and the outsized role of third-party payers (insurance companies) in health care leads to inefficient and wasteful utilization. As an example, recent academic work suggests that Medicaid's benefit to recipients per $1.00

[2] The 2008 Oregon Health Insurance Experiment provided credible estimates of the impact of Medicaid and found increased healthcare use, including outpatient care, preventive care, prescription drugs, hospital admissions, and emergency room visits. At the same time, although self-reported health improved and depression fell, there was no statistically significant impact on mortality or physical health measures (Finkelstein et al. 2012; Baicker et al. 2013).

of government spending ranges from about $0.20 to $0.40 (Finkelstein et al. 2019), while the bulk of Medicaid spending is simply a transfer to providers of uncompensated care. In another example, the ACA led to no significant initial effects on self-reported health and risky behaviors, despite large changes in insurance coverage, access, and costs (Courtemanche et al. 2018). The "wish list" by those who want a more dynamic health care market is extensive, but often boils down to far less government intervention including rolling back involvement in public health insurance, as well as more transparency in prices and costs in health care decisions which are thought to empower consumers and unleash market forces.

Given the current policy climate in the United States—such as a majority of the public viewing the ACA positively and an increasingly number of conservative states adopting Medicaid expansions through voter initiatives—the likelihood for sweeping change in the direction of less extensive government involvement seems remote (Kirzinger et al. 2022). Nonetheless, one of the core assumptions embedded in scaling back government involvement is that consumers know better than bureaucrats how to manage their health insurance and healthcare decisions. As discussed extensively in this essay, although such an assumption seems innocuous in most markets, there is evidence showing a sizable percentage of consumers make serious errors with respect to health insurance decisions. However, this does not mean bureaucrats can do better.

The goal of this essay is incremental in that it advocates for more consumer empowerment and less bureaucratic decision-making, but within the confines of existing programs and structures for government involvement. This is because of the lack of compelling empirical evidence on wholesale changes to the structure of healthcare. The remainder of this essay is arranged as follows. Section "Consumer Errors in Choosing Health Insurance" outlines some recent evidence from some highly stylized situations that show consumer make errors in health insurance plans. Section "Will Bureaucrats Successfully Advocate for Consumers?" explains—specifically through an example from Kentucky Medicaid's transition to managed care–how bureaucratic solutions can go awry, especially with behavioral economic strategies like nudges. Section "Recent Policy Proposals and Concluding Thoughts" concludes by examining recent proposals involving greater bureaucratic involvement using behavioral economics in these settings.

Consumer Errors in Choosing Health Insurance

Whether purchasing insurance in the private market, choosing Medicare or Medicaid plans, or picking among plans offered by an employer, many consumers face a menu of health insurance plans with different cost-sharing arrangements and provider networks, along with underlying uncertainty about future health shocks and a lack of transparency in prices for services or procedures. In addition, even the savviest consumers rarely investigate the "Explanation of Benefits" booklet that further clarifies the minutiae of how the insurance plan operates. Put differently, health insurance is a complex financial product that covers various health expenditure. Thus, it may not be surprising that many consumers make what appear to be mistakes in choosing plans.

Consider an individual shopping for private health insurance on the Federally Facilitated Marketplace. In 2022, a 50-year old in Miami, Florida would be presented with 221 available health insurance plans on HealthCare.gov, including 82 bronze plans, 100 silver plans, 34 gold plans, and 5 platinum plans. Assuming the individual earned $41,000, putting the person just over 250% of the poverty line, a premium tax credit amounting to $406 per month would be applied. After this substantial subsidy, monthly premiums would range from $60 to $1412. In addition, annual deductibles on some plans are as high as $8700. There are 10 distinct insurance companies offering coverage with different provider networks. Many of the bronze and silver plans have low premiums, but significant out-of-pocket exposure. Pauly (2017) notes that the maximum deductible for either bronze or silver plans was $6250 in the early years of the ACA, with an average deductible of $1536 for a silver plan and $1888 for a bronze plan. For an individual that encountered significant health expenses, this would result in sizable out-of-pocket expenditures relative to income, often more than 20% of income for individuals with large negative health shocks. He also notes that many of the incentive structures "weren't chosen based on any strong behavioral evidence, especially in terms of coverage or the premiums being charged, but rather were based on round number examples and what fits into a budget." Given the salience of premiums—which are paid each month with certainty, "some choose the cheapest bronze plan just to punch their ticket to avoid the mandate rather than the more heavily subsidized silver plan." The thrust of Pauly's article suggests this choice toward low premium plans may be a mistake, given the uncovered out-of-pocket exposure.

One early, compelling example that suggests individuals make mistakes is Abaluck and Gruber's (2011) examination of the Medicare Part D program. Among elders who enrolled in a Medicare Part D plan in 2006, only 12.2% choose the lowest-cost plan (accounting for both premiums and out-of-pocket costs); individuals could save nearly 31% of their total spending on average by choosing the lowest-cost plan. The authors find most Medicare Part D plan choices are off the "efficient frontier" meaning individuals could have lowered either their mean costs or the variance by picking a different plan. The authors estimate models of insurance choice with several testable implications and find large divergences from what would occur if individuals made fully informed and rational decisions about plan choice. Specifically, individuals underweight out-of-pocket spending relative to premiums; they overweight plan characteristics beyond their own circumstances; and they do not fully appreciate the risk-reducing aspects of plans for themselves (the "pure insurance" component of the plan).[3] Although in principle, there could be sizable welfare gains for seniors from restricting choices to plans on the efficient frontier, the authors question whether policymakers could effectively distinguish such plans.

Errors also occur in the employer health insurance setting. Bhargava et al. (2017) analyzed employee decisions in which a large U.S. Fortune 100 firm asked its employees to "build" their own insurance plan across

[3] Related, Finkelstein et al. (2019) estimate that the "pure insurance" component of Medicaid (reallocation toward states of the world with high marginal utility) is positive but sensitive to methodology, with the authors concluding that the transfer component (increases in resources to the individual) represents a large share of recipient's willingness-to-pay for Medicaid.

four cost-sharing components: deductible, copayment, coinsurance, and out-of-pocket maximum. The 48 plans were otherwise identical with respect to quality. Given the premium levels, many plans were "financially dominated" because other plans were less expensive regardless of how much medical care the employee required. This may not have been obvious to all employees, however, because the web interface allowed employees to "build" a plan, and then new plans were iteratively added to the comparison page. To see all 48 plans, employees would have to access a web page that was not prominently displayed. The authors found that for nearly every high-deductible plan, the additional premiums required to reduce the deductible exceeded the maximum possible out-of-pocket savings provided by the lower deductible, so no belief about health-care needs or standard preferences for avoiding risk could rationalize the choice. Of the 36 lower-deductible plans available, 35 were dominated in this fashion. The majority of employees selected financially dominated plans, where the average employee opting into a dominated plan could have saved \$372 a year by choosing an otherwise equivalent plan with a higher deductible. The authors conclude that a lack of basic insurance competence played a significant role in the demand for dominated plans.

Another interesting example comes from Handel (2013), where he examines a large private firm in the United States that compelled employees to actively re-enroll in one of five health insurance options when it introduced an entirely new set of three PPO plan options (and two HMO options). At the time of the initial reform, enrollment in any of the plans could be rationalized depending on expected medical utilization and no plan was dominated. In subsequent years, employees would remain by default into their previously chosen plan, even as costs changed. The PPOs shared the same provider network and only differed from one another by premiums and cost-sharing characteristics (deductible, coinsurance, and out-of-pocket maximums) that determined the mapping from total medical expenditures to employee out-of-pocket expenditures. For the three PPOs, individual-level deductibles were \$250, \$500, and \$1200. As premiums changed over time, some PPO plans became dominated for some employees in that for any amount of medical expenses, the total employee expense was higher than for another plan. For example, the PPO with the \$250 deductible was strictly dominated for a low-income family compared to the same PPO with the $500 deductible, due to substantially higher premiums. Handel (2013) finds both strong evidence of inertia (which could be rationalized by high switching costs or inattentiveness), but also evidence of errors. New employees who joined the firm after some PPO plans became dominated were less likely to join such dominated plans (and were making an active choice), yet 11% of new hires still chose the PPO with the $250 deductible. This choice was costly; for a low-income family choosing this plan, they lose at least $1000 relative to the plan with the higher deductible due to much higher premiums. In addition, the role of initial defaults and inertia becomes clear; for the subset of employees who would be unambiguously better off by switching to another plan, only a small fraction actually switched after one or two years.

In summary, across a variety of "clean" settings where mistakes can be convincingly documented, there is strong empirical evidence that many consumers make mistakes, and those mistakes often carry on for at least several years.

Will Bureaucrats Successfully Advocate for Consumers?

Many studies that document consumer mistakes in health insurance choices advocate for policies to refocus consumer attention, or more consequentially default consumers into certain health plans (with the freedom to switch), or most consequentially restrict choice by eliminating certain plans altogether. For example, Bhargava et al. (2017) discuss decision aids or standardization to allow consumers to be better shoppers. Handel and Kolstad (2015) discuss a more extreme version—"smart defaults"—that potentially switch consumers to a new plan during open enrollment (but with the freedom to switch out) when the regulator has substantial confidence that a consumer is enrolled in a poor plan match. Abaluck and Gruber (2011) discuss how eliminating Medicare Part D plans that are not on the efficient frontier could improve welfare if policymakers could identify such plans.

Many of these solutions to consumer mistakes involve "nudges," most importantly changing defaults in the "choice architecture" of decision-making. The enduring impact of defaults is one of the contributions of behavioral economics and was popularized in the highly influential book *Nudge* (Thaler and Sunstein 2008). They describe a "nudge" as any aspect of the choice architecture that alters people's behavior in a predictable way without forbidding any options or significantly changing their economic incentives. The classic example of a nudge is the decision of an employer to "opt-in" or "opt-out" employees from a 401(k) plan while allowing the employee to reverse that choice; the empirical evidence strongly suggests that opting employees into such plans dramatically raises 401(k) participation (Madrian and Shea 2001).

There is no question that nudges—decision aids, standardization, or even altering the default insurance choices (with the option to switch)—can have powerful effects on the eventual health insurance choice, often due to inattention or inertia. Kentucky Medicaid switched from fee-for-service to statewide managed care in 2012 (Marton et al. 2017). During the 90-day open enrollment period immediately prior to 2012 rollout of managed care, enrollees were assigned by the algorithm to one of three managed care plans—Wellcare, Coventry, or Spirit. The auto-assignment algorithm designed by the state accounted for the enrollee's historical physician relationships, consistency of household members assigned to the same plan, load balancing across plans, and capitation payments made by the state to managed care organizations. Kentucky Medicaid recipients have strong incentives to switch to the highest quality managed care plan—presumably plans with larger networks and greater access—because cost-sharing is near zero for all three plans from the enrollee's perspective. Nonetheless, initial assignment dramatically affected the ultimate choice of plan. For those initially assigned to Wellcare or Coventry, approximately 95% remained in the plan during the first year of managed care. Even in Spirit—which had well-documented access problems—more than 57% of those initially assigned to the plan remained in it.

In summary, initial defaults—as illustrated with Kentucky Medicaid—have very sizable effects on eventual consumer choices. Yet do these bureaucrat-designed defaults guarantee that consumer mistakes will be remedied? Or might nudges compound these problems? Thaler and Sustein (2008) devote approximately two pages (out of 253 pages of text) to the concepts of "evil nudgers" and "bad nudges." They note "In offering supposedly helpful nudges, choice architects may have their own agendas. Those who favor one default rule over another may do so because their own economic interests are at stake" (Thaler and Sunstein 2008: p. 239). They strike an optimistic tone for nudges in public programs. With respect to government nudges, their view is "On the face of it, it is odd to say that the public architects are always more dangerous than the private ones. After all, managers in the public sector have to answer to voters, and managers in the private sector have as their mandate the job of maximizing profits and share prices, not consumer welfare."

Despite their optimism for nudges, the Kentucky context provides a compelling example of a "bad nudge" and possibly "evil nudgers." Given enrollee incentives to choose the highest quality plan, the initial default was decidedly inferior for those assigned to the Spirit-managed care plan. For example, Spirit was not able to contract with Appalachian Regional Healthcare, a dominant provider in eastern Kentucky due to unsuccessful rate negotiations. Thus, the quality of the Spirit plan would certainly be viewed as lower than other MCOs in eastern Kentucky because enrollees would have trouble receiving services from the region's dominant provider. Spirit's difficulties in eastern Kentucky were widely reported in the press and would lead to greater awareness of differences in MCO provider network quality in that region, as compared to the rest of the state. Among Kentucky Medicaid enrollees who made an active decision to switch during the open enrollment window in 2011, the recognition of the stark gap in plan quality was apparent. Nearly 43% of those assigned to Spirit switched, compared to 5% assigned to other plans. Strikingly, out of the 37,510 individuals in eastern Kentucky initially assigned to Coventry or Wellcare (two managed care plans that had reasonable quality), only 108 actively switched to Spirit during open enrollment. This is in accordance with Spirit's quality problems in eastern Kentucky, suggesting there is little doubt that assignment to it was a low-quality match for virtually all participants.

If the Spirit plan was bad for Medicaid recipients, why did the state initially assign nearly 40% of enrollees to it? For many groups of Medicaid recipients in many regions of the state, Spirit's capitation rates were lower than for the other two plans, thus saving the state money. Compared with assigning enrollees to the highest quality plan, Kentucky's assignment algorithm saved the state over $31 million annually. The state's auto-assignment algorithm most heavily weighted cost savings and plan balancing (making sure all three plans had a critical mass of consumers) and placed less weight on the quality of the enrollee-plan match. The presence of inertia contributed to the success of the state's cost-minimization strategy, as more than half of enrollees assigned to even the lowest quality plans (Spirit) did not opt-out. While this was beneficial for taxpayers or a budget-conscious state government, it is precisely the bad nudge that Thaler and Sunstein describe.

Even if bureaucrats are not "evil nudgers" in other contexts, one needs to fundamentally question the competence of those who might design such nudges. Consider, for example, the two cases of mistakes highlighted here with employer-provided health insurance. A natural question is how did such detrimental choices emerge on the menu in the first place, and would we trust such designers to provide good guidance? Bhargava et al. (2017) notes "while a full discussion of the genesis of plan pricing is beyond the scope of the article, in an earlier working paper, we show that the observed prices appear roughly consistent with what would have been expected from the application of average cost pricing, a common strategy for pricing insurance, to the firm's plan menu given plausible assumptions of employee sorting." From Handel (2013), "It is important to note that the existence of dominated plans for these select groups was unknown to the firm at t_1. The firm determined total premiums and subsidies over time separately from the t_0 decision on health plan characteristics, such that the firm did not analyze these features in combination with each other at t_1 and t_2 as we do here." Such statements—that completely summarize the thought process behind offering dominated options in these two studies—do not inspire confidence that such companies would do well in designing decision aids or defaults.

Although there are certainly cases when nudges can improve outcomes, one should not dismiss the idea that choice architects have motives beyond maximizing utility for the clientele or lack the competence to correctly guide consumers. This concern tends to be acknowledged but minimized in many discussions of behavioral economic interventions.

Recent Policy Proposals and Concluding Thoughts

A variety of proposals continue to advocate for different defaults in choice architecture. As part of the well-known project "1% Steps for Health Care Reform," one proposal by Ndumele and Wallace (2022) suggests states use "smart defaults when auto-assigning Medicaid enrollees to managed care plans. States have an opportunity to leverage auto-assignment as a tool to better understand the efficiency of the plans in their market and then as a tool to steer enrollees into plans that constrain spending without reducing enrollee satisfaction or health. For example, research suggests that auto-assigning Medicaid enrollees into narrower network plans that include their usual providers can lower cost without harming enrollee satisfaction or health." The authors estimate that such actions could lower Medicaid costs by up to $9.2 billion. Interestingly, the authors note that the auto-assignment experience in New York to narrow networks did reduce enrollee satisfaction and the quantity of care consumed (including preventive services). The findings from Kentucky Medicaid in the Marton et al. (2017) study suggest that such algorithms—often lacking transparency—may provide the kind of "bad nudge" discussed in Thaler and Sunstein (2008) where choice architects may have their own agendas that differ from the client. Moreover, the Ndumele and Wallace proposal clearly acknowledges "the diversity of approaches likely reflects, in part, the competing priorities of policy makers in different states." Their proposal is silent on an algorithm that entails higher quality for Medicaid recipients (perhaps through more expansive networks) but entails higher costs.

If we acknowledge that consumers make mistakes in choosing health insurance, and that nudges that change default enrollment can do harm, are there remaining solutions consistent with free choice? One possibility is to give consumers the opportunity to make mistakes but then correct them. For example, open enrollment periods usually occur once per year (unless there is a triggering event such as job loss or change in family structure), meaning that mistakes take some time to correct. Although there will be higher administrative costs from allowing greater flexibility to switch plans, the benefit would be allowing consumers to match with more appropriate plans. Another possibility—embedded in some of the studies that discuss such mistakes—is greater information provision. Information dissemination has a public good characteristic, so there may be a role for centralized provision. Even with provision, however, it is unlikely that a one-size-fits-all approach to conveying the information will be effective. Even with more personalized information—such as in a novel randomized experiment conducted by Marzilli Ericson et al. (2017)—where information about savings on insurance premiums from switching was presented, although shopping on the Marketplace increased but plan switching did not.

References

Abaluck J, Gruber J (2011) Choice inconsistencies among the elderly: Evidence from plan choice in the Medicare Part D program. Amer Econ Rev 101:1180–1210.

Baicker K, Taubman SL, Allen HL, Bernstein M, Gruber JH, Newhouse JP, Schneider EC, Wright BJ, Zaslavsky AM, Finkelstein AN (2013) The Oregon experiment—Effects of Medicaid on clinical outcomes. New Engl J Med 368:1713–1722.

Bhargava S, Loewenstein G, Sydnor J (2017) Choose to lose: Health plan choices from a menu with dominated option. Q J Econ 132:1319–1372.

Center for Medicare and Medicaid Services (2022) NHE fact sheet: Historical NHE, 2021. Center for Medicare and Medicaid Services, Baltimore.

Courtemanche C, Marton J, Ukert B, Yelowitz A, Zapata D (2017) Early impacts of the Affordable Care Act on health insurance coverage in Medicaid expansion and non-expansion states. J Pol Anal Manag 36:178–210.

Courtemanche C, Marton J, Ukert B, Yelowitz A, Zapata D (2018) Early effects of the Affordable Care Act on health care access, risky health behaviors, and self-assessed health. South Econ J 84:660–691.

Cutler DM, Reber SJ (1998) Paying for health insurance: The trade-off between competition and adverse selection. Q J Econ 113:433–466.

Finkelstein A, Hendren N, Luttmer E (2019) The value of Medicaid: Interpreting results from the Oregon health insurance experiment. J Polit Econ 127:2836–2874.

Finkelstein A, Taubman S, Wright B, Bernstein M, Gruber J, Newhouse JP, Allen H, Baicker K, Oregon Health Study Group (2012) The Oregon health insurance experiment: Evidence from the first year. Q J Econ 127:1057–1106.

Handel BR (2013) Adverse selection and inertia in health insurance markets: When nudging hurts. Amer Econ Rev 103: 2643–2682.

Handel BR, Kolstad J (2015) Getting the most from marketplaces: Smart policies on health insurance choices. Brookings Institution, Washington, DC.

Kirzinger A, Montero A, Hamel L, Brodie M (2022) 5 charts about public opinion on the Affordable Care Act. Kaiser Family Foundation, San Francisco.

Madrian BC, Shea DF (2001) The power of suggestion: Inertia in 401(k) participation and savings behavior. Q J Econ 116:1149–1187.

Marton J, Yelowitz A, Talbert JC (2017) Medicaid program choice, inertia and adverse selection. J Health Econ 56:292–316.

Marzilli Ericson KM, Kingsdale J, Layton T, Sacarny A (2017) Nudging leads consumers in Colorado to shop but not switch ACA marketplace plans. Health Affair 36:311–319.

Ndumele C, Wallace J (2022) Improving auto-assignment in Medicaid managed care. 1% steps for health care reform, New Haven.

Pauly MV (2017) Should lower-income people be allowed to buy insurance with high cost sharing? Amer J Health Econ 3:1–9.

Thaler RH, Sunstein CR (2008) Nudge: improving decisions about health, wealth, and happiness. Yale University Press, New Haven.

11

Challenges to Market-Based Healthcare for Consumers, Insurers, and Society

Tina Marsh Dalton

Introduction

On the spectrum between government provision of health care versus market-based approaches, the U.S. stands lonely on the extreme among its industrialized country counterparts. Even with large portions of care funded federally through Medicare and Medicaid, our employer-based insurance and individual insurance market system puts over 67% of the population in a market-based environment[1] and most providers of care, regardless of payer, are private firms. For most consumer goods, a market

[1] The U.S. Census reported the percentage of the U.S. which was privately insured at 67.3 in 2018 and 68 in 2019 (Keisler-Starkey and Bunch 2020).

T. M. Dalton (✉)
Wake Forest University, Winston-Salem, NC, USA
e-mail: daltonc@wfu.edu

A. L. Kassens and J. C. Hall (eds.), *Challenges in Classical Liberalism*, Palgrave Studies in Classical Liberalism,
https://doi.org/10.1007/978-3-031-32890-9_11

is a great way to improve welfare, allowing buyers and sellers to meet in equilibrium without costly and inefficient central planning and with constant competition to spur innovation. However, health care is not a run-of-the-mill consumer good, as we shall see below, and we observe a vastly different approach taken by the bulk of modern healthcare systems. Among OECD countries, more than 70% of health spending is publicly funded, on average. Only two out of the 36 OECD countries spend at or below the U.S.'s 50% level, with eight countries providing over 80% of their healthcare through public provision, including Norway and Luxembourg at 85%.[2] "Everyone else is doing it" is rarely a good rule of thumb for life choices, and health care should be no exception. However, here we will discuss particular challenges to market-based provision of health care that must be addressed, which may indeed be better served with a centralized, government approach.

We will examine these challenges from three angles—the consumer, the insurer, and society.

Consumers

Consumers of health care are faced with two major questions. First, will and when will I get sick? Second, if I do get sick, how should I treat my condition?

Are You in Control of Your Future Health?

The consumer's first question, will and when will I get sick, is really about uncertainty. In contrast to other essential goods like basic food and shelter, which arrive predictably three times a day or perhaps at bedtime, healthcare needs are more uncertain. "Will I get sick?" The answer to this question is a strong "well…maybe." At a fundamental level, the question is asking, "how much do I control my future health?" The struggle to make "maybe" more precise undergirds the debate on how much a

[2] OECD (2020). Note that not all 38 OECD countries were included in the report.

market-based system, with an individual willingness to pay driving the allocation of care, will be satisfying to the population.

In the U.S., the current top cause of death is heart disease, at about 1 in every 4 deaths (Kochanek et al. 2020). Cardiovascular disease is also hugely expensive, costing nearly $1 billion per day (American Heart Association 2018). According to the American Heart Association, an estimated 80% of cardiovascular diseases, including heart disease and stroke, are preventable. Three of the other top 10 causes of mortality—diabetes, kidney disease, and lower respiratory diseases—share similar preventable causes.

Insurance covering these top killers, which are often late onset and thus covered by Medicare, can lead to moral hazard. Moral hazard is the idea that people who are insulated from risk, such as the financial risk of medical treatment, will act in a way that can increase the probability of this bad event happening, since they are off the hook for much of the sting of its consequences. Market-based approaches might be able to counteract moral hazard in this area through pricing if individuals can qualify for cheaper premiums by making costly prevention investments, such as good lifestyle choices.

In contrast, consider the second big leader in U.S. deaths—cancer (Kochanek et al. 2020). Some major cancers are viewed as highly preventable, such as lung cancer. However, there is a larger role in cancer for genetics and a popular view of "luck." The third highest reason for death in the U.S. is unintentional injuries, where the idea of luck plays a larger role. For medical needs that can be ascribed more to bad luck than prevention, the social view of the problem often prefers a "fairness" approach. This philosophical view matches the "veil of ignorance" paradigm. This paradigm asks what system you would prefer to be in place before you know what kind of draw you will get in life or, in our case, your health status. Since you don't know your draw ahead of time, you'd like any person that gets the unlucky draw of a bad health outcome to be well taken care of. Our current market-based system inevitably leads to higher lifetime costs for individuals with bad health outcomes, since willingness to pay is used to match consumers and services. This violates the "fairness" and "veil of ignorance" norms.

You may ask, wait a minute, I aggravatingly encounter bad luck (and its accompanying costs!) in many areas of life—why should health care be a particular concern? To consider this, let's examine two other major market-based insurance systems—those for car and home insurance.

In these settings, a large portion of the possible bad events can be mitigated through individual actions. If you don't want to risk a large repair bill in an accident, you buy a compact economy car instead of a Lamborghini. Similar to health, you can engage in maintenance on that economy car to avoid future problems—regular oil changes, yearly inspections, etc. In your home, you perform regular preventative maintenance, and you can be forewarned about possible problems through inspections and flood assessments and walk away from a lemon. Although you still face the risk of a careless Lamborghini hitting *you*, you can control where and when you drive, and courses exist in defensive driving.

In health, choice of vehicle is sadly not an option. Some of us may have inherited a Lamborghini genetic code and others an economy car, but switching between the two is less feasible. Additionally, there is no disposal and renewal of insured property. You can replace your old car when it becomes unreliable. If only we could do the same with depreciating health capital! This exposes an individual's health to larger risks not in their control, in comparison to home or automobile choices.

Given a large amount of uncertainty that is non-preventable in health, let's move to a bird's eye view and ponder the kind of insurance that would address the concerns of uncertainty under a "veil of ignorance" norm. Consider Type I diabetes. Distinct from Type II, this is a chronic metabolic disease affecting approximately 1.6. million Americans where the pancreas no longer produces necessary insulin (American Diabetes Association 2018). This creates a life-long need for daily blood glucose monitoring and insulin injections and eventually leads to other (expensive) interventions from a lifetime of increased stress on the circulatory system. Sometimes called "juvenile" diabetes because of its common onset in children, its causes are currently largely a mystery, meaning prevention is not a conscious choice.

The fundamental role of insurance is to protect an enrollee from expensive, but uncertain events. In the current market-based U.S.

system, plans are chosen on a yearly basis, with new enrollment periods each year. In the case of Type I diabetes, there is actually no uncertainty for a bulk of yearly medical needs—glucose testing equipment and several daily injections of insulin, for which patient demand is highly inelastic. Leaving aside issues of high price levels, does the lack of uncertainty mean these patients have no need for insurance? In this case, the uncertainty exists over a more expansive time period—beginning around the onset age in childhood and going well into middle age.

A more relevant question then is, "what is the *time period* over which we would like insurance?" Under the veil of ignorance, an average person really would like insurance over long periods of their life, not just a year. "Will I be healthy up to age 40, or will I get some bad luck and end up with a rare expensive condition?" A better insurance contract would be one that controls for uncertainty over large periods of life, not merely the within-year shocks.

The same arguments could be made for long-term health even with good preventive care. "Old age" may be inevitable, but the list of possible bad outcomes can vary—Alzheimer's' Disease, Dementia, reduced mobility, failing eyesight, and complex home care needs, to name a few. We might not know which one but can be fairly certain that at least one and maybe several will arrive if we last that long. Again, this kind of outcome doesn't need insurance on a theoretical basis—if you live past 50, you will face old age outcomes with near certainty. However, certainty within a life stage isn't maybe what we'd like insured. We would like to insure across a lifetime, from when we are young and healthy to when we are old and sick.

Given such an expansive time frame for an insurance policy and the values of the veil of ignorance viewpoint, government provision is naturally positioned to satisfy these needs. Why? First, the veil of ignorance viewpoint is explicitly discarding willingness to pay during a year as an allocation mechanism, in favor of average pricing to hedge against bad luck over a lifetime. Second, with voluntary enrollment, individuals in a private market may choose to disenroll from their initial choice after they discover their personal outcome happened to be above average. This is not insurmountable through contract design, but government provision renders enrollment mandatory. Third, the veil of ignorance prescribes equal charges per individual over long periods of time which equal the average individual cost within the population; individuals getting a bad draw are subsidized by those with a good draw. This kind of average cost collection is more directly implemented through general taxation.

Do You Know What You're Getting When You Consume Health Care?

The second major challenge for a consumer in insurance markets is answering, "how should I treat my condition when I do get sick?" There is a huge burden of asymmetric information for the consumer in health-care markets. Just to begin practicing medicine, an average primary care practitioner has been engaged in schooling for 11 years. Specialists add 1–3 more years onto this count (Emanuel and Fuchs 2012). Compared with this preparation, the average patient severely lacks comprehensive and accessible information on treatment options and quality.

Now, for many people, this same asymmetry exists in cars or in houses! For this, the private market has developed a myriad of tools. You can submit your new house to a barrage of inspections and tests and many services exist to discover the history of your used car, besides a simple second opinion from your trusted mechanic. How does this compare to health care markets?

First, quality is hard to assess and report in health care. Although there have been recent efforts to create quality report cards for consumers, these remain imperfect. The large quantity of information used to communicate quality through these report cards is often overwhelming for consumers (Peters et al. 2007; Jung et al. 2011). As report cards evolve, research has found patients often prefer summary measures, such as composite scores. These are easier to report but dilute the diversity of information on different quality dimensions (Hibbard et al. 2002). Often, consumers only respond to extremes of the distribution, such as very high composite scores or very low scores (Perraillon et al. 2019; Scanlon et al. 2002). The nursing home industry began publicly reporting quality information in 1998, but research finds that consumers respond very little to published information (Werner et al. 2012). In comparison to automobiles and homes, quality of health outcomes may be more multidimensional than the number of years that a car runs or harder to monitor over time—it is more invasive to check out your artery flow than your shower drain.

Secondly, besides the difficulties in reporting information, research shows that healthcare consumers consistently choose suboptimal plans and care—that is, they "make mistakes." One reason may be poor health literacy, particularly in the elderly population, which makes absorbing and using information difficult (Gazmararian et al. 1999). Economists have started euphemistically calling this mismatch in the choice problems as *behavioral hazard*. This growing literature shows that consumers often "leave money on the table." There are many potential causes, but primary explanations are inertia, lack of information or trouble processing this information, choice biases overweighting certain parts of an insurance plan, or non-rational optimization, such as present-biased choice (Handel and Schwartzstein 2018; Bhargava et al. 2017). One study of insurance plan choice estimated the average consumer would overpay by $1694 because of incomplete knowledge of choices compared to the fully informed consumer (Handel and Kolstad 2015). Parallel to the composite quality scores, consumers often focus on one dimension of a plan without accounting for differences in other out-of-pocket costs, overweighting premiums by a factor of 5 to 1 relative to expected out-of-pocket spending (Abaluck and Gruber 2011). Finally, the complex structure of plan pricing creates a dynamic optimization problem that is too complex for enrollees, leading to behavioral hazard such as heavy future discounting or pure myopia, where enrollees completely disregard the year-long pricing scheme and focus solely on the price they face at that moment of purchase (Aron-Dine et al. 2015; Brot-Goldberg et al. 2017; Einav et al. 2015; Dalton et al. 2020).

Both of these concerns may imply a role for a centralized, transparent, and trusted authority to provide regulatory quality baselines and reporting for the market. A centralized approach reduces the burden of search costs which would exist in a market-based approach of competing quality reporting services. Additionally, information is often non-rival, meaning that, once it is produced, many consumers can simultaneously consume it at no additional cost. If high levels of transparency are socially optimal, as in the case of infectious disease, this also means provision should be non-excludable, or economist-speak for "free." This can obviously be a problem for a market-based approach. These dual characteristics are often more simply served through direct government provision.

Insurers

We now flip our perspective to the insurer side of health insurance. The two biggest challenges facing market provision of insurance are adverse selection and the downsides caused by not having a closed system.

The Ever-Present Specter: Adverse Selection

The omnipresent concern for any insurance structure is the specter of *adverse selection*. Adverse selection results from the galling detail that those who seek out health insurance are usually the sick! This is correspondingly inseparable from insurance markets themselves. A simple illustration of the resulting problem is this: If an insurer offers a premium for a health insurance plan based on the average consumer in a market, by construction, approximately half the consumers in the market will find this plan a bargain and half will consider it too expensive. Accordingly, the healthy half will decline to enroll, the sicker half will sign up, and suddenly the realized average cost to the insurer has risen dramatically. Even adjusting this illustration for enrollees' risk aversion, the eventual predicted outcome still leaves the insurer making a loss on realized plan enrollment. If the insurer cannot charge individual consumers premiums based on the individual consumers' expected costs, the only defense left to the insurer is to provide (now expensive) plans geared toward the sicker consumers—leaving healthy consumers high and dry and priced out of the market.

A straightforward market solution to this is to allow pricing for pre-existing conditions. This allows insurers to match costs and revenues and facilitates plan offerings for healthy individuals. However, now we have run against the social problem of luck, since payments would be higher for the unlucky. Another solution is an individual mandate, requiring all consumers to purchase insurance,[3] but here the government is required to enforce the mandate.

Even Bigger Pickle: Not a Closed System

I argue there is an even bigger problem than adverse selection for market provision, often left out of the broad policy discussion. Market provision of insurance does not provide the closed system that government provision achieves.

For health outcomes not attributed to luck, prevention plays an important role. This takes the form of yearly checkups and screenings at appropriate ages and for appropriate groups. This also includes non-medical interventions to encourage healthy behaviors in nutrition, exercise, and other lifestyle attributes. However, the input of prevention in the health production function has a long wait time until the largest (that is, most cost-saving) rewards are reached. If prevention is encouraged and rewarded in a consumer in her 30s, when will this pay off? Perhaps by her 50s by preventing heart disease and Type 2 diabetes? 20 years? Good behaviors accumulate over a lifetime to create a better health stock at age 75 versus the counterfactual poor prevention counterpart—no heart disease or diabetes with the accompanying chronic prescriptions, the ability to be active and independent in daily activities which reduces fall risk, maintenance of cognitive abilities forestalling the need for home aid. Here the return-on-investment for prevention hits least at least 45 years later.

Some preventive health investments do have large payoffs within the short period of a year. Investments in maternal health such as routine visits and screenings during the pregnancy can prevent low birthweights, associated with complications in delivery and during the postnatal period. However, even these short-term payoffs are accompanied by major long-term payoffs in the form of improved socioeconomic

[3] Note this is the approach of the Affordable Care Act (2010) in the U.S. and its model, the Swiss health care system.

outcomes in education, employment, and income, which in turn are positively correlated with adult health.[4]

What's the balance of medical costs today versus benefits in the long term? In the U.S., nearly all private market plans enroll for a period of a year. Although the literature shows that enrollees are reluctant to change plans often, called consumer inertia, adverse selection tells us that consumers switch plans if their healthcare needs change enough to overcome these switching costs.[5] In the current system of employer-based insurance and geographic pricing, consumers switch plans as they switch jobs or change locations. What's more, all consumers eventually partially or entirely transition out of any private plan onto Medicare at 65, just as they enter the most expensive phase of their life. This means that an insurer who covers or encourages preventive care in youth is unlikely to see the rewards of this investment, which will accrue slowly over the next 20 to 40 years.

Thus, our current multipayer framework in the U.S. is not a closed system. When consumers can move between insurers, many of the linked costs and benefits are not contained within any one insurer's problem. We can think of this as a "Prisoner's Dilemma." This famous dilemma structure is used to illustrate many settings in economics and political science. Imagine there are two criminals who have been brought in for questioning based on a petty offense. However, the interrogating detectives suspect them of a larger crime. Sitting in separate rooms, unable to communicate with each other, the criminals are pressed to confess their larger crime. But, the detectives are clever. They offer each individual a deal: Rat out your friend and confess the large crime, and we'll let you go. The betrayed partner will then get a life sentence, but the rat goes free. Alternatively, the criminal can remain silent and loyal, but she will still serve a short sentence for the petty offense. The same deal is

---

[4] Currie and Hyson (1999) showed low birthweight children were less likely to pass standardized academic tests. Almond (2006) found lower graduation rates and Field et al. (2009) showed prenatal supplementation increased educational attainment. Currie and Moretti (2007) showed low birthweight decreased the likelihood of living in a wealthy neighborhood and Currie and Hyson (1999) found corresponding correlations with increased unemployment.

[5] Common explanations for this inertia are inattention to plan details, hassle costs of searching new plans, and desire for provider continuity. See Abaluck and Adams-Prassl 2021; Handel 2013; or Drake et al. 2021.

offered to her partner. If both remain silent, they will merely serve the short sentence and then be able to return to their life of crime unassailed. However, if both succumb to the lure of immediate freedom and rat out their partner, the detectives will be able to convict them both of the large crime and lock them up for good.

Even if you yourself aren't a hardened criminal, hopefully you can see the difficulty here. Although cooperating and remaining silent would be better in the long term for both than dual confessions, the short-run benefit of being set free versus serving a short sentence can sway the individual decision toward confess, relegating them both to the worst outcome. The important piece to notice is that prison sentences are assigned individually, not jointly, so the individual is not incentivized to account for benefits to all players.

This dilemma has parallels to prevention efforts and insurance markets. In this case, all insurers (and patients, while we're at it) would be better off if their fellow insurers generously covered preventive care. The pool of consumers would be healthier overall, leading to lower costs for insurers on long-term and chronic illnesses. However, if preventive costs are expensive, any individual insurer has incentive to defect from this plan. If no other insurers defect, then the culpable plan would save costs today, yet still reap most of the future benefits as long as consumers move plans frequently. Yet, sadly, since each insurer is facing the same incentives, this makes the dominant choice for all to defect, and preventive care is emphasized less than would be optimal overall.

Of course, we see some criminal partnerships enduring over time, so how is the dilemma commonly solved? The most common way to address the Prisoner's Dilemma is to play over and over, so that cooperative actions are rewarded over time. However, in the case of insurance, this approach faces several difficulties. First, a good competitive market for insurance would have many players, by design, making it hard for individual insurers to coordinate on policy or share profits, even if antitrust legislation weren't in place. Second, moving from one insurance plan to another is a voluntary consumer decision. There is no way to predictably repeat the game. The flow of patients receiving preventive care can't be controlled by an individual insurer to another. Thirdly, tracking the flow of patients would be difficult because of the length of time involved and privacy concerns. Finally, the most damning current problem is that the old and especially sick are covered by government insurance. There's certainly no incentive to invest and coordinate now, if you know the government pays for the worst outcomes or takes over just as the cost-savings would be reaped!

How do we see this in practice? As we discussed in the consumer's problem, many of the top causes of death in the U.S., and accordingly the top expenses, are from preventable diseases. A major prevention input in these cases is lifestyle changes, not increased testing, screening, or medical interventions. These lifestyle changes can be influenced through smoking cessation and nutrition counseling. However, in the U.S., only 20% of office visits for cardiovascular disease, diabetes, or high cholesterol in 2015 included counseling about diet (Kahan and Manson 2017). Nutrition and behavioral counseling have traditionally been non-reimbursed services. Although the 2010 Affordable Care Act mandates coverage for nutrition counseling for patients with heart disease risk factors and obesity, private insurer benefits are inconsistent, and coverage is often unclear to providers and their patients.

One way this problem has been addressed in private markets is through government mandates on preventive care. This solves the coordination problem, since all plans must then offer basic preventive services, but requires high monitoring costs. A more comprehensive solution leads us to the simplicity of "closing the system" through national universal provision. National provision wipes out both the concerns of adverse selection and "closing" the system. First, since all consumers are in the insurance pool by legal mandate, there is no adverse selection by definition. Sick people aren't disproportionately opting in and healthy people aren't opting out since all possible individuals are covered statutorily. Secondly, "birth to death" coverage tracks all costs and benefits through one system and approximates balancing both prevention and long-term cost savings by having young and old expenditures within one national plan.

Society

Norms and values play an outsized role in the market for health care. Although it is clear that markets are the most efficient way to allocate goods based on willingness to pay, the fact remains that society often rejects these allocation criteria in health care compared to other sectors.

"Health Care Is a Human Right"

Especially as health care costs rise, a common cry in the U.S. has been that everyone is entitled to basic care. In context, this often turns out to mean the best and plenty of it. This norm is going to present a problem for markets, where the whole point is to equate willingness to pay for a good with the cost of care. Willingness to pay depends on demand, but also on income and budgets, which may be quite insufficient for the magnitude of expenses associated with conditions such as cancer.

Why the calls for equal access? What is different about health care than other basics of life, such as food, clothing, shelter, and transportation? Government food assistance programs similarly cover basic food needs, which may themselves lead to health outcomes. However, we don't observe cries for equal access to designer clothing or individual car ownership—both of which would represent high-quality characteristics in their categories—compared with healthcare demands. One reason might be the luck component, that cancer could happen to anyone equally, so the ability to address this bad draw should also be equally available.

A bigger differentiating factor might be our inability to dispose of and renew our health capital. In other essential components of living such as clothing, housing, and transportation, an individual might start out in a low-quality product but has hope of eventually upgrading. Initial low-quality clothing or transportation doesn't translate into persistent problems after switching to a high-quality product. Housing may share this quality only to a lesser extent, depending on factors such as crime and environmental hazards. However, low-quality health care early on does translate into persistent health problems in the long term.[6] As such, society often wants care to be provided by "deservingness," which likely means some combination of willingness to pay and other factors such as age, disadvantaged situations, and the unexpectedness of the condition. Price allocation is unlikely to match society's preferred "deservingness" ranking, and in fact, might be fundamentally opposed in cases where lack of income is a positive contributor to "deservingness."

Even a casual student of economics should understand that government allocation of health care cannot unwind the basic underlying economics of the market. One common failure of government provision is long waiting lines for care. Foregoing market allocation and keeping administrative prices low creates excess demand for care and leads to shortages. These must be allocated through time, since price has been removed as an allocation method. For example, 18% of patients surveyed in 2016 in Canada had to wait 4 months or more for an elective surgery, compared to 4% in the U.S. Norway and New Zealand rank high as well, at 15% of patients waiting 4 months or more. All three of these systems are publicly funded universal health care financed through general taxation (Schneider et al. 2017). However, switching to a non-monetary payment for care might still be in line with a social desire for a regressive system that gives an extra advantage to those with less money but more time.

No Treatment Is Not a Credible Threat

The largest stumbling block to a true voluntary private market system of insurance is the fact that social norms do not stomach withholding treatment from a needy consumer.

To avoid future costs, a prudent individual would invest in good health behaviors today. These future costs include both the happiness

[6] Almond (2006) focused on prenatal exposure to the 1918 Influenza Pandemic, estimating that children of infected mothers were 15% less likely to graduate high school and wages were between 5 and 9% lower. Kelly (2011) found similar effects, though modest, for exposure to the 1957 "Asian flu" in Britain on test scores. In a developing context, Field et al. (2009) show prenatal iodine supplementation in Tanzania raised educational attainment by half a year of schooling.

lost from poor quality of life, but also financial medical costs from necessary treatments. As far as we believe individuals are optimizing over their lifetime according to their own decision-making framework, these should be baked in already. Even given current medical technology, individuals cannot avoid reduced mobility or pain from a heart attack, given one occurred. The thornier problem for insurance markets arises in future financial costs. Market-based insurance can indeed offer financial incentives today for proof of regular preventive care or healthy lifestyles in exchange for reduced financial risk. Absence of proof of preventive activity, insurers could require significant cost-sharing or refuse treatment for preventable expenses, for example. But, therein lies the problem. In health care, no treatment is not a credible threat. Physicians have been trained to help patients for medical needs, not to evaluate their ability to pay. Perhaps happily, most cultural systems' social norms don't accept the idea of leaving a person to suffer when you have the ability to relieve this suffering. As such, there is negative social pressure for not treating patients who do not have the means to pay. Without this credible threat, however, the incentive system for voluntary, private insurance suffers.

As a parallel example, during the COVID-19 pandemic, businesses incurred massive losses due to the shutdowns. Many businesses carried business interruption insurance. However, standard policies for this type of insurance explicitly exclude virus events, insuring mainly structural damage such as fire or flooding. There was still a healthy crop of lawsuits of businesses against insurers trying to require claim payouts for the losses (including by the band Metallica!) By April 2021, over 1500 suits had been filed since March 2020 in state and federal courts. In two-thirds of these cases, the policy explicitly included a virus exclusion clause (Friedman 2021). Although judicial interpretations of the true source of interruption are still in play, the rush of lawsuits and media coverage highlights the social pressures surrounding insurance payouts even for explicitly noncovered events.

Well-functioning consumer good markets are based on what is called *excludable* goods. This means the private business can prevent a consumer from using the good if she doesn't pay for it. Without the excludability characteristic, the market will not function well, since consumers have little incentive to purchase the good yet still may obtain the product. Without a credible threat of exclusion, the incentive system for voluntary, private insurance suffers.

Conclusion

A high-quality and cost-efficient healthcare system is a key input for a flourishing economy. A healthy population is more productive, innovative, and leads new generations to be the same. At the same time, a cost-efficient system ensures that scarce resources are used for other important inputs such as education and technological advancement. A market-based system works well for many aspects of economic production. However, there are a few characteristics of health care which must be addressed by any proposed solution—market-based or not.

On the consumer side, information asymmetries on quality for consumers persist in healthcare. The pace of technological advancement has continued to outpace the increase in accessible consumer information and medical literacy remains a problem. Centralized information on quality, either through direct-to-consumer information or through mandated standards, is important to improve healthcare outcomes and reduce unnecessary spending.

On the provider side, both a solution to adverse selection and the incentive to create a preventive environment would exist in a centralized system. Given the current chronic illness environment in developed countries, the need to realign incentives in order to encourage healthy behaviors has become increasingly pressing.

Finally, any overarching approach needs to reconcile different views of how much individuals are able to influence their own health and to what extent society wants to share in these costs. The current market-based system of insurance focuses on short periods of time, often merely a year. In reality, the most expensive uncertainties faced by an individual exist on a broader span of years or decades. A system which address the concerns and uncertainties of the true span of time in which health capital is created will do a better job of aligning incentives with medical needs and generating the peace of mind which insurance was designed to create.

References

Abaluck J, Adams-Prassl A (2021) What do consumers consider before they choose? Identification from asymmetric demand responses. Q J Econ 136:1611–1663

Abaluck J, Gruber J (2011) Choice inconsistencies among the elderly: Evidence from plan choice in the Medicare Part D program. Am Econ Rev 101:1180–1210

Almond D (2006) Is the 1918 influenza pandemic over? Long-term effects of in utero influenza exposure in the post-1940 U.S. population. J Polit Econ 114:672–712

American Diabetes Association (2018) Economic costs of diabetes in the U.S. in 2017. Diabetes Care 41:917–928

American Heart Association (2018) Federal priorities, CDC prevention programs. American Heart Association, Dallas

Aron-Dine A, Einav L, Finkelstein A, Cullen M (2015) Moral hazard in health insurance: Do dynamic incentives matter? Rev Econ Stat 97:725–741

Bhargava S, Loewenstein G, Sydnor J (2017) Choose to lose: Health plan choices from a menu with dominated option. Q J Econ 132:1319–1372

Brot-Goldberg ZC, Chandra A, Handel BR, Kolstad JT (2017) What does a deductible do? The impact of cost-sharing on health care prices, quantities, and spending dynamics. Q J Econ 132:1261–1318

Currie J, Moretti E (2007) Biology as destiny? Short- and long-run determinants of intergenerational transmission of birth weight. J Labor Econ 25:231–264

Currie J, Hyson R (1999) Is the impact of health shocks cushioned by socioeconomic status? The case of low birthweight. Am Econ Rev 89: 245–250

Dalton CM, Gowrisankaran G, Town RJ (2020) Salience, myopia, and complex dynamic incentives: Evidence from Medicare Part D. Rev Econ Stud 87:822–869

Drake C, Ryan C, Dowd BE (2021) Sources of inertia in health plan choice in the individual health insurance market. University of Minnesota, Working Paper

Einav L, Finkelstein A, Schrimpf P (2015) The response of drug expenditure to nonlinear contract design: Evidence from Medicare Part D. Q J Econ 130:841–899

Emanuel EJ, Fuchs VR (2012) Shortening medical training by 30%. JAMA-J Am Med Assoc 307:1143–1144

Field E, Robles O, Torero M (2009) Iodine deficiency and schooling attainment in Tanzania. Am Econ J-Appl Econ 1:140–169

Friedman B (2021) COVID-19 business interruption insurance litigation—one year later. Nat Law Rev XI: 23 April

Gazmararian JA, Baker DW, Williams MV, Parker RM, Scott TL, Green DC, Fehrenbach SN, Ren J, Koplan JP (1999) Health literacy among Medicare enrollees in a managed care organization. JAMA-J Amer Med Assoc 281:545–551

Handel BR, Kolstad, JT (2015) Health insurance for 'humans': Information frictions, plan choice, and consumer welfare. Am Econ Rev 105:2449–2500

Handel BR (2013) Adverse selection and inertia in health insurance markets: When nudging hurts. Am Econ Rev 103: 2643–2682

Handel BR, Schwartzstein J (2018) Frictions or mental gaps: What's behind the information we (don't) use and when do we care? J Econ Perspect 32:155–178

Hibbard JH, Slovic P, Peters E, Finucane ML (2002) Strategies for reporting health plan performance information to consumers: Evidence from controlled studies. Health Serv Res 37:291–313

Kahan S, Manson JE (2017) Nutrition counseling in clinical practice: How clinicians can do better. JAMA-J Am Med Assoc 318:1101–1102

Keisler-Starkey K, Bunch LN (2020) U.S. Census Bureau current population reports, P60-271, health insurance coverage in the United States: 2019. U.S. Government Printing Office, Washington, DC

Kelly E (2011) The scourge of Asian flu: In utero exposure to pandemic influenza and the development of a cohort of British children. J Human Res 46:669–694

Kochanek KD, Xu J, Arias E (2020) Mortality in the United States, 2019. National Center for Health Statistics, Data Brief No. 395

Jung K, Feldman R, Scanlon D (2011) Where would you go for your next hospitalization? J Health Econ 30:832–841

OECD (2020) Focus on public funding. OECD, Paris

Perraillon MC, Konetzka RT, He D, Werner RM (2019) Consumer response to composite ratings of nursing home quality. Amer J Health Econ 5:165–190

Peters E, Dieckmann N, Dixon A, Hibbard JH, Mertz CK (2007) Less is more in presenting quality information to consumers. Med Care Res Rev 64:169–190

Scanlon DP, Chernew M, McLaughlin C, Solon G (2002) The impact of health plan report cards on managed care enrollment. J Health Econ 21:19–41

Schneider EC, Sarnak DO, Squires D, Shah A, Doty MM (2017) Mirror, mirror 2017: International comparison reflects flaws and opportunities for better U.S. health care. The Commonwealth Fund, New York

Werner RM, Norton EC, Konetzka T, Polsky D (2012) Do consumers respond to publicly reported quality information? Evidence from nursing homes. J Health Econ 31:50–61

Part VI

Technology

12

Coping with Technological Disruption

Adam Thierer

Introduction

Is the disruptive nature of technological change worth it? It may seem like a silly question, but if the costs associated with innovation exceed the benefits, then perhaps society should slow or stop the pace of change. Luckily, while cost–benefit analysis is not an exact science, it does not need to be as it pertains to technological change. By any fair and sensible accounting methodology, the aggregate benefits of technical progress far outweigh its costs, as this chapter aims to show.

It is nonetheless true that innovation defenders sometimes make for poor champions of their cause. When confronted with claims that technological change too easily upends well-established norms, laws, institutions, or cultures, some innovation boosters casually retort: *Well,*

A. Thierer (✉)
Street Institute, Washington, DC, USA
e-mail: AThierer@rstreet.org

A. L. Kassens and J. C. Hall (eds.), *Challenges in Classical Liberalism*, Palgrave Studies in Classical Liberalism,
https://doi.org/10.1007/978-3-031-32890-9_12

get over it. Some of these tech defenders imply that resistance to change is futile and that the affected parties simply need to get with the program.

That is a horrible response to concerns about technological innovation, which can indeed be a gut-wrenching process for many individuals and organizations. When the Schumpeterian "gales of creative destruction" blow in, someone's settled status quo is going to be *un*settled—if not obliterated. They will understandably want to know why they should go along with the new order.

On the other hand, most people understand we cannot shut the door on technological change and that, by its very nature, progress demands a certain degree of disruption. Despite today's growing "techlash" among politicians and academics, most citizens still appreciate the benefits innovation provides to society. A May 2021 poll conducted by Data for Progress and Vox revealed that 71 percent of likely voters agreed with the tech-optimist statement: "Technology is generally a force for good" that has delivered innovations "that have improved our quality of life" (Desmas 2021).

Despite such general support, technological change is constantly being challenged and efforts to slow progress are omnipresent. Those defending it will need to do a better job communicating the benefits of innovation while also considering additional strategies for countering its occasional downsides. "Just get over it" will not do.

This chapter outlines a better approach to responding to tech critics and others worried about technological disruption. The framework advocated here is rooted in rational optimism about the prospects for innovation to continue to change life for the better, but also an understanding that concerns about disruptive effects must be addressed.

Resistance to Change Comes Naturally, but so Does Experimenting

Psychologists and behavioral economists have noted that status quo bias or loss aversion provides powerful explanations for why many people and institutions oppose change. These biases reflect an innate, and entirely understandable, desire by many to hold on to what one already has instead of accepting new ideas or developments. In this sense, resistance to technological change might be considered normal.

Most people refuse to settle for the status quo, however, because they possess an equally powerful desire to build and improve. Benjamin Franklin once noted, "man is a tool-making animal" by his very nature. Similarly, Samuel C. Florman (1994: p. 6), an engineer and tireless defender of innovation, observed that, "the elementary pleasure of solving technical problems and successfully completing constructive projects" is "as old as the human race." Technological innovation is simply the by-product of the human need to experiment and find new and better ways of getting things done.

History provides countless examples of these competing human desires for stability and experimentation colliding constantly and creating tensions between defenders of both values. "The quickest way to find out who your enemies are is to try doing something new," noted Calestous Juma (2016) in opening his book, *Innovation and Its Enemies: Why People Resist New Technologies*. Juma's book includes detailed case studies of "the tensions between innovation and incumbency" and reveals a reoccurring pattern of well-established institutions (churches, governments, guilds, labor unions, etc.) resisting new technologies through the ages. His wide-ranging histories included coffee, margarine, farm machinery, electricity, mechanical refrigeration, recorded music, transgenic crops, and genetically engineered salmon. A basic pattern emerged in each case: initial resistance, gradual adaptation, and then eventual assimilation of a new technology into society (Thierer 2013). Eventually people found ways to adapt to technological change by employing a variety of coping mechanisms, new norms, or other creative fixes. But not without a fight.

Whether one sympathizes with concerns about technological disruption or not, these issues will always be with us and need to be confronted repeatedly. In some cases, change will come so fast as to make this problem moot. In the mid-twentieth century, for example, there existed an entire profession of people known as "calculators." With the help of their trusty slide rules, they did the hard math for companies and government agencies that required exceptional computational capabilities. Then mainframes and microchips came along, and mechanical calculators replaced the human ones very quickly. There wasn't much time for a resistance to form computerized calculators. However, the more important part of that story is what next: people set to work making better calculating machines. The resulting computer revolution continues today, and that sector provides what many believe are some of the best jobs in the nation.

Usually, the opposition to change is more formidable and requires a combination of strategies to address and overcome. In particular, industrial incumbency often entails deep ties to lawmakers and political institutions. This can entrench the status quo for remarkably long periods of time and create lasting, unnatural market power. "Time and again, the losing interest groups created by scientific progress or technological change have been able to convince politicians to block, slow, or alter government support for scientific and technological progress," says Mark Zachary Taylor (2016: p. 213), author of "*The Politics of Innovation.*"

The challenge for innovation defenders is to repeatedly make their case for the benefits of technological development while also considering strategies to address opposition to change, including fears about various forms of disruption. What follows is a sketch of how to achieve this.

The Case for Innovative Dynamism and Rational Optimism

There are good reasons to be optimistic about the future and the role innovation will play in making it better. This optimism is not based on a Pollyanna outlook or a naïveté about the downsides of technological change, however. As science writer Matt Ridley (2010) argues, it makes more sense to embrace *rational optimism* when defending innovation. This is an approach rooted in empiricism and a close review of the historical record, which rational optimists believe clearly identifies five unambiguous benefits of innovation (Thierer 2019a).

1. Innovation Enriches Us Economically

Technological innovation is "widely considered the main source of economic progress" (Mokyr et al. 2015: p. 31). In a 2019 white paper co-authored with my Mercatus Center colleague James Broughel, we cataloged the voluminous body of academic evidence documenting the positive relationship among technological progress, economic growth, and overall social welfare (Broughel and Thierer 2019). The only real dispute in that extensive literature is exactly *how much* technological innovation drives growth.

Economic growth is important because it translates to meaningful improvements in the daily lives of humans. Innovation and growth provide more goods and services, of a constantly improving quality, typically for steadily falling prices. But the fruits of innovation and growth are even more profound than that. Elsewhere, I have documented some of the leading indicators making it clear how innovation has enriched us (Thierer 2020a: pp. 19–52), or how as a *Wall Street Journal* headline put it in 2019, "The World Is Getting Quietly, Relentlessly Better" (Ip 2019)[1]:

- **Life expectancy**: From 1800 to 2017, average life expectancy more than doubled, from just 31 years all the way up to 72 years (Rosling 2018: p. 55).
- **Extreme poverty**: In 1800, 85% of humanity was surviving on less than $2 a day. By 1966, that number had fallen to 50%. As of 2017, just 9% of the world's population was living in such extreme poverty (Rosling 2018: p. 52). "Today almost everybody has escaped hell," Hans Rosling asserts, noting that in just that past 20 years, "[e]xtreme poverty has dropped faster than ever in world history" (Rosling 2018: pp. 52–53). According to Max Roser (2018), "on average, every day

[1] Ip (2019) notes: "Poverty around the world is plummeting; half the world is now middle class; and illiteracy, disease and deadly violence are receding. These things don't make headlines because they are gradual, relentless and unsurprising. That is why they are worth highlighting. The problems the world faces are far smaller than those it has already overcome and can be solved the same way: not by betting on miracles but by patiently applying knowledge and tools we already possess."

for the past 25 years 137,000 fewer people were living in extreme poverty than the day before."

- **Infant mortality**: Since 1960, child deaths have fallen from 20 million a year to 6 million in 2016 (Roser 2018). During this time, innovations in maternal health and neonatal medicine have pushed the age of viability lower and allowed for the treatment of previously deadly diagnoses.
- **Vaccines:** Not that long ago, immunizations against deadly diseases were uncommon. But from 1980 to 2016, the share of 1-year olds globally who got at least one vaccination jumped from just 22% to 88% (Rosling 2018: p. 63). Meanwhile, the recent COVID pandemic resulted in the remarkably rapid rollout of multiple vaccines to address the disease, far faster than most predicted was possible (Heath and Garcia-Roberts 2021).
- **Information and communication**: The number of new music recordings rose from almost zero in 1860 to 6.2 million per year by 2015 (Rosling 2018: p. 62). New movies grew from nothing in 1900 to 11,000 per year by 2015 (Rosling 2018: p. 62). And in just the past three decades, Internet access grew to reach almost 50% of the world's population by 2017, and 65% of people globally now have a mobile phone (Rosling 2018: p. 63). Much of this has been driven by the plummeting cost of computing. Data transit prices, for example, fell from about $1,200 per Mbps (megabits per second) in 1998 to just $0.02 per Mbps in 2017 (Wallensten 2018).

These wonderful developments occurred primarily because of the relentless nature of technological change. Disruptions were worth enduring because they led to substantial improvements in human welfare.

Tech critics sometimes claim all the choices and improvements spawned by technological innovation are unnecessary or unneeded, and they sneer at the supposed materialistic "cult of convenience" created by abundance (Morozov 2015). A related complaint with roots in Marxist theory is that citizens get overwhelmed by the supposed "paradox of choice" (Schwartz 2004), or the idea that too many choices overwhelm us. They lament the supposed "anxiety" or "alienation" of the masses due to technological change.[2]

These responses are ultimately unpersuasive and even somewhat elitist. Most people rightly regard more choices and greater convenience as tremendous benefits. A rational optimist can concede that some new choices will indeed force trade-offs on society but can also point to the fact that ongoing experimentation with new and better ways of doing things has repeatedly improved the human condition in profound and measurable ways.

2. Innovation Gives Us the Ability to Pursue Lives of Our Own Choosing

Technological innovation is worth defending not only because it delivers the goods, but also because it also gives us a greater chance to live lives of our own choosing. As Rosling (2018: p. 64) argued, the goal of expanding innovation opportunities and raising incomes "is not just bigger piles of money" or even more leisure time. "The ultimate goal is to have the freedom to do what we want" (Rosling 2018: p. 64). This freedom to pursue lives of our own choosing has been made easier thanks to technological change.

Consider this in the context of "Maslow's pyramid," which describes a five-level hierarchy of human needs. Innovation helps us achieve our needs at each level, from the most basic survival and safety-related needs. By doing so, innovation opened the possibility that we might satisfy higher needs on Maslow's pyramid, such as belonging, self-esteem, and self-actualization.[3] In other words, living a life of your own choosing. "Technology and the pursuit of improvement are ultimate expressions of freedom, of the capacity of humans to reject the limitations of their

[2] For a critique of such thinking, see Florman (1994: p. 16), "Anxiety and alienation are the watchwords of the day, as if material comforts made life worse, rather than better."

[3] Gillespie (2019): "Prosperity is central to most human values. A wealthier world helps you be more creative."

past and their experience, to transcend the boundaries of their biological capacities and their social traditions," noted Robert Friedel (2010: p. 543), author of *A Culture of Improvement: Technology and the Western Millennium.*

3. Innovation Enriches us Culturally

Innovation—especially commercial innovation—often gets a bum rap for supposedly not being concerned with matters of art, culture, or higher learning. What is most perplexing about this claim is that it ignores how continuous technological improvements helped address basic human tasks, thus freeing up extra time and resources to spend on other pursuits. Returning to Maslow's pyramid, we can posit that self-actualization, however defined, is not something one had a lot of time to worry about when toiling in fields or forests, struggling to figure out how to put the next meal on the table.

As innovation helped us take care of our base needs, it allowed us to pursue many other goals or values that our ancestors could have only dreamed about. Most specifically, innovation and economic growth allowed humans to be more creative and has benefited creators of all varieties. "A commercial society is a prosperous and comfortable society, and offers a rich variety of niches in which artists can find the means to satisfy their creative desires," argued Tyler Cowen (2008: p. 16) in his 2008 book, *In Praise of Commercial Culture.*

Indeed, there are more outlets for people to both find what they want and express themselves than ever before. Consider how television and movies have gone from limited-run "appointment viewing" (i.e., you either saw it at a specific schedule place and time, or you didn't see it at all), to ubiquitously and instantly available across a constantly expanding array of platforms. In 2002, there were 182 scripted original series across broadcast and cable TV (Andreeva 2021). Less than two decades later, almost 500 scripted shows were being produced annually. Every conceivable niche creator or consumer can now enjoy the sort of content they desire. Of course, disruption was a major part of this story. Much of this growth has coincided with a complete reinvention of the television and motion picture industry, with an ongoing explosion of online platforms and the "app-ification" of branded entertainment media. Meanwhile, our phones have "morphed into the Swiss Army knife of gadgets" (Bajarin 2013) and allow us to create and consume whatever sort of culture we want. Old ways of doing things—think video rental stores—came and went very fast. Others—like first-run movies in cinemas—are still with us but fading away as our only option.

The growth of the internet and the explosion of different sites and platforms has allowed the emergence of niche communities and allowed us to become "pro-sumers"—both producers and consumers of news, information, art, entertainment, and much more (Gillmor 2004). We now enjoy an unparalleled cornucopia of cultural opportunities as we have migrated from a world of information poverty to information abundance (Murphy 2019). "There has never been a better time to be a reader, a watcher, a listener, or a participant in human expression," notes Kevin Kelly (2016: p. 165).

4. Innovation Expands the Horizons of Our Humanity

Increasingly, tech critics rally under the flag of *humanism* and suggest that technological change is undermining or even "reengineering" our humanity (Frischmann and Selinger 2018). This a peculiar argument in that it suggests that humans are incapable of mastering the tools they create or adapting to change. It is also wrong to suggest that those supporting technological change are somehow anti-human (Thierer 2018a).

This is not to say innovation does not alter our humanity in important ways. Richard Longworth of the Chicago Council on Global Affairs, notes that all innovations from the Gutenberg press to the internet, "forced us to rethink humanism, not only to adjust it to the new technology but to ensure that it eventually commanded this technology (Longworth 2015)." The human experience has evolved in response to each new technology as we assimilated them into our lives and came to depend upon them. The need for a phone, camera, or computer in each home was originally viewed with puzzlement and even contempt. Each of them quickly became viewed as an essential part of the human experience. We adopted them and adapted to them (Thierer 2014).

As already noted, there are few things more fundamentally human than crafting tools to solve important problems and to better our lives and the lives of our loved ones and others around us. "Individual creativity and expertise have always arisen in the context of the collective battle to solve the problems of everyday survival," says Norman Lewis (2018). Once those needs are satisfied, innovation opens the door to even more forms of human flourishing. We build new and better technologies precisely to support and extend our humanity, not to undermine it.

Tech critics stress "the centrality of humankind to the universe" when criticizing certain types of innovation and change (Wieseltier 2015). But one can simultaneously believe in the sanctity of each human as well as the notion that technological innovation is central to humankind's ability to improve itself. The challenge is to figure out how to make our tools serve us and society, and also how to mitigate the problems associated with them—usually by building even more and better tools to do so.

Technological change enhances our humanity in even more profound ways. Innovation quite literally expands the horizons of our humanity when it brings to the suffering of others at a distance to our attention and gives us a chance to do something to address it. American historian Thomas L. Haskell (1985: p. 356) once observed how "our feeling of responsibility for the stranger's plight, though nowhere near strong enough to move us to action, is probably stronger today than it would have been before the airplane." He noted that modern technologies such as information and communication services have acted to "change the moral universe in which we live (Haskell 1985: p. 356)." He found that:

> Technological innovation can perform this startling feat, because it supplies us with new ways of acting at a distance and new ways of influencing future events and thereby imposes on us new occasions for the attribution of responsibility and guilt. In short, new techniques, or ways of intervening in the course of events, can change the conventional limits within which we feel responsible enough to act. (Haskell 1985: p. 356)

Innovation is central to human betterment not simply because it betters *us*, but because it allows us to better the lot of our fellow humans. Innovation expands our responsibility for each other and allows us to better act upon what Adam Smith (1759) called our "fellow-feeling," or our innate moral sensibility and sympathy for others. Historically, that fellow-feeling was limited by the geographic and technical realities. But Haskell astutely observed that modern innovations in communications and transportation opened our eyes to the needs of others at a distance. It shifted and expanded our moral universe for the better.

5. Innovation Provides a Check on Power

A final general benefit of technological innovation—and the one that is most often overlooked—is that it provides a check on various forms of public and private power. In my book, *Evasive Entrepreneurs and the Future of Governance*, I argued that innovative acts might be viewed as peaceful mini-revolts that can help bring about positive change through small acts of technologically enabled creativity (Thierer 2020a). This happens on both the creator and consumer side of innovation when people push back against the status quo.

On the creator side, it has been said that by their very nature, entrepreneurs are "kindled by a streak of rebellion" (Carlen 2016: p. 2) and in "the business of breaking the settled mold" (Gilder 1984: p. 246). On the consumer side of things, innovations provide people with additional "voice" and "exit" options beyond politics to protest or push back against things they disagree with—government policies, corporate choices, or anything else (Thierer 2020b).

Thus, we might consider innovation a form of "checks and balances" that helps society keep the powerful in check. Concerning government power, innovation can push back against laws and regulations that have failed to keep pace with the times or have grown burdensome, unwieldy, inefficient, or even unjust. For private actors, innovation can challenge static markets or entrenched incumbents, many of whom work with policymakers to defend their turf (Mitchell 2012).

Practical Solutions to Overcoming Opposition to Progress

It is not enough to make the empirical case for embracing innovation, however. Rational optimists need to consider constructive strategies to address opposition to technological change, without derailing the benefits cited above. Here I consider three general ideas for how to do so.

1. Flexible Tech Governance Options and "Soft Law"

Innovation critics often worry about emerging technologies not only being highly disruptive but also very difficult to govern using traditional legal and regulatory mechanisms. That is primarily due to the so-called pacing problem, which refers to the growing gap between the pace of technological change and the more incremental nature of policymaking efforts (Thierer 2018b). Still, some forms of technological governance will always be necessary. Where "existential" risks are present—risks that threaten immediate, irreversible, tangible harm—some precautionary restraints will be needed (Thierer 2020c). Luckily, the potential dangers of associated with most innovations do not rise to this level, however. Only a small class of technologies (nuclear, chemical, biological) usually pose such a serious threat that they require preemptive restraints.

Flexible governance mechanisms are better suited for most concerns surrounding emerging technology. Increasingly, policymakers are coming to rely on "soft law" to put some guardrails on technological developments (Thierer 2020d). Soft law includes a wide variety of informal, collaborative, and constantly evolving governance mechanisms that differ from hard law in that they lack the same degree of enforceability.[4] These mechanisms can include multi-stakeholder processes, industry best practices and standards, agency workshops and guidance documents, and various educational efforts (Hagemann et al. 2018).

---

[4] Marchant and Allenby (2017: p. 108) define soft law as "a variety of nonbinding norms and techniques," which include "instruments or arrangements that create substantive expectations that are not directly enforceable, unlike 'hard law' requirements such as treaties and statutes."

Soft law is part of a growing "responsible innovation" movement that is dedicated to finding practical, iterative, and collaborative solutions for challenges surrounding new technologies (Thierer 2017). Moreover, soft law tools are often able to address fast-moving technologies and sectors because traditional rulemaking is hindered both by the pacing problem and the overly rigid, top-down nature of traditional regulatory systems. Marc Saner (2013: p. 106) argues, "the control paradigm is too limited to address all the issues that arise in the context of emerging technologies." By the control paradigm, he generally means traditional administrative agencies and the regulatory processes they utilize.

Soft law approaches are already being tapped regularly for driverless cars, commercial drones, mobile medical applications, and more. While each of these technologies promises to be disruptive in different ways, regulators have been bringing together a diverse array of affected parties to formulate best practices for developers and users. The resulting efforts to create "privacy-by-design," "safety-by-design," and "security-by-design" mean that best practices are baked-in to technological design processes. This is a way of introducing what some call "anticipatory ethics" into the early stages of tech development in the form of various guardrails (Johnson 2011: p. 64).

Some will say soft law is not enough. Indeed, sometimes more formal, and legally binding regulations may be needed. But because traditional hard law approaches are proving too slow and onerous, it is forcing policymakers to reconsider how to govern fast-moving tech sectors going forward. Soft law tools offer a way to address the occasional downsides of disruptive technologies without foreclosing innovation opportunities.

Importantly, soft law operates alongside many other traditional governance mechanisms, including common law remedies (product liability, design defects law, assorted torts and class action claims) as well as federal and state consumer protection agencies (such as the Federal Trade Commission), which police "unfair and deceptive practices" and other harms. This is a balanced approach to addressing concerns about the misuse of new technologies.

2. Risk Education and Progress Studies

While the historical record clearly shows positive gains associated with technological innovation, these improvements sometimes fly below the radar or are simply taken for granted by a great many people. Innovation has made many important but risky things quite mundane. For example, thanks to ongoing advances in medical procedures and health technologies, there has been a dramatic decline in infant mortality and mothers dying during childbirth—so much so that it is hardly news anymore. But could there be any greater continuing innovation success story than this? Improvements like that need to be celebrated repeatedly.

Alas, such innovation benefits are easily overlooked while even the slightest fears about new technologies are regularly magnified well out of proportion. Journalists often use sensational, panic-inducing headlines and news reports when discussing breaking technological developments. Thus, innovation faces a timeless problem: bad news sells while good news often gets less attention (Jarvis 2015). The focus shifts to hypothetical worst-case scenarios instead of the many best-case scenarios that are the far more likely outcomes (Thierer 2016: p. 2).

This isn't just a problem with mainstream media or clickbait news sites, either. Pessimism about technology is reflected in popular culture narratives found in books, movies, and TV shows. While it may be the case, as *The New Yorker*'s Jill Lepore (2017) argues, that we live in "A Golden Age for Dystopian Fiction," the relentless techno-pessimism seen in pop culture negatively affects real-world debates about innovation by priming the public to expect only the worst from technology's continued advance. Education—about innovation in general and technological risk in particular—can help address this.

Progress studies refer to a "broad-based intellectual movement focused on understanding the dynamics of progress, or targeting the deeper goal of speeding it up" (Collinson and Cowen 2019). Patrick Collison and Tyler Cowen argue such a field of science is needed because progress is understudied. The goal would be not only to better determine what technological progress has given humanity, but also how to get even more of it. Progress studies would incorporate many disciplines—political science, history, economics, law, psychology, communications theory, and others—to analyze the relationship between technology, society, culture, and politics. The hope would be to better convey what we already know to be most effective in advancing the progress and prosperity of peoples, cultures, institutions, and nations (Thierer 2019b).

Turning to specific concerns about various technological risks, improved risk communication, and technological literacy efforts can help better inform individuals about complex science and technology issues. These efforts should be aimed at better informing the public about risk trade-offs and the many potential future benefits of emerging technologies. "Learning how to communicate to the general public is an important aspect of reducing distrust [in new technologies]," argued Juma (2016: p. 312).

Some regulatory agencies have tapped risk education techniques in the past, but they were often treated as secondary priorities relative to their regulatory efforts. The Food and Drug Administration (FDA), for example, has outlined comprehensive risk education strategies in its 2009 *Strategic Plan for Risk Communication* (Food and Drug Administration 2009) as well as its 2011 report on *Communicating Risks and Benefits: An Evidence-Based User's Guide* (Fischhoff et al. 2011). The agency has also tapped a variety of other public education campaigns and strategies. But these efforts have been limited in scope and much more of the FDA's "educational" efforts consists simply of explaining to companies and the public how to comply with its voluminous body of regulations.

Nonetheless, stepped-up innovation and risk educational efforts can help better communicate the benefits of technological innovation and create an ongoing dialog with those concerned about the disruptive effects associated with it.

3. Transitional Strategies/Assistance

When technological disruption threatens to create serious sectoral upheaval and job loss, many workers, labor unions, and affected industries will work to slow or stop it. Some transitional strategies or support mechanisms may be needed to ensure that technological progress can continue to produce life-enriching benefits

Historically, however, the disruption of various skills and professions eventually improved overall living standards, including those whose skills or jobs may have been affected initially because of it. Even as technological advances eliminated older professions and sectors, they simultaneously opened many other opportunities that were unanticipated. For every worker who lost a job due to innovation, new sectors and jobs developed that usually offered workers better wages, a safer work environment, and often more leisure time.

This process never ends. A 2014 Deloitte survey of the impact of technology and jobs over the past 200 years found that "[t]echnology has transformed productivity and living standards, and, in the process, created new employment in new sectors" (Stewart et al. 2014: p. 9). This is because human needs and wants constantly change and, therefore, "[t]he stock of work in the economy is not fixed; the last 200 years demonstrates that when a machine replaces a human, the result, paradoxically, is faster growth and, in time, rising employment" (Stewart et al. 2014: p. 10).[5] For example, the second half of the last century saw the gradual disappearance of switchboard operators, elevator attendants, and bank cashiers just as new professions and skills became evident, like computer scientists, software engineers, robot technicians, and AI programmers.

Of course, the promise of a better future will come as little consolation for those being disrupted in real time. Moreover, some sectors and professions will possess enough political leverage that they will act to limit technological advances in their field. Overcoming this opposition may require some transitional strategies or assistance to ensure innovation can continue.

When the field of aviation was deregulated by the Carter Administration and Congress in the late 1970s, entry restrictions and price controls were eliminated and a nationwide air marketplace was allowed to develop for the first time. In this case, industry and labor opposition to

[5] They continue on to note that "[m]achines will take on more repetitive and laborious tasks, but seem no closer to eliminating the need for human labour than at any time in the last 150 years. It is not hard to think of pressing, unmet needs even in the rich world: the care of the elderly and the frail, lifetime education and retraining, health care, physical and mental well-being."

change was overcome and the regulatory body overseeing aviation (Civil Aeronautics Board) was abolished. Many rural policymakers feared the disruption of regional airports and air service because of deregulation. To assuage their concerns, the Essential Air Service program was created to ensure that many of those smaller markets continue to receive air service. Regardless of the efficiency of the program, its creation allowed airline liberalization and innovation to advance.

In the field of media and communications, Congress has been forced to repeatedly cut deals with the powerful broadcast sector to free up valuable electromagnetic spectrum for other uses. Historically, television broadcasters had been given large swaths of valuable spectrum through federal licenses, which were supposed to come with various "public interest" conditions. In practice, this arrangement ended up meaning that broadcasters had free and nearly perpetual use of that spectrum, even though they weren't using it very efficiently. When new potential uses for that spectrum developed (especially cellular communications), Congress had to come up with schemes to transition the broadcasters off older spectrum to ensure wireless innovation could occur.

Purely from the perspective of economic efficiency, these deals were sub-optimal. It would have been better to move the broadcaster off that spectrum more rapidly, and perhaps even without any compensation since they had acquired it without charge and benefited from it enormously thanks to decades of regulatory protection from competition. But the optimal solution was also politically impossible because resistance to change ran so high both in industry and in Congress, which has many members concerned about losing political influence over the sector. It became necessary to "make them an offer they can't refuse" by offering the broadcast sector some sort of transitional assistance in exchange for the freeing up of more spectrum for other wireless innovations (Thierer and Esbin 2009).

Similar deals may need to be cut to ensure autonomous vehicle innovation continues. For the past several sessions of Congress, lawmakers have tried to create a federal framework for driverless vehicles. Currently, no overarching law exists governing this market and a patchwork of state policies has filled the void. Bipartisan agreement exists in favor of a national framework for autonomous vehicles, but special interests (tort lawyers and truck drivers) have pushed back and contributed to inaction on this front.

Recently, the president of the Transportation Trades Department for the AFL-CIO told Congress that autonomous vehicles place "millions of jobs at risk" and demanded that trucks be exempted from any legislation to accelerate the deployment of self-driving vehicles (Shepardson 2021). Chances are that the only way Congress will be able to overcome labor opposition to driverless trucks is to ensure that current truck drivers are guaranteed a seat in the cab for a certain period of time, even if they are no longer operating the vehicle. Alternatively, lawmakers might have to offer them some other form of transitional assistance or retraining programs.

Again, these solutions are not optimal from the perspective of economic efficiency; they will be quite costly and potentially even counter-productive by discouraging the movement of labor to new and more highly valued professions. On the other hand, if progress is ever to happen on driverless vehicles—progress that could result in significant cost savings and safety improvements—then some sort of deal will probably need to be cut to overcome labor opposition. These deals should be limited in duration so that such special privileges are not perpetual in character.

Of course, there already exist many other types of general welfare support mechanisms to address unemployment, and there are growing calls for some sort of universal basic income to address technological disruption. These "safety net" programs and proposals entail a variety of trade-offs and costs that is beyond the scope of this essay. The fundamental problem with transitional strategies or assistance that are overly generous is that they could act as a disincentive for the disrupted to more rapidly seek out alternative business or employment opportunities. But, again, such support mechanisms at least keep the door open to ongoing innovation efforts while addressing concerns about the distributional effects associated with technological progress.

Conclusion

Technological innovation will always be the target of critics who fear how it might disrupt a given economic, cultural, or governmental status quo they think is worthy of preservation. Supporters of technological change should push back against the preservationist instinct with a combination of evidence, empathy, and smart solutions.

Rational optimists ask tech skeptics to appreciate the undeniable relationship between innovation, economic growth, and human betterment. But tech defenders owe the critics respectful answers when it comes to the various challenges associated with technological change. Both sides should reject overly nostalgic accounts of some supposedly "good 'ol days" or better bygone eras and instead look toward building a better future together.

References

Andreeva N (2021) Peak TV: Scripted originals dipped in 2020 for the first time since FX launched tally amid pandemic. Deadline, 29 January.

Bajarin T (2013) The smartphone is the Swiss Army knife of gadgets. Time, 18 November.

Broughel J, Thierer A (2019) Technological innovation and economic growth: A brief report on the evidence. Mercatus Center, Arlington.

Carlen J (2016) A brief history of entrepreneurship: The pioneers, profiteers, and racketeers who shaped our world. Columbia University Press, New York.

Collinson P, Cowen T (2019) We need a new science of progress. The Atlantic, 30 July.

Cowen T (2008) In praise of commercial culture. Harvard University Press, Cambridge.

Desmas J (2021a) Voters already love technology-they don't need anti-China messaging to get there. Vox, 3 May.

Fischhoff B, Brewer NT, Downs JS (2011) Communicating risks and benefits: An evidence-based user's guide. Food and Drug Administration, Washington, DC.

Food and Drug Administration (2009) Strategic plan for risk communication. Food and Drug Administration, Washington, DC.
Friedel R (2010) A culture of improvement: Technology and the Western millennium. MIT Press, Cambridge.
Frischmann B, Selinger E (2018) Re-engineering humanity. Cambridge University Press, Cambridge.
Florman SC (1994) The existential pleasures of engineering. St Martins Griffin, New York, 2nd edition.
Gilder G (1984) The spirit of enterprise. Simon and Schuster, New York.
Gillespie N (2019) Tyler Cowen's gospel of prosperity. Reason, March.
Gillmor D (2004) We the media: Grassroots journalism by the people, for the people. O'Reilly Media, Inc., Sebastopol.
Hagemann R, Huddleston Skees J, Thierer A (2018) Soft law for hard problems: The governance of emerging technologies in an uncertain future. Colorado Tech Law J 17:37–130.
Haskell TL (1985) Capitalism and the origins of the humanitarian sensibility, part 1. Amer Hist Rev 90: 339–361.
Heath D, Garcia-Roberts G (2021) Race to the vaccine. USA Today, 31 January.
Ip G (2019) The world is getting quietly, relentlessly better. Wall Street Journal, 2 January.
Jarvis J (2015) Optimism doesn't sell. Medium, 25 May.
Johnson DG (2011) Software agents, anticipatory ethics, and accountability. In: Marchant KE, Allenby BR, Herkert, JR (eds) The growing gap between emerging technologies and legal-ethical oversight: The pacing problem. Springer, Dordecht, 61–76.
Juma C (2016) Innovation and its enemies: Why people resist new technologies. Oxford University Press, New York.
Kelly K (2016) The inevitable: Understanding the 12 technological forces that will shape our future. Viking, New York.
Lepore J (2017) A golden age for dystopian fiction. New Yorker, 5 and 12 June.
Lewis N (2018) The enduring wisdom of the crowd. Spiked, 24 October.
Longworth R (2015) A misguided view on technology and humanism. Chicago Council on Global Affairs, 20 January.
Marchant GE, Allenby B (2017) Soft law: New tools for governing emerging technologies. B Atom Sci 73:108–114.
Mitchell MD (2012) The pathology of privilege: The economic consequences of government favoritism. Mercatus Center, Arlington.

Mokyr J, Vickers C, Ziebarth NL (2015) The history of technological anxiety and the future of economic growth: Is this time different? J Econ Perspect 29:31–50.
Morozov E (2015) The taming of tech criticism. The Baffler 27, March.
Murphy R (2021b) This is what peak culture looks like. Works in Progress, 20 May.
Ridley M (2010) The rational optimist: How prosperity evolves. Harper Collins, New York.
Roser M (2018) Memorizing these three statistics will help you understand the world. Gates Notes, 26 June.
Rosling H (2018) Ten reasons we're wrong about the world—And why things are better than you think. Flatiron Books, New York.
Saner MA (2013) The role of adaptation in the governance of emerging technologies. In: Marchant KE, Abbott KW, Brown JE (eds) Innovative governance models for emerging technologies. Edward Elgar, Northhampton, 92–107.
Schwartz B (2004) The paradox of choice: Why more is less. Ecco, New York.
Shepardson D (2021) U.S. labor leader calls for human drivers in automated vehicles. Reuters, 18 May.
Smith A (1759) Theory of moral sentiments. A Millar in the Strand, London.
Stewart I, De D, Cole A (2014) Technology and people: The great job-creating machine. Deloitte LLP, London.
Taylor MZ (2016) The politics of innovation: Why some countries are better than others at science and technology. Oxford University Press, Cambridge.
Thierer A, Esbin B (2009) An offer they can't refuse: Spectrum reallocation that can benefit consumers, broadcasters and the mobile broadband sector. Progress Snapshot Release 5.13, Progress & Freedom Foundation, Washington, DC.
Thierer A (2013) Technopanics, threat inflation, and the danger of an information technology precautionary principle. Minn J Law Sci Tech 14:312–350.
Thierer A (2014) Muddling through: How we learn to cope with technological change. Medium, 30 June.
Thierer A (2016) Permissionless innovation: The continuing case for comprehensive technological freedom. Mercatus Center, Arlington.
Thierer A (2017) Are 'permissionless innovation' and 'responsible innovation' compatible? Technology Liberation Front, 12 July.
Thierer A (2018a) Is it 'techno-chauvinist' and 'anti-humanist' to believe in the transformative potential of technology? Medium, 18 September.

Thierer A (2018b) The pacing problem and the future of technology regulation. The Bridge, 9 August.
Thierer A (2019a) Countering threats to innovation with rational optimism. Technology Liberation Front, 29 April 2019.
Thierer A (2019b) Is there a science of progress. AIER, 8 August.
Thierer A (2020a) Evasive entrepreneurs and the future of governance: How innovation improves economies and governments. Cato Institute, Washington, DC.
Thierer A (2020b) Voice, exit, and innovation. Cato Unbound, 10 August.
Thierer A (2020c) Existential risk and emerging technology governance. Technology Liberation Front, 5 August.
Thierer A (2020d) Soft law in ICT sectors: Four case studies. Jurimetrics 61: 79–119.
Wallensten (2018) Cloud computing: Co-invention for the masses. Technology Policy Institute Blog, 19 July.
Wieseltier L (2015) Among the disrupted. New York Times, 7 January.

13

Law Controlling Technology

Ryan Calo

Outside of the Federal Trade Commission, the agency primarily responsible for protecting the American consumer, stand two Art Deco sculptures entitled *Man Controlling Trade*. The sculptures depict giant horses, each straining to gallop forward but held back by a muscular man pulling with all his strength. The image is a fitting symbol of the FTC's past (Carter 2017). The agency arose in an America much closer to an industrial revolution, where markets and machines presented a visceral danger and the sheer size of corporations seemed frightening. Lawmakers interested in reigning in industry spoke in stark, moralistic terms, which is why the FTC's enabling legislation empowers the Commission to pursue acts and practices deemed "unfair" or "deceptive."[1]

[1] 15 U.S.C. § 45(a)(1).

R. Calo (✉)
University of Washington, Seattle, WA, USA
e-mail: rcalo@uw.edu

A. L. Kassens and J. C. Hall (eds.), *Challenges in Classical Liberalism*, Palgrave Studies in Classical Liberalism,
https://doi.org/10.1007/978-3-031-32890-9_13

A hundred years into its existence, the FTC faces a very different environment. Companies aren't trusts to be busted but multivalent platforms—global innovation ecosystems of limitless ambition. The Commission itself is held back by inadequate resources, a lack of technical expertise, a skeptical Supreme Court,[2] and a requirement to conduct what amounts to a cost–benefit analysis before determining something is unfair—a standard initially self-imposed by the Commission to assuage critics and later codified by Congress in the days of Newt Gingrich.[3] Thus hobbled, if unbowed, the FTC must address a range of new, information-based harms, emanating from the primary economic drivers of American commerce.

Despite the complexity that has unfolded over the course of a century, new entrants to technology policy could be forgiven for viewing the relationship between government and technology in similar terms to *Man Controlling Trade*. Public policy discourse around technology still counterpoises two forces: those of precaution and permission. The Precautionists would hold the horse of progress fast until it can be proven safe. The Anti-Precautionists would let the horse go—and clean up after it, as needed. The Precautionist worldview is traceable to European environmental regulators who first proposed a "precautionary principle" for innovation that persists in Europe to this day (Holm and Stokes 2012). The Anti-Precautionists grow out of a Neoliberal/libertarian tradition that might be summed up in the ethos of "permissionless innovation" (Thierer 2016).

The purpose of this chapter is to challenge the dichotomy of precaution and permission in two ways. The first challenge is descriptive. Critiques of precaution, and defenses of permission, rest on evidence that is oddly thin. Examples of precaution thwarting innovation are surprisingly few and many purported hurdles to technology governance evaporate upon inspection. The second challenge is normative. The rhetoric of precaution and permission articulates no normative baseline by which to justify legal intervention or forbearance, beyond a dry

[2] *E.g., AMG Cap. Mgmt. v. Fed. Trade Comm'n*, 141 S. Ct. 1341 (2021) (limiting the Commission's power to seek disgorgement, restitution, or other equitable monetary relief).

[3] 15 U.S.C. § 45(n).

pragmatism. The proper posture of law toward emerging technology is neither banning nor blessing, but a methodical process of inventorying broken promises and unmet expectations. The role of law and policy is not to restrain the horses of progress but to yoke them to societal interests.

Almost from its inception in German environmental policy of the 1970s, the precautionary principle has been wrapped up in concerns over science and technology. What else but these powerful forces are capable of devastating consequences for humanity if left unchecked? Early candidates for precaution thus included nuclear power and energy, chemical pesticides, and genetic engineering. Of course, in reality, any sufficiently ambitious societal change—and the occasional humble one—is capable of a massive impact on human flourishing. The effects of China's one-child policy (Feng et al. 2016),[4] Clinton-era welfare reform (Ehrenfreund 2016),[5] oil import quotas in the 1960s (Priest 2012),[6] the Wage Stabilization Act of 1942 (Mihm 2017),[7] and the fairness doctrine (Hazlett and Sosa 1997),[8] are but a few examples. But precaution as a principle has largely been deployed and debated in the context of science and technology.

Longstanding critiques of the precautionary principle are similarly tied to technical and scientific innovation. In an era enamored with the power of science and technology to promote progress, the idea of proceeding with utmost caution can be a hard sell. We assume an unfettered industry free to innovate at will yields rapid progress. Virtually every research paper or report—even those ultimately urging caution—rush to concede at the outset that the emerging technology under consideration stands to

4 "China's one-child policy will be remembered as one of the costliest lessons of misguided public policymaking" Feng et al. (2016: p. 84).

5 Due to Clinton-era welfare reform, "[p]eople receiving federal welfare payments fell by half in four years," and "[d]eep poverty increased among families and unemployed adults" (Ehrenfreund 2016).

6 Priest (2012) argues that "Eisenhower's 1959 imposition of mandatory import quotas on oil" sped depletion at home.

7 Mihm (2017) explains that the Wage Stabilization Act of 1942 led to employers offering healthcare benefits.

8 Hazlett and Sosa (1997) argue that the fairness doctrine acted as a "tax on controversial speech."

improve our world. Indeed, most technologies hold some potential for harm and for good, if not in equal measure.

And yet, the evidentiary basis for the claim that precaution impedes progress is curiously thin. This can be seen in the paucity of examples available to critics of precaution. Were technophobia-fueled precaution so prevalent and dangerous, one might suppose there would be many examples of its ills, expanding year by year. The number of examples in the literature has, if anything, dwindled. Anti-Precautionists still cite nuclear power as a road not taken in clean energy and continue to lament the slow start of genetically modified organisms (GMOs) due to unfounded public concerns (Thierer 2019).[9] Recent evidence of toxicity has taken the shine off of a third favorite example, the internet,[10] and the prospect of regulation of artificial intelligence seems far off to serve as a replacement. Two or three bedtime stories are not going to keep frightening the children.

It is far from self-evident that precaution "costs lives" (Thierer 2019). But can precaution really be done well? Anti-Precautionists don't think so. The so-called pacing problem posits that law cannot keep up with technological change. When lawmakers try, they get things wrong, because neither the trajectory nor the impact of technology is knowable in advance. This intuition finds support in an unlikely alliance between libertarian intuitions that regulation will always backfire, and decades of work in science and technology studies asserting that the societal impacts of technology are a function of complex, non-deterministic forces.

Yet, technology is far from the only social fact to occasionally outpace the law. In 1919, the Eighteenth Amendment garnered a supermajority in the House and Senate and was ratified by forty-six states. Over the

[9] E.g., Thierer (2019) explaining that, in the nuclear context, "the precautionary principle has had significantly negative direct costs in the form of increased electricity costs as well as increasing carbon emissions, due to forced continued reliance on fossil fuels" and that "anti-GMO resistance among environmental activists and regulatory officials held up the diffusion of" golden rice, which solved a deathly nutrient deficiency, for over ten years.

[10] Ironically, the internet is today the chief vehicle by which misinformation about nuclear power and GMOs spread. See, e.g., Jiang and Fang (2019: p. 327), who state "On the mechanism of diffusion of rumours on Weibo, we observed that 'evidence' that directly or indirectly purported to show that GM soybeans cause cancer was added to the rumours and that the rumours were 'assimilated' into people's perception through the stigmatization of GMOs and through conspiracy theories."

decade that followed, the ban on alcohol rapidly lost support until the Constitution was amended again to reverse it. At other times in American history, it has been commonplace to remark upon the relative speed of life over law, as evidenced by a passage in the 1946 Pulitzer-prize winning novel *All the King's Men* in which Robert Penn Warren's (1946: p. 204) memorable character Willie Stark likens the law to a blanket that is too small for the bed or a pair of pants "you bought last year for a growing boy." Stark's diagnosis of the law generally reads like a paraphrase of the pacing problem: "The law is always too short and too tight for growing humankind. The best you can do is do something ... and by the time the law gets on the books you would have done something different" (Warren 1946: p. 204).

Meanwhile, law often keeps up with technology just fine. There are historical examples, like outer space exploration. The United States signed the Outer Space Treaty in 1967, a mere eight years after the first photograph of Earth was taken from orbit.[11] But one need not look to history at all to see evidence of law running beside technology at a light jog. I have been reading about the imminent introduction of driverless cars for decades. They are being tested in many states, sometimes under laws that have been on the books for years.[12] The Department of Transportation is turning the light green.[13] The primary issue with mainstreaming driverless cars is that *robotics is hard*, not that lawmakers are putting on the brakes.

Technology has no greater tendency to outpace law than any other social fact. What is unique about technology is not that technology is different, but that policymakers treat it as such. Technology is surrounded by a kind of policy force field, forestalling intervention even in the face of sustained public scrutiny. This force field emanates from a political economy that fetishes innovation and a policy apparatus

---

[11] Sarah [sic] (2019): "On August 7, 1959, the Explorer 6 satellite launched.... Approximately a week into the mission, it captured and transmitted the first photograph of Earth via satellite while orbiting over Mexico."

[12] E.g., Nev. Rev. Stat. § 482A (2017).

[13] For example, in its letter replying to Google about gaps in federal legislation affecting driverless vehicles. Letter from Paul Hemmersbaugh, Chief Counsel, Dep't Transp., to Chris Urmson, Dir. Self-Driving Car Project, Google (on file with the Nat'l Highway Traffic Safety Administration).

desperately lacking in technical acumen. (The same Congress that codified the cost–benefit requirement for unfairness defunded the Office of Technology Assessment, an agency that had helped Congress channel technology since the 1970s [U.S. Government Accountability Office 1977]). Proponents of permissionless innovation often talk of "technopanic," wherein the public experiences disproportionate fears over a new technology (Thierer 2013). Far more commonplace in my experience is "techno-paralysis." People fear phenomena they don't understand but, sometimes for the same reasons, make few concrete attempts to address them.

There are other arguments to be levied against precaution. Critics allege, for example, that precaution lends itself to economic protectionism.[14] Thus, a foreign economic rival of the United States—such as Russia or Europe—may urge or impose precaution on an American innovation if it threatens local incumbent industries. Examples include the fan favorites GMOs as well as internet search and social media. The converse turns out to be true as well. At the time of this writing, United States domestic policy around artificial intelligence revolves around a narrative that the government cannot put guardrails around AI lest we fall behind rivals such as China. Regardless, the problem of protectionism is protectionism itself, which can be expressed in any number of policies, from tariffs and trade barriers to selective enforcement.[15]

The case against precaution is not self-evident. But neither is pure precaution very defensible. The precautionary principle, in its strongest (hence, weakest) form, would disallow *any* innovation until proponents could demonstrate the absence or harm. This is, admittedly, an impossible standard to meet. It also happens to be almost nowhere in evidence. Ours is a system of negative liberties, under which something is lawful unless it is not. If you want to know whether you may wear a hat while

[14] Wiener and Rogers (2002: p. 339), for example, note "In particular, economic protectionism may explain some of the complex pattern of relative precaution."

[15] Soesastro (2011: p. 35) argues that global trade "could become a fundamental part of the solution to the global economic crisis" because "it could help reverse the growing economic nationalism that is manifested in various forms of trade and financial protectionism." Baldwin and Evenett 2011: pp. 1, 5) argue that "protectionism in government procurement is an old problem" and that "[p]rotectionism is creeping into national policies and trade volumes are collapsing."

riding a bicycle on a Sunday, you look up whether there's a law against it. True precaution would involve speculating as to the impacts of emerging technology prior to dissemination and banning it on this basis—a status reserved to stem cell research, for a time, and the neutrino bomb.

Precaution in practice takes different forms. A version of precaution plays out in common law torts. Since the days of Judge Learned Hand, courts in the United States perform a kind of negligence calculus, implicitly comparing the probability and extent of loss to the burden associated with mitigation in determinations of negligence.[16] Similarly, in determining whether to hold a new activity to a strict liability standard, courts ask how useful the activity is and how amenable it may be to risk mitigation. This standard can change over time: as the technology matured, hot air ballooning went from a strict liability regime to negligence, as what constituted reasonable practice became clear. These and other tort doctrines are designed to stand less in the way of useful innovation, especially where the innovator has taken steps to mitigate potential harm.

What strikes me most about Anti-Precautionist discourse is the refusal to acknowledge the wide range of interventions. Take, for example, federalism. In American jurisprudence, it is commonplace to defend federalism on the basis that states act as "laboratories of democracy."[17] Devolving control to individual states, the argument runs, allows for experimentation with different rules. If the rules work, they can be emulated in other states or even at the federal level. If they fail, then at least the damage is limited to a portion only of the nation's citizens. Not only are states free to experiment but also smaller units such as cities and counties. Even within cities there is the prospect of "zones" where, for example, drug laws are not enforced.

Most law and technology scholars understand this principle well. For example, Margot Kaminski argues expressly that states should set drone policy so that the nation might compare approaches to balancing values

---

16 *United States v. Carroll Towing Co.*, 159 F.2d 169, 173 (2d Cir. 1947) ("[T]he owner's duty... to provide against resulting injuries is a function of three variables: (1) The probability that she will break away; (2) the gravity of the resulting injury, if she does; (3) the burden of adequate precautions.").

17 *New State Ice Co. v. Liebmann*, 285 U.S. 262, 311 (1932) ("It is one of the happy incidents of the federal system that a single courageous state may, if its citizens choose, serve as a laboratory.").

such as safety, privacy, and free speech.[18] Ugo Pagallo, Sofia Ranchordás (2021), and others call attention to the prospect of legal experimentation in the governance of data protection and artificial intelligence.[19]

Policymakers have, in fact, adopted a number of different approaches to drone regulation, driverless cars, and many other emerging technologies. Some have enacted moratoria or outright bans on certain applications technology—for example, facial recognition. Outside the United States, governments from Japan to Europe have experimented with regulatory sandboxes in which experimentation with new technology is permitted but only within particular contexts. There are myriad other responses available to address facial recognition or other aspects of AI, including requirements to be transparent, strict liability standards for harm, or regulations on use by specific actors or in specific contexts.

Curiously, however, for those who glorify innovation, critics of the precautionary principle almost completely ignore legal experimentation. They write as though the only possibility were permission everywhere or nowhere.[20] The pacing problem similarly assumes that officials can but stand by helplessly as technology spreads across the nation before having any sense of whether regulation is indicated. Yet all it takes is a single, entrepreneurial jurisdiction to, for example, require a ride-sharing company to be licensed by a taxi and limousine commission prior to operating before society would have pretty good data on the impact of precaution. Of course, social-culture contexts are not fungible and some technological phenomena may require scale and longevity before their full impacts are understood. But generally speaking, the prospect that *every* jurisdiction will entirely ban a technology in such a way that no one realizes its benefits is remote.

---

[18] Margot E. Kaminski, *Drone Federalism: Civilian Drones and the Things They Carry*, 4 Calif. L. Rev. Cir. 57 (May 2013).

[19] Pagallo et al. (2019) argue that "[T]hese forms of legal experimentation go hand-in-hand with the creation of lawfully de-regulated special zones, that is, a sort of living lab for the empirical testing and development of AI and robotics."

[20] There was next to no mention of federalism in Collingridge (1982), Thierer (2013), Juma (2016), Downes (2009).

This chapter has thus far been largely descriptive. The stark universe in which technology invariably and uniquely outpaces law, in which technology is banned everywhere and nowhere, in which fear of technology leads to regulation instead of avoidance, fails to match the complex reality. Or, at a minimum, the Anti-Precautionists are far from meeting their evidentiary burden. A final part begins to describe the normative considerations at the heart of technology policy—what we should be debating instead of what we are.

To think of the debate in terms of precaution or permission is often to treat all of technology policy as a risk analysis with the simplest of inputs. Technology is either too threatening to human well-being to allow, or else too beneficial to constrain. Technology on this view becomes a kind of force or entity—not unlike a giant horse—that officials either hobble or unleash on the basis of moral reasoning about nuanced as an Excel spreadsheet.

What technology does, in practice, is change human affordances—what we do and how we do it.[21] Some of these changes are knowable in advance, others, revealed with time. Changes to human affordances can challenge assumptions of law and policy. In Lawrence Lessig's (2006: p. 25) words, changes to technology can reveal "latent ambiguities" in law and legal institution. Once upon a time, people drove cars. Departments of Motor Vehicles were charged with testing drivers and granting or denying permission to operate a vehicle. Now cars drive themselves. Does a car need a "license"? How might that work? Changes to human affordances can also raise societal or legal expectations. One day, using a robot to conduct surgery is negligent. The next, it's negligent to do the surgery by hand. (Maybe one day it will be negligent to drive a car.) Police and prosecutors are able to sift through enormous volumes of data using artificial intelligence to find evidence of crimes. But perhaps they now owe a greater duty to defendants and defense attorneys to turn up exculpatory evidence.[22]

---

[21] For a discussion of affordances and how they relate to law, see Calo (2017).

[22] *Brady v. Maryland*, 373 U.S. 83 (1963).

The task of government in all this is not an easy one. Policymakers must monitor new technology and attempt to ascertain the shifts in affordance that accompany it. They must articulate a normative baseline against which to assess that shift. And they must root around in their toolkit for the best set of interventions, including sometimes none at all. Each of these challenges requires the dedication of time and expertise. Monitoring new technology requires not just technical acumen, but the wherewithal to build and maintain relationships with the people and institutions—academic, industrial, independent, indigenous—that are the sources of innovation. Ascertaining how technology shifts human affordance requires a structured imagination, working knowledge of history, and close observation of the present.

Normative base-lining, in the sense of justifying a legal intervention by reference to a source of moral or legal authority, can be easy enough. Where, as often, technology undermines a constitutional or statutory guarantee—such as the right to due process before a deprivation of liberty or property—policymakers have a ready reason to intervene and restore the status quo ex ante. A rather more difficult challenge is ascertaining when new affordances do or should raise societal expectations (Calo and Citron 2021). At some point, the widespread availability of new technology raises the bar on the government itself (McGinnis 2013: p. 2).

Finally, policymakers convinced that a guarantee or expectation has been displaced or eclipsed will have to choose from among a broad regulatory toolkit—be it subsidy, sandbox, sunset, ban, rule, or standard—to address the development. There will be mistakes. But policymakers can learn from these mistakes, and from the jurisdiction right next door that may have approached the issue differently. It is a curious position, that of the Anti-Precautionist, that sees the benefit of innovation everywhere but governance.

Government as presently configured is not always adept at these tasks. But that deficit is contingent, not inevitable. Nothing about technology or the nature of governance necessitates a binary choice between reflexive prevention or default permission. We are not living in the world of *Man*

Controlling Trade, if such a simple world ever existed. Rather, each significant development in technology represents an invitation to inventory our values and an obligation to "muddle through" their societal impacts as best as contemporary methods allow (Lindblom 1959; Calo 2021).

References

Baldwin R, Evenett S (2011) Introduction and recommendation for the G20. In: Baldwin R, Evenett S (eds) The collapse of global trade, murky protectionism, and the crisis: Recommendations for the G20. Centre for Economic Policy Research, London, pp 1–12

Calo R (2017) Privacy, vulnerability, and affordance. In: Selinger E, Polonetsky J, Tene Omer (eds) Cambridge handbook of consumer privacy, Cambridge University Press, New York, pp 198–206

Calo R, Citron, DK (2021) The automated administrative state: A crisis of legitimacy. Emory Law J 70: 797–846

Calo R (2021) Modeling through. Duke L J 71:1391–1423

Collingridge D (1982) The social control of technology. St Martin's Press, New York

Carter E (2017) Man controlling trade. Atlas Obscura, 19 September

Downes L (2009) The laws of disruption: Harnessing the new forces that govern life and business in the digital age. Basic Books, New York

Ehrenfreund M (2016) How welfare reform changed American poverty, in 9 charts. Washington Post, 22 August

Feng W, Gu B, Cai Y (2016) The end of China's one-child policy. Stud Fam Plann 47:83–86

Hazlett TW, Sosa DW (1997) Was the fairness doctrine a "chilling effect"? Evidence from the post-deregulation radio market. J Legal Stud 26:279–301

Holm S, Stokes E (2012) Precautionary principle. In: Chadwick R (ed) Encyclopedia of applied ethics, 2nd edition, Elsevier, New York, pp 569–575

Jiang S, Fang W (2019) Misinformation and disinformation in science: Examining the social diffusion of rumours about GMOs. Culture Sci 2:327–340

Juma C (2016) Innovation and its enemies: Why people resist new technologies. Oxford University Press, New York

Lessig L (2006) Code 2.0. Basic Books, New York
Lindblom CE (1959) The science of muddling through. Pub Admin Rev 19:79–88
McGinnis JO (2013) Accelerating democracy. Princeton University Press, Princeton
Mihm S (2017) Employer based healthcare was a wartime accident, Chicago Tribune, 24 February
Pagallo U, Casanovas P, Madelin R (2019) The middle-out approach: Assessing models of legal governance in data protection, artificial intelligence, and the Web of Data. Theory Pract Leg 7:1–25
Priest T (2012) The dilemmas of oil empire. J Am Hist 99:236–251
Ranchordás S (2021) Experimental regulations and regulatory sandboxes—law without order? Law Method: 1–23
Sarah [sic] (2019) 60 years ago first satellite image of Earth. Kennedy Space Center: The Payload Blog, 7 August 2019
Soesastro H (2011) East Asia must share Obama's leadership to keep trade open. In: Baldwin R, Evenett S (eds) The collapse of global trade, murky protectionism, and the crisis: Recommendations for the G20. Centre for Economic Policy Research, London, pp 35–36
Thierer A (2013) Technopanics, threat inflation, and the danger of an information technology precautionary principle. Minn J Law Sci Tech 14:312–350
Thierer A (2016) Permissionless innovation: The continuing case for comprehensive technological freedom. Mercatus Center, Arlington
Thierer A (2019) How many lives are lost due to the precautionary principle? Mercatus Center, Arlington
U.S. Government Accountability Office (1977) The office of technology assessment. Government Printing Office, Washington, DC
Warren RP (1946) All the king's men. Harcourt, Brace & Company, New York
Wiener JB, Rogers MD (2002) Comparing precaution in the United States and Europe. J Risk Res 5:317–349

Part VII

Recreational Drugs and Alcohol

14

Legalize and Deregulate for Innovation

Angela K. Dills and Jeffrey A. Miron

Introduction

Drug, alcohol, and cigarette uses are associated with many personal and social harms. Much discussion assumes that the substance use causes these harms, rather than just being associated with them. In some cases, this view has merit: drug, alcohol, or tobacco use can have adverse effects on the user or others. But in many instances, this use reflects underlying issues, so targeting substance use is likely ineffective. Most importantly, attempts to suppress use generate a broad range of harmful, unintended

A. K. Dills (✉)
Western Carolina University, Cullowhee, NC, USA
e-mail: akdills@email.wcu.edu

J. A. Miron
Harvard University, Cambridge, MA, USA
e-mail: miron@fas.harvard.edu

A. L. Kassens and J. C. Hall (eds.), *Challenges in Classical Liberalism*, Palgrave Studies in Classical Liberalism,
https://doi.org/10.1007/978-3-031-32890-9_14

consequences. Thus, a free or at least substantially freer market in drugs, alcohol, and tobacco would improve a wide variety of societal outcomes.

A large fraction of adults consumes illicit drugs and tobacco and most adults use alcohol in the United States and globally. In the United States, in 2019, roughly 20% of the population aged 12 and older used illicit drugs, about half (51.1%) used alcohol, and 21.1% used tobacco in the past month (Substance Abuse and Mental Health Services Administration 2020). Globally, 5.5% of adults aged 15–64 used drugs in the past year (United Nations Office on Drugs and Crime 2019), about 43% of those 15 and over are currently alcohol drinkers (World Health Organization 2018: p. 39), and 20.7% smoked tobacco (World Health Organization 2017).

Drug, alcohol, and tobacco markets are highly regulated in the United States. Marijuana and other drugs are illegal according to federal law. The government schedules marijuana, heroin, and ecstasy as Schedule I drugs, which means the government believes they have "no currently accepted medical use and a high potential for abuse." Cocaine, methamphetamines, oxycodone, and fentanyl are Schedule II drugs, meaning ones that (according to the government) have "a high potential for abuse, with use potentially leading to severe psychological or physical dependence."[1] Legal penalties for consumption and production differ by scheduling level. Current marijuana laws differ by state.[2] As of January 2021, 31 states and the District of Columbia have decriminalized the possession of marijuana; 36 states and the District of Columbia have adopted medical marijuana laws, with ease of obtaining medical marijuana approaching legalization in some states; and 15 states and the District of Columbia have legalized recreational marijuana. In addition, Oregon voted in November 2020 to decriminalize possession of small amounts of all controlled substances.

We focus first on the potential benefits and harms likely to follow a shift from the current regime of drug prohibition to one where drugs are manufactured, purchased, and sold in a free market.

[1] Controlled Substances Act 21 U.S.C. § 812.

[2] State laws from Marijuana Policy Project (2021a, b, c).

Prohibitions Versus Legal Markets

What would happen if drugs and other substances were sold in legal markets? Prohibitions modestly reduce, but do not eliminate, the consumption of the prohibited good. Underground or grey markets emerge because consumers desire the restricted products and producers profit from satisfying consumers' wants and needs. Consumption and production of the good then occur in underground, illicit markets. Most of the negative effects associated with illicit drugs arise from operating in illicit markets. These negative effects include violence, reduced quality control, corruption, and disparate harms to minority communities. Deregulating and legalizing will improve a range of other public health features, more than offsetting any potential costs from modestly increased consumption. These include product innovations toward safety and quality, reduced violence, and improved community relations with the police.

The production and sale of most scheduled drugs occurs illicitly. For example, many use prescription opioids non-therapeutically, obtaining drugs diverted from legal sources via dealers or friends (Cicero et al. 2011). Prohibitions raise the costs of producing and distributing, while also penalizing use, raising the effective price. But on both a priori grounds, and available evidence, the impact of such policies on use appears to be modest: they mainly create underground or grey markets, which supply a large fraction of those who wish to use (Dills and Miron 2004; Dills et al. 2005; Anderson and Rees 2014). Removing drug prohibitions likely will result in only small changes in price. Although illicit producers incur added costs for bribery, evading detection, and legal penalties, shifting to legal production brings new costs in complying with labor and environmental laws (Miron 2003).

The relationship between drug use and harms to others suggests at worst small effects and in many cases beneficial effects from easing legal access to drugs. Research shows that some crimes decreased following states' adoption of medical marijuana laws (Morris et al. 2014; Dragone et al. 2019). Further, traffic fatalities fell in response to state medical marijuana laws (Anderson et al. 2013) and had no change following state recreational marijuana laws (Hansen et al. 2020). Medical marijuana laws reduced suicides among men aged 20–39, possibly because marijuana helped them "cope with stressful life events" (Anderson et al. 2014). Some of the observed effects of softening marijuana laws appear due to decreased alcohol consumption; people switch to less harmful substances when laws treat those substances more evenly. Recent synthetic control evidence shows that Colorado's recreational marijuana law reduced opioid overdose rates (Alcocer 2020).

Many are concerned about the health effects of drug use for consumers: in 2019, more than 70,000 people died from a drug-overdose, primarily opioids (Wilson et al. 2020). But drug overdoses are more common when substances are illegal, possibly due to changes in product quality. Portugal, for example, experienced a large decline in drug-related deaths following their decriminalization of drug possession (Hughes and Stevens 2007).

Product quality suffers under prohibition for two main reasons: innovations to avoid criminal penalties, and government interventions. Under prohibition, traffickers and consumers prefer substances that are easier to conceal. Mandatory minimum sentencing, for example, delineates sentencing based on the quantity of substance on one's person. This leads to sales of higher potency products, making it easier to overdose. Drug entrepreneurs also innovate to avoid drug scheduling laws, creating new substances not technically covered in the law (Redford 2017). We discuss innovation under various regimes in more detail below. Operating in underground markets reduces the incentives for quality control. Consumers are less able to regularly interact with the same supplier, limiting reputational pressures on suppliers. Lack of access to the judicial system to sue a supplier, say, for fraud further reduces incentives for quality control.

Government enforcement also leads to harmful products being sold as recreational substances. Using U.S. government funds for the War on Drugs, the Mexican government sprayed marijuana fields with the plant-killing chemical, paraquat, which can be fatal even in modest quantities (Kornbluth 1978). Paraquat-tainted marijuana was then sold in the United States. The DEA and state law enforcement agencies also sprayed domestic marijuana fields with paraquat (*New York Times* 1982, 1988). During federal alcohol prohibition, consumers used legally produced industrial alcohol to make bootleg liquor. To scare consumers, the federal government required industrial alcohol to increase its percentage of methanol, leading to a deadly product when diverted to bootleg liquor and killing 10,000 (Lopez 2014).

Legalizing drugs will affect government budgets by reducing enforcement expenditures and increasing tax revenues. Current enforcement expenditures total more than $47 billion every year; fully legalizing would generate an estimated $58 billion in federal, state, and local tax revenues annually (Miron 2018). The enforcement costs stem from funding the Drug Enforcement Agency and criminal justice expenditures from arresting, trying, and incarcerating people convicted on drug offenses. Other costs from enforcing drug laws include lost wages and productivity of those incarcerated, career changes required and degrees foregone due to felony drug records, and costs to families left behind while serving one's sentence. Other countries incur some of the costs of U.S. drug policy: for example, the thousands of deaths at the hands of Mexican cartels, and the harms to farmers from U.S. funded poppy eradication efforts in Afghanistan (Coyne and Hall 2017).

Enforcement of prohibition is expensive and can be counterproductive. Violence arises more often in markets where government strongly enforces prohibitions. Much of this enforcement focuses on the supply-side by interdicting drug traffickers. The resulting supply reductions increase the product's price but, given inelastic demand curves, only somewhat decrease consumption. The result is higher expenditures on and revenues from the product, increasing its attractiveness to entrepreneurs. Higher profits for successful entrepreneurs intensify competition. Underground businesses resort to violence to resolve disputes, given their inability to rely on the non-violent legal system. We observe greater violence in countries and time periods with more enforcement (Kulick et al. 2016; Miron 1999, 2001).

The government disproportionately enforces its War on Drugs against minority communities. Past-year drug use rates are comparable between whites (21.7%), blacks (21.9%), and Hispanics (19.1) (Substance Abuse and Mental Health Services Administration 2020: Table 1.23B). Arrest rates for drug possession, however, are substantially higher among blacks and Hispanics than among whites. In one studied county, whites are more likely than blacks and Hispanics to be cited and released; blacks and Hispanics are more likely to be booked into jail, convicted, and serve time than whites (Camplain et al. 2020). National figures on arrests for drug law violations and prisoner characteristics similarly show disproportionate high arrest rates and imprisonment rates for drug offenses for blacks and Hispanics (U.S. Department of Justice 2020: Table 49). Police brutality of black communities is linked to the War on Drugs and its police strategies of stop-and-frisk and SWAT teams (Cooper 2015).

For those concerned about substance use disorders, prohibitions inhibit people's willingness to seek treatment. For example, pregnant women with substance use disorders are more likely to seek treatment when states adopt prenatal substance use policies that include treatment and support and are not solely criminal justice-oriented (Kozhimannil et al. 2019). Treating addiction and substance use disorders like medical issues instead of crimes leads to more effectively provided care. Further, a legal regime facilitates academic and medical research on medical uses of scheduled drugs (NAS 2017).

Prohibitions only modestly reduce consumption. Because prohibitions drive consumption and production into underground markets, however, prohibitions lead to a variety of harms: increased violence, reduced product quality, reduced substance use disorder treatment, reduced medical research, and a disparate impact on minority communities. Further, prohibitions are expensive—both in their cost of enforcement and in the loss of tax revenue.

Legal Markets with Modest Regulation Versus Free Markets

Legal markets with modest regulations may not be ideal, but they are a significant improvement over underground markets. We next consider likely changes were states to shift from legal markets with modest regulations to free markets.

Alcohol, tobacco, and recreational marijuana currently are taxed and regulated more than other products. Colorado, for example, imposes an additional 15% excise tax and an additional 15% sales tax on recreational marijuana, collecting almost $30 million per month (Fritts 2019).[3] Similarly, recreational marijuana generated $70 million in tax revenue in the first year of sales in Washington, $10 million per month in Oregon, and $50 million monthly in California.

Alcohol is taxed highly at the federal level and again at the state level. Federal excise tax rates are roughly 21 cents per ounce of pure alcohol in distilled spirits, about 10 cents per ounce of pure alcohol in beer, and about 6 cents per ounce of pure alcohol in wine (Congressional Budget Office 2022). States' distilled spirits taxes range from untaxed to $32.52 per gallon (in Washington); wine from $0.20 per gallon to $3.26; beer is taxed federally and then again by states, constituting roughly 40% of the retail price of beer (Cammenga 2019a, b, c). States also regulate where and when consumers can purchase alcohol. In some states, like Arizona and California, beer, wine, and distilled spirits can be purchased in grocery stores. Other states require separate stores for distilled spirits sales (Georgia, Oklahoma) or for distilled spirits and wine sales (Connecticut, New York). In seventeen states, a government alcohol control board controls the sale of distilled spirits and, in some cases, wine.[4]

Tobacco similarly faces high and diverse tax rates. The federal cigarette tax is $1.01 per pack. The average state cigarette excise tax rate is $1.88 per pack ranging from 37 cents in Georgia to $4.35 in New York and Connecticut. Some localities add taxes with Chicago, IL imposing the highest combined tax rate of $7.16 per pack (Campaign for Tobacco Free Kids 2020).

A move to free markets implies removing additional state and federal taxes on marijuana, alcohol, and tobacco and regulations restricting their sale and consumption, but still allowing standard, neutral sales taxes that apply broadly. Do these laws work as intended? That is, do these restrictions on alcohol and drug markets reduce the consumption and abuse of alcohol and drugs?

---

3 See also Colorado Department of Revenue (2021).

4 The seventeen control states are Alabama, Idaho, Iowa, Maine, Michigan, Mississippi, Montana, New Hampshire, North Carolina, Ohio, Oregon, Pennsylvania, Utah, Vermont, Virginia, West Virginia, and Wyoming. Mississippi, New Hampshire, Pennsylvania, and Wyoming also control the sale of wine (National Alcohol Beverage Control Association 2020).

In principle, restrictions on production, distribution, sale, and use might significantly reduce the amounts produced and consumed, along with the negative effects that use sometimes generates. Taxes raise the costs. Age restrictions raise the cost of obtaining age-restricted substances for young people who cannot legally purchase the product. In economics language, all these policies aim to restrict supply and shrink demand, which should lead to a lower equilibrium quantity. This no doubt happens to some degree.

As with prohibitions, however, consumers and producers do not fully comply with legal restrictions. Age restrictions are one example. Age restrictions do seem to prevent some young people from consuming those substances (Yörük and Yörük 2011). However, almost 20% of people aged 12–20 years old report consuming alcohol in the past 30 days, even though none are old enough to legally purchase alcohol (Substance Abuse and Mental Health Services Administration 2020). Similarly, some 4% of people aged 12–17 report consuming tobacco products, although not yet of legal age.

Higher alcohol tax rates raise alcohol prices and lower consumption (Sharma et al. 2017). Similarly, higher tobacco tax rates raise alcohol prices and lower consumption (Chaloupka et al. 2011). However, society must trade-off any potential benefits of reduced consumption with the increased incentive to avoid taxation and operate illicitly. If taxes and regulations are significant, it becomes profitable for firms to avoid taxation and regulation by operating in a gray market. Onerous taxation or regulation drives producers and consumers to underground markets to avoid those regulations, leading to similar harms, discussed above, associated with illicit markets. Also, taxes and restrictions harm those who consume without harming themselves or others.

Many legal products are also sold in underground markets. Illicit alcohol is a significant part of the global market as producers seek to avoid taxation and dry laws (Skehan et al. 2016). In 2019, 46 state and territory Attorneys General issued a letter to eBay, Facebook, and Craigslist to take down online posting of alcohol products (National Association of Attorneys General 2019). The complaint notes that these sales are "unlicensed, unregulated, and untaxed." Grey markets in cigarettes are common in the United States because tax rates differ across jurisdictions. Entrepreneurial smugglers buy in lower tax locations and sell for a profit in higher tax locations. In high-taxed states, illicit tobacco makes up 20% of the market (*The Economist* 2015). New York's high cigarette tax rate has led to 58% of cigarettes sold in the state being sold illegally to avoid taxation; (*The Economist* 2015); Eric Garner was killed by New York Police Department officers arresting him for selling untaxed cigarettes (Carrega, 2019).

Illicit markets in alcohol and tobacco include counterfeit, untaxed versions of name brand products. However, these products tend to be adulterated versions of the name brand product sold under a counterfeited label. Counterfeit alcohol products are more common in high-tax locales (Skehan et al. 2016); lead leached from home stills for moonshine, and methanol content in illicit products, generate more dangerous products. Counterfeit tobacco products, sold to avoid high-tax rates, have been adulterated with fillers including human excrement (LaFaive and Nesbit 2013).

High-tax rates and substantial regulatory burdens increase the potential to profit from tax avoidance, arbitrage across differing tax regimes, and regulatory avoidance. These regimes distort producers' incentives toward evasion and occupy justice system resources, adding to any harms created by the substances themselves. Removing the onerous taxes and regulations would refocus criminal justice resources and entrepreneurial efforts toward more productive endeavors.

Innovation Under Regulation and Prohibition

Entrepreneurs seek innovations that increase profits. In free markets, this requires producing products with characteristics, including prices, that meet consumers' needs. In regulated markets, profit-making additionally requires entrepreneurs to consider which regulatory and tax structure is most beneficial. In drug, alcohol, and tobacco markets, entrepreneurs invest in products and production processes that allow them to avoid taxation, avoid detection when selling illegal products, and reduce the penalties associated with the products they sell. Differential tax rates among classes of alcohol, scheduling of controlled substances and associated laws, and a variety of other regulations on alcohol and drug markets influence the behavior of producers.

Under the current regulatory regime, the forces of creative destruction and dynamism are concentrated on avoiding taxation and criminal penalties. Drug entrepreneurs invest millions in electric submarines and low-profile vessels to transport cocaine into the United States (Sutton 2020). Traffickers dig tunnels, equipped with rails and trolleys, to transport drugs and untaxed cigarettes across borders.[5] Jet skis, boats, and now drones deliver packages of illicit goods across political borders.

Investing in violent means of securing and maintaining illicit trade routes can be profitable for drug cartels but leads to significant harms around the world (Miron 1999, 2001). Drug cartels in Mexico, for example, have led to the deaths of 85,000 people (Coyne and Hall 2017). Homicide rates during federal prohibition display increased violence around markets for bootlegged alcohol (Owens 2014). Violence also occurs in underground U.S. and global tobacco markets (Kulick et al. 2016).

Given the challenges with transportation and evading detection, entrepreneurs invest in drugs that can be produced closer to home. For example, heroin and other opioids are produced from the gum of opium poppies, primarily and visibly grown in Afghanistan and Latin America (Pappas 2017). The costs of either transporting from the Middle East without detection or growing domestically an easy-to-observe crop lead entrepreneurs to invest in synthetic opioids such as fentanyl. These synthetic opioids are produced in easier-to-conceal laboratories.

Entrepreneurs also invest in substances that better avoid detection or lead to lower criminal sanctions. Prohibitions and taxes lead producers and consumers to prefer higher potency, easier-to-conceal substances (Thornton 1998). More potent drugs are typically cut with other substances prior to retail sale. However, this leads to drugs sold with unknown potency, and consumers more likely to overdose. Federal drug

[5] On narcotics, see Solis (2018). On cigarettes, see Michalopoulos S (2016).

scheduling led entrepreneurs to develop new drugs to avoid being "covered" by the drug scheduling (Redford 2017). These new drugs, like fentanyl-analogs and bath salts, are more dangerous to consumers, and a variety of analogs were sold under the same street name, reducing product information for consumers. Legalizing scheduled substances would lead to drugs sold in clearly labeled doses, with known quality and potency.

For legal, but highly taxed products such as alcohol and tobacco, producers innovate to take advantage of differential tax rates. Alcohol producers innovate in ways conscious of the differential tax rates for distilled spirits, wine, and beer. For example, White Claw—a carbonated, flavored seltzer water—is taxed under the lower beer tax rates and not the higher spirits tax rates. Beverage companies don't sell bottled vodka sodas (taxed as spirits), but brewed beverages like Zima, White Claw, and Mike's Hard Lemonade (taxed as beer) (Barro 2019).

Under a legal regime, entrepreneurs would innovate in ways that benefit consumers, producing better products. The history of tobacco products demonstrates producers' attempts to provide safer products for consumers with filters, lower-tar versions, and, more recently vaping (Lehrer 2017). We might see new delivery methods and new products. The 2018 Farm Bill legalized hemp farming and distribution; entrepreneurs responded by developing and selling hemp-derived products with Delta-8-THC, a psychoactive substance reported to alleviate pain (Richtel 2021). Perhaps ways to vape marijuana instead of smoking it will enter the market, or opioids will be sold packaged with clean needles.

Conclusion

Currently, state and federal regulations and rules greatly restrict the kinds of substances individuals can consume. Legalizing drugs and deregulating alcohol and tobacco would save money and improve a variety of societal outcomes. The current complex and stultifying regulatory regime around the sale and consumption of alcohol, tobacco, and drugs means a lot of entrepreneurs' focus is on innovation to avoid the regulatory regime. Legal, less regulated markets would allow innovators to focus on the types of products consumers prefer.

References

Alcocer JJ (2020) Exploring the effect of Colorado's recreational marijuana policy on opioid overdose rates. Public Health 185:8–14

Anderson DM, Rees D (2014) The legalization of recreational marijuana: How likely is the worst-case scenario? J Policy Anal Manage 33:221–232

Anderson DM, Hansen B, Rees D (2013) Medical marijuana laws, traffic fatalities, and alcohol consumption. J Law Econ 56:333–369

Anderson DM, Rees D, Sabia J (2014) Medical marijuana laws and suicides by gender and age. Am J Pub Health 104:2369–2376

Barro J (2019) How tax policy gave us White Claw. Intelligencer, 4 September

Campaign for Tobacco-Free Kids (2020) State cigarette excise tax rates and rankings. Campaign for Tobacco-Free Kids, Washington, DC

Camplain R, Camplain C, Trotter RT, Pro G, Sabo S, Eaves E, Peoples M, Baldwin JA (2020) Racial/ethnic differences in drug-and alcohol-related arrest outcomes in a southwest county from 2009 to 2018. Am J Pub Health 110(S1):S85–92

Cammenga J (2019a) How high are beer taxes in your state? Tax Foundation, Washington, DC

Cammenga J (2019b) How high are wine taxes in your state? Tax Foundation, Washington, DC

Cammenga J (2019c) How high are spirit taxes in your state? Tax Foundation, Washington, DC

Carrega C (2019) 5 years after Eric Garner's death, a look back at the case and the movement it sparked. ABC News, 16 July

Chaloupka FJ, Straif K, Leon ME (2011) Effectiveness of tax and price policies in tobacco control. Tob Control 20:235–238

Cicero TJ, Kurtz SP, Surratt HL, Ibanez GE, Ellis MS, Levi-Minzi MA, Inciardi JA (2011) Multiple determinants of specific modes of prescription opioid diversion. J Drug Issues 41:283–304

Colorado Department of Revenue (2021). Data and reports: Marijuana data. Colorado Department of Revenue, Lakewood

Congressional Budget Office (2022) Increase all taxes on alcoholic beverages to $16 per proof gallon and index them for inflation. Congressional Budget Office, Washington, DC

Cooper HL (2015) War on drugs policing and police brutality. Subst Use Misuse 50: 1–7

Coyne CJ, Hall AR (2017) Four decades and counting: The continued failure of the war on drugs. Cato Institute, Policy Analysis No 811

Dills A, Miron JA (2004) Alcohol prohibition and cirrhosis. Am Law Econ Rev 6:285–318

Dills A, Jacobson M, Miron JA (2005) The effect of alcohol prohibition on alcohol consumption: Evidence from drunkenness arrests. Econ Lett 86:279–294

Dragone D, Prarolo G, Vanin P, Zanella G (2019) Crime and the legalization of recreational marijuana. J Econ Behav Organ 159:488–501

Fritts J (2019) How high are taxes on recreational marijuana in your state? Tax Foundation, Washington, DC

Hansen B, Miller K, Weber C (2020) Early evidence on recreational marijuana legalization and traffic fatalities. Econ Inq 58:547–568

Hughes CE, Stevens A (2007) The effects of the decriminalization of drug use in Portugal. The Beckley Foundation, Discussion Paper

Kornbluth J (1978) Poisonous fallout from the war on marijuana. New York Times, 19 November

Kozhimannil KB, Dowd WN, Ali MM, Novak P, Chen J (2019) Substance use disorder treatment admissions and state-level prenatal substance use policies: Evidence from a national treatment database. Addict Behav 90:272–277

Kulick J, Prieger J, Kleiman MAR (2016) Unintended consequences of cigarette prohibition, regulation, and taxation. Int J Law Crime and Just 46:69–85

LaFaive MD, Nesbit T (2013) Higher cigarette taxes create lucrative, dangerous black market. Mackinac Center for Public Policy, Midland

Lehrer E (2017) The rise of vaping has nothing to do with big tobacco. The Hill, 22 April

Lopez G (2014) The US government once poisoned alcohol to get people to stop drinking. Vox, 8 August

Marijuana Policy Project (2021a) Decriminalization. Marijuana Policy Project, Washington, DC

Marijuana Policy Project (2021b) Medical marijuana overview. Marijuana Policy Project, Washington, DC
Marijuana Policy Project (2021c) Cannabis legalization. Marijuana Policy Project, Washington, DC
Michalopoulos S (2016) 'Cheap whites': The new trend dominating tobacco black markets. Euractiv, 3 October
Miron JA (1999) Violence and the US prohibitions of drugs and alcohol. Am Law Econ Rev 1:78–114
Miron JA (2001) Violence, guns, and drugs: A cross-country analysis. J Law Econ 44:615–633
Miron JA (2003) The effect of drug prohibition on drug prices: Evidence from the markets for cocaine and heroin. Rev Econ Stat 85:522–530
Miron JA (2018) The budgetary effects of ending drug prohibition. Cato Institute, Washington, DC
Morris RG, TenEyck M, Barnes JC, Kovandzic TV (2014) The effect of medical marijuana laws on crime: Evidence from state panel data, 1990–2006. PLOS ONE 9: e92816
National Alcohol Beverage Control Association (2020) Control state directory and information. National Alcohol Beverage Control Association, Arlington
National Academies of Sciences, Engineering, and Medicine; Health and Medicine Division; Board on Population Health and Public Health Practice; Committee on the Health Effects of Marijuana: An Evidence Review and Research Agenda (2017) The health effects of cannabis and cannabinoids: The current state of evidence and recommendations for research. National Academies Press, Washington DC
National Association of Attorneys General (2019) On-line sale of alcohol (combined letters from Attorneys General). National Association of Attorneys General, Washington, DC
New York Times (1982) Florida will spray marijuana. New York Times, 13 July
New York Times (1988) Paraquat is sprayed on marijuana in Texas. New York Times, 20 July
Owens EG (2014) The American temperance movement and market-based violence. Am Law Econ Rev 16:433–472
Pappas S (2017) Massive poppy bust: Why home-grown opium is rare. LiveScience, 24 May
Redford A (2017) Don't eat the brown acid: Induced 'malnovation' in drug markets. Rev Austrian Econ 30:215–233
Richtel M (2021) This drug gets you high and is legal (maybe) across the country. New York Times, 27 February

Sharma A, Sinha K, Vandenberg B (2017) Pricing as a means of controlling alcohol consumption. British Med Bull 123:149–158

Skehan P, Sanchez I, Hastings L (2016) The size, impacts, and drivers of illicit trade of alcohol. In: Illicit trade: Converging criminal networks. OECD Publishing, Paris

Solis G (2018) Drug smuggling, and the endless battle to stop it. USA Today

Substance Abuse and Mental Health Services Administration (2020) 2019 national surveys on drug use and health detailed tables. Substance Abuse and Mental Health Services Administration, Rockville

Sutton HI (2020) Rare electric narco submarine seized in Colombia. USNI News, 16 November

The Economist (2015) Smuggled smokes: Nannies v Al Capone. The Economist, 12 February

Thornton M (1998) The potency of illegal drugs. J Drug Issues 28:725–740

United Nations Office on Drugs and Crime (2019) World drug report 2019. United Nations Office on Drugs and Crime, Vienna

U.S. Department of Justice (2020) Crime in the U.S. 2019. Federal Bureau of Investigation, Washington, DC

Wilson N, Kariisa M, Seth P, Smith H IV, Davis NL (2020) Drug and opioid-involved overdose deaths—United States, 2017–2018. MMWR-Morbid W 69:290–297

World Health Organization (2017) WHO report on the global tobacco epidemic, 2017: Monitoring tobacco use and prevention policies. World Health Organization, Geneva

World Health Organization (2018) Global status report on alcohol and health 2018. World Health Organization, Geneva

Yörük BK, Yörük CE (2011) The impact of minimum legal drinking age laws on alcohol consumption, smoking, and marijuana use: Evidence from a regression discontinuity design using exact date of birth. J Health Econ 30:740–752

15

Individual's Demand for Bad Health: Tradeoffs in Alcohol and Illicit Drug Regulations

Armineh Zohrabian

Introduction

The first mandate of any national government is to provide security for its people from external and internal threats. If it cannot provide this security, then none of the other mandates have a meaning. Based on the same logic, if any products, institutions, or events constitute a threat to people's security, government involvement is warranted. The issues of alcohol and illicit drugs may seem far less severe than threats to national security. Still, the recent experiences with the opioid epidemic and deaths of despair in many communities across the U.S. (Case and Deaton 2015) have made the debates around government roles in alcohol and drug regulation ever more relevant.

Is it the government's role to be involved in disease prevention to protect individuals from any causes of premature death? Should the

A. Zohrabian (✉)
University of Arkansas for Medical Sciences, Little Rock, AR, USA
e-mail: AZohrabian@uams.edu

A. L. Kassens and J. C. Hall (eds.), *Challenges in Classical Liberalism*, Palgrave Studies in Classical Liberalism,
https://doi.org/10.1007/978-3-031-32890-9_15

government invest in programs designed to help the most vulnerable people and reduce social inequities? From an economics viewpoint, the answer is more complex than from a public health viewpoint. Would the invisible hand that made free markets work also apply to alcohol and illicit drugs? Are individuals who use illicit drugs or consume excessive amounts of alcohol better off when their demand is met?

The government's roles and responsibilities have been debated over the centuries. The views range from anarchists, who believe in the abolition of the state, to totalitarian socialists, who support full state control of the economy and society. Most individuals' views are between these two extremes, and they can vary widely. The traditional economic principles of limited government's roles are grounded in the seminal works of Adam Smith (The Wealth of Nations [1776]), Friedrich Hayek (The Constitution of Liberty [1960], and The Road to Serfdom [1948]), and Milton Friedman's work (Is Capitalism Humane? 1977). Although Friedman's work refuses anything that restricts an individual's freedom to choose, Hayek's studies mention communities repeatedly, implying that government may have a role in serving communities' interests. The latter may apply to the recent opioid epidemic and deaths of despair that have devastated communities across the U.S.

In his *An Inquiry into the Nature and Causes of the Wealth of Nations* ([1776] 2007), Adam Smith stated that the government's roles in society should be limited but well defined: *national defense*, *administration of justice*, and *public goods*. In other words, the government should protect its citizens from threats and aggressions and supply public goods that the free market may not provide. Today, governments in Western democracies have more responsibilities that involve public education, government-provided or -funded health care, old-age pensions, and security-net programs for the most vulnerable as a part of being a humane society. Furthermore, government taxing and spending as a percentage of aggregate output have risen, and regulations of the private economy have increasingly become more complex.

Policy formulation unavoidably involves tradeoffs involving social values that are impossible to measure or compare (liberty, public health, individual responsibility, compassion, etc.). Health protection, economic impact, and reducing or not exacerbating inequities are tradeoffs that can rarely be determined through simple social consensus (Arrow 1963). In pluralist democracies, this process is negotiated among many groups through the political system as a competitive process involving voters, their elected representatives, interest groups, and others.

The recent public health crises and the developments in behavioral economics may indicate a more expanded role for the government in preventing and reducing harm from excessive alcohol and illicit drugs. Furthermore, the evolution in better understanding of the addictive nature of these substances and the role of socioeconomic factors in addiction also may support government programs that consider socioeconomic realities and inequalities (Heather and Segal 2015). Overall, accurate and trustworthy information is essential for any progress in this challenging field of balancing individual liberty and preventing or reducing harm from alcohol and illicit drugs.

Rationales for Government Regulation: Market Failure, Equity, and Social Justice

Risky Health Behaviors as Leading Actual Causes of Death

Excess alcohol and illicit drugs are risky behaviors that are among the top ten leading actual causes of death in the U.S. (McGinnis and Foege 1993; Mokdad et al. 2004). Causes of death are often categorized as diseases, such as cardiovascular diseases and cancer. Still, these diseases are consequences of the actual causes of death, e.g., smoking, alcohol, or sedentary lifestyle. In a powerful study, McGinnis and Foege (1993) looked at excess mortality, combining epidemiological and mortality data with death certificate data to reach an astonishing conclusion: the leading actual cause of death was our own behavior: smoking, obesity, and excessive alcohol use (Phelps 2016). Over decades, tobacco has been the leading actual cause of deaths (400,000 and 435,000 annual deaths for 1990 and 2000, respectively), followed by poor diet/physical inactivity (300,000 and 365,000 annual deaths for 1990 and 2000), while excessive alcohol consumption was responsible for 100,000 and 85,000 annual deaths in the U.S. in 1990 and 2000, respectively (McGinnis and Foege 1993; Mokdad et al. 2004). In 2020, the COVID-19 pandemic introduced a new leading cause of death, i.e., the SARS-COVID-19 virus (Ahmad and Anderson 2021). Nevertheless, heart disease and cancer still lead the list, and increases in unintentional injury deaths, the fourth leading cause, were driven mainly by drug overdose deaths.

The impact of risky health behaviors, such as drug poisoning and long-term alcohol excessive use, has been profound in the U.S. Unlike other high-income countries, age-adjusted mortality in the U.S. plateaued in 2010 and increased in 2015. As a high-income country, the magnitude of annual mortality increases in the U.S. was extremely unusual. Between 1999 and 2014, public health successes, including HIV treatment and smoking cessation, contributed to declining premature mortality in Hispanic and black individuals, and Asians and Pacific Islanders, ages 25–64 years old (Shiels et al. 2017). However, this progress was largely negated in young and middle-aged white individuals (25–49 years) and American Indians and Alaska Natives, primarily because of potentially avoidable causes such as accidental deaths (primarily drug poisonings), chronic liver disease, and cirrhosis (mainly caused by long-term alcohol excessive use), and suicide (Shiels et al. 2017).

Externalities

From a public health perspective, the knowledge that alcohol and drugs are among the leading actual causes of premature death provides sufficient rationale for government regulation. From an economic perspective, market failures, including externalities and information deficiencies, are the strongest rationales for government regulations.

Risky health behaviors pose risk not only to the individual's health, but they also involve direct and indirect external costs for others in the society. External costs arise when a person or a group does not bear all the costs of their actions. Some of the costs are borne by others or society at large. The costs that a person bears as a consequence of his or her actions are called internal (private) costs. External costs are not considered in a person's decision-making because others bear them.

Possible external costs of any health-related behavior primarily derive from public or private group health insurance and events directly causing harm to others (e.g., traffic crash or crime and violence under the influence of alcohol or drugs). External costs are relevant on the grounds of fairness and efficiency. They become an issue of fairness when someone pays unwillingly or unknowingly for the actions of others. Grounds of economic efficiency apply when paying the full costs of their action leads to an overall higher level of efficiency by a change in personal behavior, i.e., the benefits are more than the losses associated with the change, regardless of who gains or loses.

Among the three risky behaviors—smoking, alcohol, and poor nutrition/sedentary lifestyle—excessive alcohol has had the highest external costs (Zohrabian and Philipson 2010), resulting in $249 billion, or $2.05 per drink, in external costs (Sacks et al. 2015). An effective method of decreasing excessive alcohol consumption, youth consumption, and related harms such as traffic fatalities is to increase alcohol taxes (Babor 2010; Chaloupka et al. 2002; Elder et al. 2010; Wagenaar et al. 2010; Xuan et al. 2015). Alcohol tax increases are passed on to consumers, resulting in shelf price increases of equal or greater magnitude than the tax itself. Although such taxation has historically been motivated primarily by revenue generation, governments increasingly use these taxes to discourage unhealthy consumption and reduce crimes.

Behavioral economics models, such as time-inconsistent preferences, hot brain/cold brain models of decision-making (Bernheim and Rangel 2004), biases, and bounded rationality (Kahneman 2011), to name a few, provide additional grounds for government intervention. Some individuals may view these interventions as beneficial. For example, Gruber and Koszegi (2004) developed a model that was much more consistent with existing evidence on smoking decisions, i.e., a time-inconsistent formulation where excise taxes on cigarettes served a self-control function that was valued by smokers who would like to quit but could not. The authors argued that this self-control function benefited lower income groups more, since they had a significantly higher price sensitivity of smoking. Calibrations showed that, as a result, cigarette taxes were much less regressive than previously assumed, and were even progressive for a wide variety of parameter values (Gruber and Koszegi 2004). While this study was on smoking, excise taxes may also serve a similar self-control function for reducing excessive drinking because of the similarities in terms of their addictive nature and not being necessities of life.

It is useful discussing how these potential externalities have not been resolved yet. Aligning the private costs of risky behaviors with the social costs appear to be straightforward to implement. A glimpse into the differences and similarities between tobacco and alcohol industry may provide some insight. There have been significant differences in the tax policies for smoking and alcohol. Despite the enormous external costs of excessive drinking, excise taxes on alcoholic beverages have been little adjusted for decades, with an effective rate of taxation declining over the years (Blanchette et al. 2020). On the other hand, from 2002 to 2009 cigarette tax rates were increased for 88 times by 46 states, D.C., and several U.S. territories. This difference may be explained by the difference in the political influence of the two industries (Sloan 2004), but there is another important difference. For alcohol, harm and particularly externalities were believed to arise from only excessive consumption. An occasional drink was thought to even have health benefits. However, recent studies challenge this understanding, offering new information that there may not be a safe level of alcohol (Griswold et al. 2018), and the perception of benefits of alcohol may be a consequence of a systematic error in the prospective studies (Fillmore et al. 2007).

Taxation has another economic aspect. There is gain, i.e., surplus, to people when the prices they pay for products they enjoy is less than their maximum willingness to pay for them. When taxation increases prices, consumer's response will likely be reduced consumption, involving changes in private surplus. Two economic models predict this change differently. According to the model of time-inconsistent preferences, persons with risky behaviors will be better off because taxes will serve as a self-control device helping them achieve what they eventually want to do, i.e., quit smoking, drinking, or eating excessively. On the other hand, the standard economic model predicts that those with risky behaviors will be worse off because the policy intervention will constrain their rational choices. This loss in private surplus will be due to consumers having to pay more for the amount of the product they still continue to consume, and they also will have to consume less of something they enjoy. Comparing changes in private surplus for these risky behaviors can be an important topic for future research (Zohrabian and Philipson 2010).

Lessons from Prohibition

National alcohol prohibition (N.P.) came into effect with the ratification of the 18th Amendment to the U.S. Constitution in 1919 and the passage in 1920 of the Volstead Act that prohibited the manufacture, sale, and supply of alcohol. The 18th Amendment stated that: "After a year from the ratification of this article the manufacture sale or transportation of intoxicating liquors within, the importation thereof from the United States and all territory subject to the jurisdiction thereof for beverage purposes is hereby prohibited". It defined intoxicating beverages as those that contained more than 0.5% alcohol and therefore forbade the sale of spirits, beer, and wine (Warburton 1934). Over time, N.P. was disregarded widely by most Americans and it was repealed in 1933.

The policy worked as a public health intervention, insofar as it aimed to lower alcohol consumption and ailments. At the same time, there were unintended consequences of bootlegging, violence. N.P. also played a role in the development of organized crime (Blocker 2006; Kassens 2019). Many believe, however, that these problems might have been reduced "by a better enforced and smarter policy—say, one that permitted taxed sales to adults of light wines and beer" (Hall 2010).

The generally accepted view that N.P. was a failed policy provides the basis for referring to prohibition in modern-time policy debates as lessons learned that should not be repeated. For example, proposals to reduce the availability of alcohol, increase its price, or regulate its advertising and promotion are frequently called by their opponents as "neoprohibitionist" (Cook 2007). Advocates of cannabis law reform also often refer to N.P. in support of their proposals to legalize cannabis. They argue that cannabis prohibition should be repealed because, like alcohol prohibition, it has failed to deter young people from using the drug, and the social costs of its enforcement and the foregone tax revenue outweigh any benefits (Morgan 1991; Nadelman 1989; Levine and Reinarman 1991; Wodak et al.2002).

It is noteworthy that the N.P. permitted individual possession and use, stockpiling, and limited home production of alcohol. If this leniency were allowed for cannabis, it would probably end the comparisons between the N.P. and cannabis restrictions. This year marks 50 years since President Nixon declared drugs "public enemy number one," including cannabis, leading to War on Drugs, spending of hundreds of billions of dollars in law enforcement and to the incarceration of millions of people—disproportionately Black. Today, cannabis reform is seen as a pathway to racial justice and opportunity toward reversing the effects of the War on Drugs. At the time this chapter was written (fall 2021), The Marijuana Opportunity Reinvestment and Expungement (MORE) Act—a bill to federally legalize marijuana, was approved by the House Judiciary Committee.

There are good reasons to believe that the alcohol prohibition probably reduced per capita alcohol use and alcohol-related harm. Over time, however, these benefits eroded as an organized black market developed and public support for N.P. declined. "Those who remain unconvinced by the historical evidence of its effects on alcohol use should similarly moderate their confidence in conclusions about its effects on crime, because the same type of evidence is used in each case" (Hall 2010).

There are good reasons to believe that the prohibition's benefits of reduced alcohol use could have been achieved by less restrictive alcohol policies, with fewer adverse effects (Cook 2007; Miron 1999). For example, the experience with raising minimum legal drinking age in the U.S. shows that partial prohibitions can produce substantial public health benefits at an acceptable social cost, in the absence of substantial additional expenditure on enforcement (Hall 2010).

Looking at the prohibition's effects through economic lens, we can summarize its lessons that the decline in alcohol use came at an unacceptable social and economic cost, including increased crime and corruption, disrespect for the law, and foregone tax revenue. The fact that the American people voted for Repeal in 1933 serves as evidence for these costs being unacceptable.

Lessons from Deaths of Despair and the Opioid Crisis

In the last 250 years, the U.S. saw unprecedented material progress. The free market combined with the discovery and application of useful knowledge, led to a decline in poverty and an increase in life expectancy: the latter being one of the key indicators of how well a society is doing. This increase, however, was reversed starting 2013/2014; for the first time since the 1918 Spanish flu epidemic, life expectancy at birth declined for white non-Hispanics, consequently leading to a decline in life expectancy for the whole population.

Deaths from alcohol-related liver diseases, legal and illegal drug overdoses, and suicide contributed to this almost unprecedented increase in overall mortality among middle-aged white non-Hispanics and were coined as deaths of despair (Case and Deaton 2015, 2017, 2020). In 1995/1996, there was also an increase in the mortality rate from heart disease—after many years of decline. If obesity was the cause, as many argued, some of these deaths might also be classed as deaths of despair, which would put the total deaths of despair at levels approaching deaths from cancer or from heart disease, the two major killers in midlife in the U.S. (Deaton, Congress testimony, 2017).

Opioids were a big part of this story. Supplies of opioids—the new forms of heroin, fentanyl, and prescription opioids—fueled and maintained the opioid epidemic. The cumulative total deaths from drug overdose from 2000 to 2017 was greater than the total number of Americans who died in the two world wars. Opioid deaths, like other deaths of despair, were not equal opportunity. Two-thirds of opioid epidemic victims had no more than high school education (Case and Deaton 2017). On the other hand, the percentage of accidental drug overdose deaths for whites with bachelor's degree has held constant at nine percent since the early 1990s (Case and Deaton 2020: pp. 113–114). This finding serves as one of the strongest evidence that education has a protective effect on deaths involving addictive substances.

A subtle but essential context that can be easily overlooked related to the deaths of despair is that many less-educated people have lives that are not only economically, but also socially inferior to those of their parents.

Recent literature provides evidence that subjective measures of economic distress are better predictors of drug and alcohol abuse than objective measures of financial and employment conditions (Glei and Weinstein 2019). These findings on the subjective measures of economic distress, combined with the conclusions from the deaths of despair studies, tell the story of how a better education can support not only the economic goals for the poor socioeconomic groups but also their mental and physical wellbeing.

In his 2019 Tanner Lecture, Nobel Laureate Sir Angus Deaton talked about corporate behavior, rent seeking, and individual well-being. His talk highlighted the spectacular failures of American healthcare system in preventing and protecting the public from the opioid epidemic. Despite 100-year evidence of opioids' addiction dangers, the government failed to protect the public. Pharmaceutical companies were allowed to enrich themselves by pumping out huge quantities of opioids as pain prescriptions, using Congress to stop attempts to police by the U.S. Drug Enforcement Administration and to change the law in favor of distributors. Even more shocking, it is not even clear if opioids are more effective than other methods, such as interdisciplinary methods of controlling pain (Angus Deaton, 2019 Tanner Lecture). Given that pain, mental distress, and drug misuse are intertwined, successful intervention may require addressing all three factors instead of having separate policies and programs to ameliorate one of them at a time (Glei and Weinstein 2020).

Alcohol Industry's Dark Nudges and Sludge

Nudges are relatively new interventions: they represent a change in the choice architecture, i.e., the context in which choices are presented to people (Thaler and Sunstein 2008). Nudges help achieve desirable outcomes by altering an individual's behavior without limiting their freedom to choose, as opposed to traditional government laws, regulations, taxes, or financial subsidies. The latter interventions are considered as "hard" paternalism given that they restrict people's freedom to choose (Sunstein 2014). Through nudges, public policy planners can affect people's behaviors to increase individuals' welfare while respecting their freedom of choice. This is coined by Thaler and Sunstein (2003) as libertarian or "soft" paternalism. Since then, choice architects from public and private institutions have gained considerable traction in developing and testing nudges to complement traditional policy interventions.

More recently, the term sludge was introduced, to refer to situations where the context impedes behavior by creating frictions (Sunstein 2022; Soman 2020). While nudge usually means an intervention that facilitates actions by minimizing decision friction, sludge is an intervention that deters actions by increasing decision friction (Thaler 2018). For example, searches of the alcohol-industry-funded corporate responsibility (CSR) organizations' Twitter content and website materials for the 2016–2020 period, and from previously published studies identified a range of sludge and dark nudges, i.e., nudges that can promote behaviors harming health. Sludge methods used included the positioning of information to make it more or less available, omission of relevant information, priming, and social norming effects, both of which use cognitive biases to affect decision-making and choice. For example, priming drinkers involves offering verbal and pictorial cues to drink while simultaneously appearing to warn about alcohol harms, while social norming tells consumers that most people are drinking. The ultimate goal is to present larger benefits and lower harms than they actually are (Petticrew et al. 2020).

It is possible that the public's relatively favorable alcohol sentiment, which has been one of the reasons for its historically lower rates of tax increases, will decline if the alcohol industry's dark nudges and sludge to manipulate consumers becomes widespread knowledge.

Concluding Comments

Alcohol and drugs can cause great harm to the user and society, and regulating them can be justified on several grounds. However, changing risky health behaviors is complex, involving approaches and methods from multiple disciplines, such as economics, psychology, public health, and medicine. Therefore, single-dimensional policies are a risky enterprise of unintended consequences (Vernon Smith 2016). Hence, alcohol prohibition in the U.S. seemed like a good policy and was so popular that it resulted in a constitutional amendment in 1920. The experiment lasted thirteen years, but the consequences were so unpopular that it was repealed in another amendment. "We need, but do not have, better ways of trying it before flying it" (Vernon Smith 2016).

The insights made decades ago on the tension between individual freedom and society's approaches to protect the public interests still apply. Freedom requires that the coercion of some by others in society be reduced as much as possible. "One function of government is to prevent individuals from coercing other individuals, but then government itself must be prevented from using coercion improperly. In a free society, the exercise of government's coercive power is constrained and made predictable by general rules that apply equally to all individuals, including to those who make and enforce the laws" (Hayek 1960).

Individuals' rationality and responsibility cannot function if the industry or the government attempts to manipulate the environment, e.g., by withholding vital information and making it harder for the individual to make decisions in their best interest. All these insidious forms of coercion have been observed in the actions of the pharmaceutical and alcohol industries, as evidenced by the latest opioid epidemic and the emerging dark nudges and sludge by alcohol CSR organizations.

From an economic standpoint, government agencies' requirement to proceed with regulations only if the benefits justify the costs will prevent the potential for having regulations based on dogmas, intuitions, political preferences, or interest-group power. The focus on costs and benefits attends to the real-world consequences of regulations. It casts a pragmatic, skeptical light on modern objections to the administrative state, invoking public-choice theory. The focus on costs and benefits is also a valuable effort to go beyond coarse arguments, from both the right and the left, that tend to ask this unhelpful question: "Which side are you on?" (Sunstein 2021).

Based on current knowledge, one of the essential implications for preventing harm from addictive goods is the need to reduce socioeconomic deprivation and empower individuals to have their own life plans and be free to pursue that plans. In the future, there will be better ways to identify the unintended consequences of government regulations, unlike the national alcohol prohibition and the war on drugs. One of the approaches would be to develop public policies and regulations that rely less on unreliable ex-ante projections and more on actual evaluations and by attending closely to distributional considerations—on who is helped and who is hurt (Sunstein 2021).

References

Ahmad FB, Anderson RN (2021) The leading causes of death in the U.S. for 2020. JAMA-J Am Med 325:1829–1830

Arrow K (1963) Social choice and individual values. Yale University Press, New Haven

Babor T (2010) Alcohol: No ordinary commodity—research and public policy. Oxford University Press, Oxford

Bernheim BD, Rangel A (2004) Addiction and cue-triggered decision processes. Am Econ Rev 94:1558–1590

Blanchette JG, Ross CS, Naimi TS (2020) The rise and fall of alcohol excise taxes in US states, 1933–2018. J Stud Alcohol Drug 81:331–338

Blocker JS (2006) Did prohibition really work? Alcohol prohibition as a public health innovation. Am J Public Health 96:233–243

Case A, Deaton A (2020) Deaths of despair and the future of capitalism. Princeton University Press, Princeton

Case A, Deaton A (2015) Rising midlife morbidity and mortality, U.S. whites. P Natl Acad SCI USA 112:15078–15083

Case A, Deaton A (2017) Mortality and morbidity in the 21st century. Brookings Pap Eco Ac 2017:397–476

Chaloupka FJ, Grossman M, Saffer H (2002) The effects of price on alcohol consumption and alcohol-related problems. Alcohol Res Health 26:22–34

Cook PJ (2007) Paying the tab: The economics of alcohol policy. Princeton University Press, Princeton

Deaton A (2017) Economic aspects of the opioid crisis. Testimony before the Joint Economic Committee of the United States Congress, Washington, DC, 8 June 2017

Elder RW, Lawrence B, Ferguson A, Naimi TS, Brewer RD, Chattopadhyay SK, Toomey TL, Fielding JE, Task Force on Community Preventive Services (2010) The effectiveness of tax policy interventions for reducing excessive alcohol consumption and related harms. Am J Prev Med 38:217–229

Fillmore KM, Stockwell T, Chikritzhs T, Bostrom A, Kerr W (2007) Moderate alcohol use and reduced mortality risk: Systematic error in prospective studies and new hypotheses. Ann Epidemiol 17(5 Suppl):S16–23.

Friedman M (1977) Is capitalism humane? Talk presented at Cornell University, Cornell, 27 September 1977

Glei DA, Weinstein M (2019) Drug and alcohol abuse: The role of economic insecurity. Am J Health Behav 43:838–853

Glei DA, Weinstein M (2020) Mental health, pain, and risk of drug misuse: A nationwide cohort study. Addict Behav 109:106467

Griswold MG, Fullman N, Hawley C, Arian N, Zimsen SR, Tymeson HD, Venkateswaran V, Tapp AD, Forouzanfar MH, Salama JS, Abate KH (2018) Alcohol use and burden for 195 countries and territories, 1990–2016: A systematic analysis for the Global Burden of Disease Study 2016. Lancet 392:1015–1035

Gruber J, B Koszegi (2004) Tax incidence when individuals are time-inconsistent: The case of cigarette excise taxes. J Pub Econ 88:1959–1987

Hall W. (2010) What are the policy lessons of National Alcohol Prohibition in the United States, 1920–1933? Addiction 105:1164–1173

Hayek FA (1948) The road to serfdom. George Routledge & Sons, London

Hayek FA (1960) The constitution of liberty. University of Chicago Press, Chicago

Heather N, Segal G (2015) Addiction and choice: Rethinking the relationship. Oxford University Press, New York

Kahneman D (2011) Thinking, fast and slow. Farrar, Straus and Giroux, New York

Kassens AL (2019) Intemperate spirits. Economic adaptation during prohibition. Palgrave Macmillan, New York

Levine HG, Reinarman C (1991) From prohibition to regulation: Lessons from alcohol policy for drug policy. Milbank Q 69:461–494

McGinnis JM, Foege WH (1993) Actual causes of death in the United States. JAMA-J Am Med Assoc 270: 2207–2212

Miron JA (1999) Violence and the U.S. prohibitions of drugs and alcohol. Am Law Econ Rev 1: 78–114

Mokdad AH, Marks JS, Stroup DF, Gerberding JL (2004) Actual causes of death in the United States. JAMA-J Am Med Assoc 291:1238–1245

Morgan JP (1991) Prohibition is perverse policy: What was true in 1933 is true now. In: Krauss MB, Lazear E (eds) Searching for alternatives: Drug policy control in the United States. Hoover Institution Press, Palo Alto, pp 405–423

Nadelman E (1989) Drug prohibition in the United States: Costs, consequences and alternatives. Science 245:939–947

Petticrew M, Maani N, Pettigrew L, Rutter H, Van Schalkwyk MC (2020) Dark nudges and sludge in big alcohol: Behavioral economics, cognitive biases, and alcohol industry corporate social responsibility. Milbank Q 98:1290–1328

Phelps C (2016) We have met our enemies and they are us. In: Meyer DJ (ed) The economics of health. WE Upjohn Institute for Employment Research, Kalamazoo, pp 7–34

Sacks JJ, Gonzales KR, Bouchery EE, Tomedi LE, Brewer RD (2015) 2010 national and state costs of excessive alcohol consumption. Am J Prev Med 49:e73-e79

Shiels MS, Chernyavskiy P, Anderson WF, Best AF, Haozous EA, Hartge P, Rosenberg PS, Thomas D, Freedman ND, de Gonzalez AB (2017) Trends in premature mortality in the USA by sex, race, and ethnicity from 1999 to 2014: An analysis of death certificate data. Lancet 389:1043–1054

Sloan FA, Justin GT (2004) Litigation and the political clout of the tobacco companies: Cigarette taxes, prices, and the master settlement agreement. School of Economics, University of Adelaide

Soman D (2020) Sludge: A very short introduction. Paper presented at the 2020 Nudgestock conference, Livestreamed, 12 June 2020

Smith VA (2016) Learning the most from proving yourself wrong: Three examples. Moderated by Gaus J. Presented at Monash University, Monash, 5 October 2016

Sunstein CR (2014) Nudging: A very short guide. J Consum Policy 37:583–588

Sunstein CR (2021) Some benefits and costs of cost-benefit analysis. Daedalus 150:208–219

Sunstein CR (2022) Sludge audits. Behav Pub Poli 6:654–673

Thaler RH (2018) Nudge, not sludge. Science 361:431

Thaler RH, Sunstein CR (2003) Libertarian paternalism. Am Econ Rev 93:175–179

Thaler RH, Sunstein CR (2008) Nudge: Improving decisions about health, wealth, and happiness. Yale University Press, New Haven

Wagenaar AC, Tobler AL, Komro KA (2010) Effects of alcohol tax and price policies on morbidity and mortality: A systematic review. Am J Public Health 100:2270–2278

Warburton C (1934) Prohibition. In: Seligman E (ed) Encyclopaedia of the social sciences. Macmillan, New York, pp 499–510

Wodak A, Reinarman C, Cohen P (2002) Cannabis control: Costs outweigh benefits. BMJ Brit Med J 324:105–106

Xuan Z, Blanchette JG, Nelson TF, Nguyen TH, Hadland SE, Oussayef NL, Heeren TC, Naimi TS (2015) Youth drinking in the United States: Relationships with alcohol policies and adult drinking. Pediatrics 136:18–27

Zohrabian A, Philipson TJ (2010) External costs of risky health behaviors associated with leading actual causes of death in the U.S.: A review of the evidence and implications for future research. Int J Environ Res Public Health 7:2460–2472

Index

A. L. Kassens and J. C. Hall (eds.), *Challenges in Classical Liberalism*, Palgrave Studies in Classical Liberalism,
https://doi.org/10.1007/978-3-031-32890-9

D

E

SPRINGER NATURE

GPSR Compliance

The European Union's (EU) General Product Safety Regulation (GPSR) is a set of rules that requires consumer products to be safe and our obligations to ensure this.

If you have any concerns about our products, you can contact us on ProductSafety@springernature.com

In case Publisher is established outside the EU, the EU authorized representative is:

Springer Nature Customer Service Center GmbH
Europaplatz 3
69115 Heidelberg, Germany

The manufacturer's authorised representative in the EU is Springer Nature Customer Service Centre GmbH, Europaplatz 3, 69115 Heidelberg, Germany. If you have any concerns regarding our products, please contact ProductSafety@springernature.com

Printed and bound by CPI Group (UK) Ltd, Croydon, CR0 4YY
30/09/2026
02225494-0007